Creating a Winning Business PLAN

A No-Time-for-Nonsense Guide

to Starting a BUSINESS and Raising CASH

Gregory I. Kravitt

IRWIN
Professional Publishing®
Chicago • London • Singapore

This publication is designed to provide accurate and authoritative information in regard to the subject matter covered. It is sold with the understanding that the author and the publisher are not engaged in rendering legal, accounting, or other professional service.

Kravitt, Gregory I.
   Creating a winning business plan: a no-time-for-nonsense guide to starting a business and raising cash / by Gregory Ian Kravitt.
      p.   cm.
   Includes index.
   ISBN 1-55738-471-1
   1. Prospectus writing.   2. Proposal writing in business.
I. Title.
HG4026.K6998   1992
658.15'22—dc20   92-22877
                                                            CIP

Printed in the United States of America

BB

        9 0

To Sandy, Rachel, and Josh
for their love, inspiration and support.

CONTENTS

CONTENTS

Introduction

Creating a Winning Business Plan is a sequel to *How to Raise Capital,* a book that was published in 1984 and reprinted several times thereafter. *How to Raise Capital* was used as the standard against which a Chicago-based venture capital company conducted all of its acquisition analysis. It was used by many others to draft business plans that helped raise millions of dollars of venture capital. Others followed the book's format to convince bankers that their companies were good credit risks. College instructors used the book to teach business planning techniques to their students, on both the undergraduate and graduate level. *The Economist* magazine chose *How to Raise Capital* as one of its "essential books for the international managers."

Creating a Winning Business Plan is an updated and substantially improved publication that builds on the many strengths of *How to Raise Capital.* Its no-nonsense outline format will save the user many hours over books that provide lengthy narrative about the philosophy of writing a business plan. Invaluable insight is provided into concepts and terms behind key questions. The twenty principles behind writing an effective business plan are summarized in Chapter 1 for initial background and quick reference. Both the basic presentation and back-up data are provided for each of the two sample business plans at the end of this book, to give the user a better understanding of the research and analysis process that is essential to all effective business plans.

For users of *Creating a Winning Business Plan* who want to further improve and expedite the business planning process, the author is now making available a companion computer software product that is a special application of *Lotus Agenda.* Information about how to order this product may be found at the end of this book.

PART I

Asking and Answering the Right Questions

1

The Basics of Writing a Business Plan

THE BASICS

The benefits that an individual derives from writing a business plan are many. Both the finished product and the process of gathering, compiling, and analyzing information are invaluable to the business plan writer. Specifically, the business plan helps the writer accomplish the following:

1   Determine the feasibility of a particular venture

2   Raise start-up, expansion, or turnaround capital

3   Develop a "blueprint" for the operation of an entire company, a new profit center, or a specialized division

4   Create a budget, time frame, and strategic direction against which to measure the progress of the company

5   Focus on potential problems and high-risk areas for the purpose of developing solutions and contingency plans

6   Focus on market opportunities

7   Conduct in-depth due diligence

8   Persuade prospective members of the management team, customers, and/or suppliers that the company has a promising future

Creating a Winning Business Plan is based on twenty principles. These principles are presented below to provide a foundation for the user's business plan.

1   Business isn't conducted in a vacuum. Individual goals can only be accomplished by enlisting the support of others. AN EFFECTIVE BUSINESS PLAN IS A DETAILED, FACTUALLY SUPPORTED DOCUMENT THAT PERSUADES DECISION MAKERS TO ASSIST YOU IN ACHIEVING THE GOALS OUTLINED IN YOUR PLAN. Assistance by decision makers may be

THE BASICS

in the form of capital investment, political support, resource allocation, and/or agreements to buy products/services from your company or supply products/services to your company.

2   ADDRESS YOUR AUDIENCE. Don't use overly technical jargon or concepts and don't drown the reader with detail. REMEMBER THE READER'S BACK-GROUND AND WHAT HE or SHE IS LOOKING FOR (e.g., an average annual return on investment of 40 percent, a viable plan for cashing out the investor's interest in the company, introduction to a new technology).

3   ANTICIPATE QUESTIONS. Answer the who, what, where, when, why, and how questions about your venture.

4   THE WHY EXPLANATIONS ARE MOST IMPORTANT. For example, although it is informative to point out that direct mail is your advertising medium of choice (HOW you will advertise your products/services), it's more persuasive to support your explanation with the results of your extensive research and competitive analysis (WHY you chose direct mail).

5   Wherever possible, INCLUDE AUTHORITATIVE, FACTUAL SUPPORT in your business plan. Sources for this factual support include market research, focus group data, competitive intelligence, newspaper and magazine articles, data bases, government industry data, Securities and Exchange Commission (SEC) filings, trade association reports, and transcripts of interviews with industry experts.

6   USE SPECIFICS, NOT SUPERLATIVES. Rather than stating that in your opinion the industry has good growth potential, cite a current *Wall Street Journal* article that projects an annual growth rate over the next five years of 22 percent.

7   QUANTIFY YOUR GOALS. Target the level of market share, net margin, sales growth, and/or net income that you hope to achieve.

6

THE BASICS

8   When describing a process, procedure, or a numerical relationship, a picture is often worth a thousand words. Accordingly, USE A FLOW CHART OR GRAPH TO SIMPLIFY AND HIGHLIGHT YOUR MESSAGE.

9   BE CONSISTENT. If there is contradictory information in your business plan, your credibility will suffer.

10   LIMIT YOUR BUSINESS PLAN TO 40 PAGES. Detail, additional support, illustrations, exhibits, legal documentation, appraisals, competitive intelligence, articles, reports, due diligence items, and information of secondary importance should be placed in a separate "Appendix" volume.

11   Although you may write your business plan for the purpose of persuading others that your company's future is bright, remember that you will be the greatest beneficiary of your efforts. THE BUSINESS PLANNING PROCESS FORCES YOU TO TEST YOUR ASSUMPTIONS, RESEARCH YOUR MARKET, ANALYZE YOUR COMPETITION, AND EVALUATE THE OVERALL VIABILITY OF YOUR PLAN.

12   AN EFFECTIVE EXECUTIVE SUMMARY WILL "HOOK" THE READER and draw him or her into the business plan. Conversely, an executive summary that doesn't create reader excitement may eliminate an otherwise strong business plan from further consideration.

13   Remember that the QUALITY OF MANAGEMENT IS THE MOST IMPORTANT ELEMENT IN ANY BUSINESS PLAN. The best way to document the strength of the company's management team is to summarize highlights of its members' relevant experience, achievements, and track record.

14   DIFFERENTIATE YOUR PRODUCTS/SERVICES. Don't compete directly against the strengths of companies with greater resources. Identify differences in buyer needs that match your company's capabilities. Differentiation of your products/services provides insulation against competitive rivalry by creating loyal customers who are less sensitive to price.

15   YOUR DIFFERENTIATED PRODUCTS/SERVICES MUST SATISFY UN-FULFILLED MARKET NEEDS. Innovative product/service features, different marketing and distribution methods, superior locations, attractive pricing, and/or improved technologies, are of value only when market needs are satisfied.

16   PROVIDE EVIDENCE OF MARKET ACCEPTANCE FOR YOUR DIFFER-ENTIATED PRODUCTS/SERVICES. Use actual sales, purchase orders, market research, market test results, letters of intent, testimonials, trade show inquiries, interviews with prospective customers, and/or other information that demonstrates demand for your product.

17   IN-DEPTH COMPETITIVE ANALYSIS IS AN ESSENTIAL ELEMENT OF A SUCCESSFUL BUSINESS PLAN. Understanding the competitions' strengths and weaknesses, as well as your own, is key to uncovering market opportunities, creating defenses against attacks by competitors, and developing an effective differentiation strategy.

18   IN-DEPTH CUSTOMER ANALYSIS IS AN ESSENTIAL ELEMENT OF A SUCCESSFUL BUSINESS PLAN. Understanding, constantly monitoring, and responding to your customers' needs is essential to the success of your company.

19   THE MOST IMPORTANT PART OF YOUR FINANCIAL PROJECTIONS IS THE AUTHORITATIVE SUBSTANTIATION BEHIND YOUR ASSUMP-TIONS. Projected sales should be based on evidence of demand for your products/services (e.g., actual sales, orders, market research, letters of intent). Competitive analysis and supplier interviews support the validity of your expenses.

THE BASICS

20 DEFINE THE MAJOR PROBLEMS AND RISKS ASSOCIATED WITH YOUR COMPANY. Then use those problems and risks as a launching platform to EXPLAIN YOUR WELL THOUGHT OUT SOLUTIONS AND CONTINGENCY PLANS.

Creating a Winning Business Plan is organized like a workbook. Each section contains a series of questions that, if answered thoroughly, will inform the reader about the quality of the subject company or division. Not all the questions will be applicable in every situation. *Creating a Winning Business Plan* was designed to maximize flexibility. It was written for firms that offer both products and services, as well as companies that are both new and established. Accordingly, answer questions in the context of your particular situation. The stage of the company's development and the industry to which it belongs will also determine which questions apply.

Immediately below each question, the author has provided brief comments entitled **Insight**. These **Insights** were designed to give the user a helpful perspective from which to understand what information the reader of your business plan considers valuable — and more importantly, *why* the reader considers that information valuable. The **Insight** section also provides definitions of the concepts that these questions address. These definitions will not only help the aspiring entrepreneur answer the questions completely but will also serve as a general reference about important business principles and philosophies.

Often these **Insights** describe the ideal criteria that a reader of your business plan would find attractive. For example, prospective investors look for companies that are unencumbered by lawsuits, that serve sufficiently diversified markets, and whose management has no conflicts of interest. Of course, few, if any, companies can meet all the ideal criteria described in **Insight**.

Thus the user should not rely on **Insight** as a guide to telling readers only what they want to hear. Such an approach to writing a business plan will inevitably distort the facts about a company. Experienced readers are shrewd enough to detect any attempt to gloss over the problems and weaknesses of a particular company. You are more likely to persuade readers of your venture's viability if you show them what your company's

9

THE BASICS

problems are and how you plan to rectify them. The business planner who does not thoroughly explain those problems and weaknesses will no doubt fail to gain the reader's confidence and support.

Although *Creating a Winning Business Plan* is presented in any easy-to-follow question and answer format, the document you present to decision makers should not be simply a series of questions and answers. The format of this book should be used as a tool for gathering and organizing the data that you need to prepare your business plan. With the use of the information you develop from this book's format, we encourage the user to prepare a coherent, flowing narrative around the structure provided. To show how this is done, the author has included two business plans that were prepared by his students at the Keller Graduate School of Management.

To make best use of this book, the user should answer all the questions as fully as possible. As explained, not all questions may apply to your firm's particular situation, and some sections will deserve more extensive answers than others. But before you skip a question, make sure you fully understand why you have done so: the reader of your business plan will probably want to know why you avoided that issue. All the information should be accurately presented so that readers can make a valid assessment of the risks involved and the returns on investment that can be anticipated.

We believe *Creating a Winning Business Plan* gives an aspiring entrepreneur all the tools necessary to write a quality plan. This book not only addresses the issues that readers will think are essential, but also pinpoints the key considerations a manager must face to make his or her business grow and prosper. However, like most ventures, the success of the final product will be only a reflection of the effort put into it.

2

Background

BACKGROUND

1 In a one- to three-page summary, please describe the company's products/services, their user benefits, and evidence of their acceptance by customers; management's qualifications and major accomplishments; the amount of and uses for capital required; investor benefits; market size and growth rate; and the identity of the company's market niche.

☐ ☐ ☐ ☐ ☐ ☐

INSIGHT

An effective executive summary will hook readers and draw them into the business plan. Conversely, an executive summary that doesn't create reader excitement may eliminate an otherwise strong business plan from further consideration. Accordingly, management should devote the time and effort to composing a clear and convincing overview of the company's proposal. Explain to prospective investors what makes your venture worthy of financing and what rate of return they can expect to receive from your company.

---

2 Date of submission   ☐ ☐ ☐ ☐ ☐ ☐

3 Full legal name of the company   ☐ ☐ ☐ ☐ ☐ ☐

4 Address of home office   ☐ ☐ ☐ ☐ ☐ ☐

5 Phone number   ☐ ☐ ☐ ☐ ☐ ☐

6 Date business was established   ☐ ☐ ☐ ☐ ☐ ☐

Include
Don't Include
Research
Research Complete
Draft Written
Final

BACKGROUND

□ □ □ □ □ □   **7**   If applicable, please describe the company's original product/service line and any subsequent changes that have been made.

INSIGHT

Numerous changes in a company's product/service line can be either a positive or negative indication. Management's sensitivity to rapid market evolution may justify frequent changes in the company's product/service line. Subtle changes to a functionally superior product/service line, in response to changing customer needs, should help to maintain or even increase the company's market share. Conversely, substantial ongoing changes may be symptomatic of serious problems, (e.g., management's loss of touch with the company's target market, declining demand, technical obsolescence, superiority of competitors' products).

□ □ □ □ □ □   **8**   Please provide a physical and functional description of the company's current product/service line.

INSIGHT

Remember your audience and keep your description simple. Include USER BENEFITS in your explanation of product/service features.

□ □ □ □ □ □   **9**   Please provide the following information about each of the company's products/services: distinctive character-

BACKGROUND

Include
Don't Include
Research
Research Complete
Draft Written
Final

istics that will allow the company to successfully compete with larger and better capitalized companies, susceptibility to obsolescence, overwhelming economic justification, estimated length, and current phase of "product life cycle."

INSIGHT

Investors prefer a quality product/service, at a reasonable price, that has strong user benefits and demonstrable market need. Commercial and industrial products that directly reduce costs while maintaining or increasing quality are strong candidates for investment (e.g., computerized versus manual record keeping). Your product/service should have a defensible market niche, (e.g., it should be differentiated from competing products/services in ways that better satisfy customer needs). Differences may include such things as quality, style, technology (patents), and price. Products/services with differences that are perceived rather than tangible, or that are easy to duplicate, are thought to be highly risky by prospective investors.

Susceptibility to obsolescence *— The vulnerability that a product/service has to a rapid change in consumer purchasing behavior due generally to style, technology, design, value, or quality.*

Cost effectiveness/overwhelming economic justification *— The ability of a product or service to fulfill an essential need (e.g., not susceptible to a change in style or fashion) at lower cost than the competition, while offering equal or better quality.*

Product life cycle *— Recognition of the distinct phases in the sales history of a product or service. The four stages consist of introduction, growth, maturity, and decline.*

Include

Don't Include

Research

Research Complete

Draft Written

Final

BACKGROUND

With each phase there are corresponding opportunities and problems with respect to marketing, strategy, and profit. Typically, the company suffers losses through the introduction and early growth phases due to heavy start-up, organization, research, development, advertising, and promotion expenditures. During the latter growth stages, profits are achieved as old purchasing patterns are changed and market penetration increases. The maturity and decline phases are characterized by increasing competition and decreasing profit margins.

☐ ☐ ☐ ☐ ☐ ☐ **10** Please discuss the future potential of all promising new products/services that the company is now developing.

INSIGHT

An investor looks to future cash flow for return on investment. Future potential will depend on demand for your company's product/service, and management's ability to supply/provide that product/service to the market at an economically justifiable price. Because most markets are characterized by continuous change, a company's ability to perceive new trends and to develop, produce/provide, and market new products/services is extremely important.

☐ ☐ ☐ ☐ ☐ ☐ **11** To what extent are the company, its officers, property, and products insured? Please include summaries of all policies in the appendix.

BACKGROUND

INSIGHT

Insurance, while reducing cash flow, does provide a limit on property losses and contingent liabilities. Usually, lenders and investors will not fund a company until they receive evidence of insurance.

12 What are the advantages and disadvantages of the company's present locations (e.g., proximity to customers, suppliers, labor, energy sources, transportation; tax breaks; special financial arrangements)?

□ □ □ □ □ □

INSIGHT

Growing companies offer new jobs and incremental tax revenues. Accordingly, many countries, states and municipalities offer special financial incentives to attract viable businesses.

13 What is the company's legal structure (e.g., proprietorship, partnership, corporation)?

□ □ □ □ □ □

INSIGHT

For information on which legal structure best suits the company's situation, an attorney should be consulted.

Include
Don't Include
Research
Research Complete
Draft Written
Final

BACKGROUND

☐ ☐ ☐ ☐ ☐ ☐ **14** In what state is the company incorporated?

INSIGHT

A company's state of incorporation will affect some legal considerations. An attorney should be consulted for more information on this subject.

☐ ☐ ☐ ☐ ☐ ☐ **15** In what states is the company licensed to do business as a foreign corporation?

INSIGHT

Used in this context, the term FOREIGN CORPORATION is defined as a business that is operating in a state other than the one in which the business was incorporated.

☐ ☐ ☐ ☐ ☐ ☐ **16** Describe fully all lawsuits and legal actions threatened or pending against the company, its directors, management, and/or principals. If applicable, please include copies of lawsuits in the appendix.

INSIGHT

Lawsuits seldom present anything but problems. As the plaintiff (entity seeking legal relief), a small business has to expend a great deal of time and money to protect its legal rights, unless an attorney agrees to represent the company on a contingent basis (for a percentage of any judgement or settlement actually received by the company).

For the defendant (entity against which legal relief is being sought for alleged wrongdoing), a lawsuit represents a contingent liability (potential loss).

---

17   If any employees of the company are vulnerable to future lawsuits by former employers, please describe the potential problem(s) (e.g., violation of covenant-not-to-compete, use of proprietary technology, divulgence of privileged information).   ▢ ▢ ▢ ▢ ▢ ▢

INSIGHT

Covenant-not-to-compete *— Many companies, especially high-technology firms, suffer great losses when an employee leaves to join another company. The employee often takes existing customers, costly training, and vital secrets learned from the previous employer. Employees may be prevented from using or sharing such proprietary information if they previously signed a nondisclosure agreement. They can also be prevented, within certain limitations, from using their expertise to form another competing firm if they previously signed a covenant-not-to-compete. Thus, key employees who are recruited from competing companies may be vulnerable to certain legal actions. Accordingly, an attorney should be consulted before potentially damaging actions are taken.*

Include

Don't Include

Research

Research Complete

Draft Written

Final

BACKGROUND

☐ ☐ ☐ ☐ ☐ ☐ **18** Please explain all mergers, consolidations, and reorganizations that the company has gone through.

INSIGHT

Investors will look favorably on those companies whose mergers and acquisitions have contributed to profitability and growth. Please explain the major terms of and reasons for the acquisition, such as the cost, any debt incurred during the process of merging with or acquiring the company, and the benefits that are expected to be derived from the combination of the two companies.

☐ ☐ ☐ ☐ ☐ ☐ **19** Please list all subsidiaries, divisions, and branches of the company, including names, addresses, dates established, products, functions, and percentages owned by the company. Include a structural chart in the appendix.

INSIGHT

Listing subsidiaries and divisions provides the reader with an indication of how diversified the company is. Industry leaders have the resources to minimize exposure to large revenue swings by diversifying their product lines, locations, and the markets they serve. However, smaller ventures, especially start-ups, should concentrate their resources on narrow, defensible market niches, rather than spreading themselves too thin.

---

20   Please describe, in detail, all franchise, royalty, license, and working agreements that are presently in effect. Please include copies of these agreements in the appendix.   ❏ ❏ ❏ ❏ ❏ ❏

INSIGHT

A licensee is the user or distributor of another company's name, product, technology, or business format, in exchange for compensation that is paid to the licensor (e.g., royalty, license fee). The use of an established company's name and/or business format (e.g., McDonald's, Midas, H&R Block) can substantially add to the licensee's sales volume. However, in return, that licensee is obligated to pay a royalty, which is usually a fixed percentage of sales or unit volume regardless of the incremental profitability generated by the license agreement. As the licensor, the entity that grants the use of its name, technology, products, or format in exchange for compensation, a company can add to its revenue base without incurring additional fixed cost (e.g., add to its own capacity by acquiring plant and equipment). However, granting a license to a company that does not maintain a high level of quality control could seriously damage the licensor's image.

21   Please discuss the assignability of the company's beneficial agreements (e.g., licenses, royalty agreements, franchise agreements, employment contracts, customer contracts, supplier contracts, real estate leases).   ❏ ❏ ❏ ❏ ❏ ❏

Include
Don't Include
Research
Research Complete
Draft Written
Final

BACKGROUND

INSIGHT

If a company can sell, or assign for collateral purposes, its license to use a valuable name, technology, product, or process, it will own an asset that increases both its market value and borrowing power. This hidden value is not always reflected on the company's balance sheet.

***Assignability** — The right to transfer a contractual right from one party to another. For example, a franchisor may permit a franchisee to sell (assign) its rights to a third party.*

□ □ □ □ □ □ **22** Please describe, in detail, all of the company's patents issued and pending, the proprietary content of its products/services, and any brand/trade names that it owns. Please include copies of patents and trademarks in the appendix.

INSIGHT

Patents, trademarks, and proprietary information may provide a significant competitive advantage as well as additional value that is usually not reflected on the company's balance sheet.

3

Management

MANAGEMENT

1   For each officer of the company, please provide the ☐ ☐ ☐ ☐ ☐ ☐
    following information: name, age, number of years ex-
    perience in the company's industry, number of years
    with company, responsibilities/functions of positions
    held with company; salary, bonus, ownership interest in
    the company; relevant qualities, achievements, track
    record, and education.

INSIGHT

*The quality of management is probably the most impor-
tant factor that an investor will consider. To most investors,
class A management with a class B product is preferable
to class B management with a class A product. Typically
the team should be divided along the functional lines of
the firm, (e.g., marketing, finance). The ultimate success
of any venture will depend on the abilities, experience,
track record, and commitment of the management team.
Other factors that investors favor include the following:
1) stock ownership and/or stock options that provide
management with incentives for both performance and
long-term employment by the company, 2) common long-
term goals between management and the investor group.
A management team with a primary objective to develop
state-of-the-art technologies will not be well received by
an investor group that looks for market driven prod-
ucts/services. From the investor's perspective, the company may develop innovative technologies for which a
market does not exist.*

Include
Don't Include
Research
Research Complete
Draft Written
Final

MANAGEMENT

☐ ☐ ☐ ☐ ☐ ☐ **2** In the appendix, please include resumes for all members of the management team, all members of the Board of Directors, and shareholders with a 10 percent or greater interest in the company.

☐ ☐ ☐ ☐ ☐ ☐ **3** What are the ultimate personal objectives of each officer and director, relative to the company (e.g., go public in five years, buy out other investors, build an industry-leading company, sell out to a larger competitor, make state-of-the-art technology available to the public)?

☐ ☐ ☐ ☐ ☐ ☐ **4** Please provide the following information about each director who is not also an officer of the company: name, age, other corporate affiliations, compensation by company, ownership interest in company (e.g., number of shares, warrants, stock options), relevant experience, and special contributions to management.

INSIGHT

Directors should contribute expertise, experience, and beneficial personal contacts to the company.

☐ ☐ ☐ ☐ ☐ ☐ **5** What are the strengths and weaknesses of the company's management team and its board of directors?

INSIGHT

Investors prefer a management team that can both identify and compensate for its shortcomings. Accordingly, the

MANAGEMENT

business plan should not ignore or hide the weaknesses of the company's management team and board of directors.

---

6   Please describe all significant changes in the management of the company that have occurred over the last five years.   ☐ ☐ ☐ ☐ ☐ ☐

INSIGHT

Repeated changes in the management team are viewed as an indication of instability. Occasional additions to the core management team may be viewed as a process of continual improvement depending on the capabilities of new management personnel and associated levels of compensation.

---

7   References will be contacted for the purpose of obtaining additional information about the company, its products/services, and the integrity/capability of management. For each member of the company's management team, please include several professional references in the appendix.   ☐ ☐ ☐ ☐ ☐ ☐

INSIGHT

If available, include letters of recommendation in the appendix.

Include
Don't Include
Research
Research Complete
Draft Written
Final

MANAGEMENT

☐ ☐ ☐ ☐ ☐ ☐   **8**   In the appendix, please list the organizations that will be providing professional counsel to the company (e.g., legal, accounting, advertising, public relations, banking, insurance).

INSIGHT

Quality professional help, although possibly more expensive, will increase the company's probability of success. In addition to direct benefits, professionals offer introductions to potentially helpful individuals and organizations (e.g., investors, lenders, employees, customers, suppliers, and distributors).

☐ ☐ ☐ ☐ ☐ ☐   **9**   How will the company add capable members to its management team?

INSIGHT

In addition to growing beyond their capital bases, most small businesses fail because they outgrow the capabilities of their management team. Therefore, the degree of success enjoyed by a rapidly growing business will be limited by its ability to attract and train new management.

☐ ☐ ☐ ☐ ☐ ☐   **10**   How will the management team grow and continually improve itself?

MANAGEMENT

INSIGHT

W. Edwards Deming is the individual credited for revital-izing the Japanese post World War II economy. His man-agement philosophy stresses the need for everyone and every department in a successful company to commit themselves to constant improvement. In her book, The Deming Management Method (Pedigree Books, 1986) Mary Walton discusses Dr. Deming's belief that only management can initiate improvement in quality and productivity, i.e., production workers on their own can achieve very little. In a summary of his management philosophy, Dr. Deming suggests that: 1) a company without constancy of purpose lacks a long-range plan for staying in business, 2) emphasis on short-term profits undermines quality and productivity, 3) individual perfor-mance ratings of employees discourages team work and encourages short-term performance at the expense of long-term planning, 4) management must continually look for ways to reduce waste and improve quality, 5) mobility of top management prevents commitment to long-term change, 6) judging the company's performance only on the basis of its financial statements ignores the importance of essential intangibles like customer satisfac-tion.

In order to initiate change, Dr. Deming suggests that the company follow the Shewhart Cycle: 1) study the process to decide what change might improve it, 2) carry out the test or make the change, preferably on a small scale, 3) observe the effects, 4) study test results, 5) repeat the cycle.

Include	Don't Include	Research	Research Complete	Draft Written	Final

MANAGEMENT

☐ ☐ ☐ ☐ ☐ ☐ **11** Please discuss conflicts of interest that members of the company's management team or board of directors may have (e.g., other business interests, ownership in a competing company).

INSIGHT

Conflicts of interest — *Conflicts of interest exist when an individual owes his or her loyalties to more than one firm. When such conflicts exist, the fiduciary relationship between the employer and the employee is endangered. One example of a conflict of interest would occur when an employee of one firm buys goods from a second firm, of which he or she is a member of the board of directors. Thus, his or her ability to conduct business in an unbiased manner is open to question. Such practices are vulnerable to legal action by shareholders and creditors, as well as government agencies.*

Fiduciary — *A person who has a duty created by his or her undertaking to act primarily for the benefit of another.*

☐ ☐ ☐ ☐ ☐ ☐ **12** If any member of the management team will not be devoting 100 percent of his or her time to the company, please explain why.

INSIGHT

Investors usually demand that management devote 110 percent of its efforts to the company.

MANAGEMENT

13 How will the company protect itself from the prospect of future competition with defecting members of its management team? Please include employment agreements, covenants-not-to-compete, and non-disclosure agreements in the appendix.

☐ ☐ ☐ ☐ ☐ ☐

INSIGHT

Many successful firms face competition from firms created by their former employees. Lack of protection is a liability.

14 Please evaluate the depth of the company's management team. Where applicable, explain how the management team will compensate for its lack of depth.

☐ ☐ ☐ ☐ ☐ ☐

INSIGHT

Stronger companies have sufficient depth of management to sustain the illness, disability, or loss of key individuals without suffering significant damage.

15 Please evaluate the management team's ability to cover each of the company's functional areas. Where applicable, explain how the management team will compensate for any functional weaknesses.

☐ ☐ ☐ ☐ ☐ ☐

Include
Don't Include
Research
Research Complete
Draft Written
Final

MANAGEMENT

INSIGHT

The strength of the company's management team will partly depend on the diversity of its members' backgrounds. A management team that has an abundance of marketing talent but a weak financial department will be less likely to succeed than a more balanced group.

□ □ □ □ □ □ **16** Please provide an organization chart that reflects the company's management hierarchy.

INSIGHT

An organization chart illustrates the division of responsibilities among the various members of management as well as the functional emphasis within the company (e.g., a medical practice might be proficient at delivering its services but very weak at marketing).

4

Ownership

OWNERSHIP

Include

Don't Include

Research

Research Complete

Draft Written

Final

1   In the appendix, please include all current owners (e.g.,   ☐ ☐ ☐ ☐ ☐ ☐
individuals, corporations, trusts, Employee Stock Own-
ership Plans) of the company's common and preferred
stock.

INSIGHT

*The higher the caliber of current investors, the more likely
that new investors will purchase your company's shares.*

Common stock *— Ownership rights in the company
issued to investors in exchange for cash and/or other
assets. Common stockholders have the right to elect the
company's board of directors, who in turn appoint top
management. Common stockholders have residual rights
to the net income and net assets of the company subject
to restrictions imposed by the contractual rights of creditors and other interested parties. The return on investment
available to common stockholders is not fixed in amount
or specified as to date. However, if the company is
liquidated, creditors' claims and the claims of preferred
stockholders usually have priority. Conversely, no matter
how successful the company, a creditor's return will be
limited to principal and interest. Thus, the common stockholder assumes greater risk than a creditor or preferred
shareholder, but has an opportunity for a virtually unlim-
ited return on his or her investment.*

Preferred stock *— Similar to common stock, preferred
shares are issued by the company in exchange for capital.
Although the characteristics of preferred stock may vary
widely, preferred shareholders rarely participate in the
election of the company's board of directors. Usually
preferred shareholders are entitled to a fixed dividend,
similar to interest on debt, and/or proceeds from the
liquidation of the company's assets, up to a specified*

Include

Don't Include

Research

Research Complete

Draft Written

Final

O W N E R S H I P

maximum per share. Preferred shareholders receive their share of liquidation proceeds after creditors but usually before common stockholders. The dividend preference is usually cumulative, meaning all back dividends must be paid to the preferred shareholders before common share-holders receive dividend distributions. Unlike debt, preferred stock does not entitle the holder to insist on dividend or principal payments by specified dates.

 **2**   In the appendix, please list all prospective owners of the company's common and preferred stock, and the number of shares available under warrants, conversion privileges, and employee stock bonus/option agreements.

INSIGHT

Prospective purchasers of the company's stock will want to compute their ownership position as a percentage of present and future (fully diluted) shares outstanding. This figure, when used in conjunction with the financial projections, will allow the investor to calculate return on investment.

Conversion privileges *— Used to increase the appeal of conventional debt and preferred stock to investors. Some preferred stocks have conversion privileges which allow shareholders to convert preferred shares into common shares by use of a specified formula (e.g., two shares of preferred for one share of common). Debt instruments sometimes carry similar conversion privileges (e.g., $100 of principal for one share of common).*

Warrants *— Similar to stock options, warrants entitle the holder to purchase a specified number of common shares, at a specified price, by a specified date. Warrants are*

OWNERSHIP

Include
Don't Include
Research
Research Complete
Draft Written
Final

usually offered to investors as an incentive to purchase other instruments with which the warrants are combined.

Employee stock options — Similar to stock bonuses, stock options are used as an additional form of employee compensation. An option entitles the holder to purchase a specified amount of common stock, at a specified price, by a specified date. The holder hopes that appreciation of the market price of the underlying common stock will increase beyond the specified exercise price, resulting in substantial profits for the employee. Stock options and stock bonuses provide employees with both a performance incentive and an incentive to remain with the company.

Employee stock bonuses — Generally used as an additional form of employee compensation, stock bonuses consist of shares of common stock that are given to employees as a reward for outstanding performance. Employee stock bonuses offer rapidly growing companies an opportunity to meet or exceed the compensation packages offered by larger competitors without depleting cash flow.

---

3 Please explain what protection investors have against future dilution of their ownership position (e.g., preemptive rights.) ☐ ☐ ☐ ☐ ☐ ☐

INSIGHT

Dilution — If an investor owns 10 shares out of a total outstanding of 100, he or she owns 10 percent of the company (10/100 = 10%). If the company subsequently sells another hundred shares to a third party, the investor's

Include

Don't Include

Research

Research Complete

Draft Written

Final

OWNERSHIP

position will be reduced (diluted) to 5 percent (10/200 = 5%).

Preemptive rights — *An existing stockholder is given the right of first refusal on subsequent stock offerings in proportion to his or her ownership percentage prior to the offering. For example, in the above illustration, the investor would be offered ten of the 100 new shares sold to maintain its 10 percent ownership position.*

□ □ □ □ □ □ **4** Please discuss restrictions on the transferability or collateral value of the company's shares.

INSIGHT

Restriction on transferability — *Certain securities laws restrict the sale or transfer of stock, especially stock not registered with the SEC. Since the stock of most small businesses is not registered, the market for their stock is severely limited.*

□ □ □ □ □ □ **5** In the appendix, please include buy/sell agreements that pertain to the company's shares.

INSIGHT

Properly structured, a buy/sell agreement provides for the future sale of a business upon the death or departure of one of the principals. Often financed through a life insurance plan covering the principals, the agreement provides for an orderly transfer of a business interest to a designated heir, employee, stockholder, or partner. These agreements enhance the value of the firm to investors because they assure continuity of the firm's ownership.

---

6   Do the company's shares have cumulative voting rights?   ☐ ☐ ☐ ☐ ☐ ☐

INSIGHT

Cumulative voting rights — *Under cumulative voting, simultaneous elections are held for all board positions, and each share of stock represents as many votes as there are board positions (e.g., 1,000 shares voting for five board positions would yield 5,000 total votes). Votes may be accumulated by shareholders and cast in favor of a particular candidate, thus improving minority shareholders' chances of electing at least one representative on the board of directors. If a firm does not have cumulative voting rights, each share of stock represents one vote for purposes of electing the board of directors. Separate elections are held for each board position, making it very difficult for minority shareholders to obtain representation on the board. Cumulative voting is preferred by advocates of corporate democracy, but it remains the exception rather than the rule.*

---

7   If applicable, please describe the company's Employee   ☐ ☐ ☐ ☐ ☐ ☐
Stock Ownership Plan/Trust. Include a copy of the plan in the appendix.

Include
Don't Include
Research
Research Complete
Draft Written
Final

OWNERSHIP

INSIGHT

Employee Stock Ownership Plan/Trust (ESOP/ESOT) *—
Vehicles that a company can use to shift ownership from
a small control group to the company's employees. In
addition to some very favorable tax benefits, ESOPs and
ESOTs represent an alternative method of raising equity
capital while simultaneously providing ownership incentives to employees. An attorney should be consulted for
discussion of the many complexities involved.*

5

Employees

EMPLOYEES

1 How many people have been employed by the company in each of the last three years (actual), and how many will be employed in each of the next three years (projected)?

☐ ☐ ☐ ☐ ☐ ☐

INSIGHT

All areas of your business require future planning. With some lead time, contingency plans can be prepared that either prevent or help to solve problems.

2 How easily can the size of the company's labor force be adjusted to fluctuations in sales volume?

☐ ☐ ☐ ☐ ☐ ☐

INSIGHT

Generally, the company's ability to conserve cash flow by decreasing fixed labor costs during periods of lower sales volume is a substantial asset. However, some management philosophies advocate lifetime retention of employees regardless of economic circumstances. This approach is believed to foster greater loyalty and valuable employee experience. Others argue that without the ability to reduce payroll, the company may not survive, which would leave all employees without jobs.

Include
Don't Include
Research
Research Complete
Draft Written
Final

EMPLOYEES

☐ ☐ ☐ ☐ ☐ ☐   **3**   If the company requires highly skilled employees, please discuss their functions, anticipated compensation, and the degree of difficulty involved in both locating and hiring qualified personnel.

INSIGHT

The greater the scarcity of certain key employees, the more vulnerable the company will be to crippling personnel losses. If a company relies heavily on highly skilled personnel, management must prepare a plan to attract and retain key employees. For example, a company's wages and benefits for key employees may exceed the competition's when the value of stock options and stock bonuses are included. The company's geographic location, special amenities, and the challenge of working for a young, emerging company may provide significant psychic income to employees.

☐ ☐ ☐ ☐ ☐ ☐   **4**   Please provide the history and current status of the company's labor relations, including any strikes or work stoppages.

INSIGHT

A history of strikes and work stoppages suggests that there are problems within the firm that management has failed to rectify. In any case, investors will be wary of recurring labor problems that could reduce productivity, cause work stoppages, and damage employee morale. (While you may be tempted not to disclose negative information,

E M P L O Y E E S

Include
Don't Include
Research
Research Complete
Draft Written
Final

doing so could mislead the reader or cause the reader to question the writer's honesty.)

5   Please discuss the company's historical labor turnover.   ❏ ❏ ❏ ❏ ❏ ❏

INSIGHT

Frequent labor turnover negatively impacts quality, productivity, and employee morale. Costs required to train replacement employees are substantial.

6   What percent of total employees will be skilled versus unskilled over the next three years?   ❏ ❏ ❏ ❏ ❏ ❏

INSIGHT

Skilled employees may be more difficult to locate and train, and may also demand higher salaries. Unskilled labor is usually perceived as less reliable and more transient. Accordingly, management is less likely to lay off or terminate skilled than unskilled labor during economic downturns.

7   Please describe the local labor market and how it affects the company (e.g., cost of labor relative to other parts of the country, skilled and unskilled labor availability, and union concentration).   ❏ ❏ ❏ ❏ ❏ ❏

Include
Don't Include
Research
Research Complete
Draft Written
Final

EMPLOYEES

INSIGHT

Some companies will choose their location based on the depth, quality, and average compensation level of available labor.

□ □ □ □ □ □ **8** What are the company's union affiliations?

INSIGHT

If the relationship is cooperative rather than adversarial, union affiliations can have a positive effect on the company. If unions and management believe that their goals and objectives are incompatible, labor relations will be strained.

□ □ □ □ □ □ **9** What has been the company's direct labor cost as a percent of sales during each of the last three years (actual), and what will it be in each of the next three years (projected)?

INSIGHT

If most of the company's cost of goods/services sold is attributable to labor costs, it is labor-intensive. If most of the company's cost of goods/services sold is attributable to investment in machinery, plant, and equipment, it is capital-intensive. Labor intensity may indicate an oppor-

EMPLOYEES

Include
Don't Include
Research
Research Complete
Draft Written
Final

tunity for increased productivity through automation. Also, a labor-intensive operation is sometimes thought to be more flexible during economic contractions because employees can be laid off or terminated more easily than machinery, plant, and equipment can be sold and later repurchased. Others argue that certain employee benefits, union agreements, and pension fund liabilities make both options equally unattractive.

10 How does the company's compensation program compare with competitors' (i.e., salary plus benefits/perquisites)?

☐ ☐ ☐ ☐ ☐ ☐

INSIGHT

Smaller companies that don't provide salary/wage/benefit packages comparable to those of larger competitors should direct the attention of prospective employees to other forms of compensation discussed in Insight for question Employees 3.

11 Please describe all benefits/perquisites that are made available to employees (e.g., pension plan, profit-sharing plan, bonus plan, employee stock ownership plan, life/medical insurance, subsidized lunches, on-premises employee athletic facilities). Please include copies of plans in the appendix.

☐ ☐ ☐ ☐ ☐ ☐

Include
Don't Include
Research
Research Complete
Draft Written
Final

EMPLOYEES

INSIGHT

Larger companies claim that employee benefits account for up to one-third of their employee compensation package. Although benefits have become an integral part of employee compensation for virtually all companies, management should not over-burden its cost structure with numerous expensive perks. To protect the company's long-term financial health, management should emphasize benefits that are directly tied to the company's success.

□ □ □ □ □ □ **12** Please describe the company's employee recruiting, training and development programs.

INSIGHT

Employees are an invaluable company resource that should be fully utilized through progressive recruiting, training, evaluation, and compensation programs. Training and development programs should include objective, quantifiable methods of measuring progress coupled with commensurate rewards. However, to encourage cooperation, some business consultants believe that employees should be evaluated on a team rather than individual basis. In any case, employees should feel that they are both fairly judged and rewarded against long-term objectives.

EMPLOYEES

13 How will the company continually improve the quality of its employees? ☐ ☐ ☐ ☐ ☐ ☐

INSIGHT

In reference to his management philosophy of continual improvement of employees, Dr. Deming suggests the following: 1) create constancy of purpose for improvement of product and service, 2) qualified instructors should train and retrain all employees including management, 3) supervisors should lead, not dictate or punish, 4) encourage employees to ask questions and take positions, 5) break down barriers between staff areas, 6) give employees the best supervision, materials, and equipment to promote pride of achievement.

6

Investment Criteria

INVESTMENT CRITERIA

1 What amount of financing is the company requesting from all sources for the next three years? ☐ ☐ ☐ ☐ ☐ ☐

INSIGHT

Don't understate your funding needs, or the viability of your company could be threatened when you need additional growth and/or development capital. Prospective investors may also question the competence of your financial management if you ask for less than you actually need. Staged cash infusions, as discussed in Insight for question Investment Criteria 3, usually make sense for both the company and the investor.

---

2 What is the company's preferred form of financing (e.g., senior debt, subordinated debt, convertible debt, preferred stock, common stock)? ☐ ☐ ☐ ☐ ☐ ☐

INSIGHT

The various forms of debt and equity that a company can use to fund itself each have their own advantages and disadvantages. Generally, the cost to the company for borrowed funds is predetermined at a reasonable increment over the prime rate. Unfortunately, the borrowing capacity of the company is usually limited to a percentage of its collateral value. Also, if the company misses a scheduled payment, the lender can foreclose on its collateral. Equity doesn't obligate the company to a repayment schedule. However, the marketability of the company's equity is limited by its historical and projected

INVESTMENT CRITERIA

Include
Don't Include
Research
Research Complete
Draft Written
Final

performance. Equity investors also require a higher rate of return than lenders, to compensate them for the higher risk.

□ □ □ □ □ □ **3** When will the requested financing be needed? If multiple takedowns are feasible, list schedule of dates, amounts, and purposes.

INSIGHT

Investors usually prefer to stage cash infusions rather than disbursing funds in a lump sum. This practice allows the investor to withhold future disbursements if the company does not achieve certain mutually agreed upon measurements of performance, (e.g., orders, sales, earnings), by certain specified dates.

□ □ □ □ □ □ **4** Please discuss the purpose(s) for which the requested funds will be used (e.g., general working capital needs, marketing, research and development, purchase of capital equipment).

INSIGHT

How the company spends investors' funds directly affects the level of risk associated with that investment. For example, an expenditure of funds on research and development or advertising would not produce the marketable asset value of an expenditure on real estate and machinery. Therefore, investments that will be used to pay

INVESTMENT
CRITERIA

Include
Don't Include
Research
Research Complete
Draft Written
Final

for intangibles are thought to be riskier than those that will be used to purchase hard assets.

---

5 On a fully diluted basis, approximately what percent of the company's stock is the present ownership group offering to its investors?

❏ ❏ ❏ ❏ ❏ ❏

INSIGHT

Some investors prefer at least 51 percent of the company's shares, or an option to acquire at least 51 percent, in order to have the ability to exercise control. Management may want an option to repurchase a controlling interest in the company based on a mutually agreed upon price or formula.

***Fully diluted** — Assumes that all warrants, options, conversion rights and bonus plans are exercised. Thus, in the earnings-per-share calculations, the number of shares is the sum of the number of shares actually outstanding plus shares potentially outstanding.*

---

6 What annual rate of return is the company offering to equity investors?

❏ ❏ ❏ ❏ ❏ ❏

INSIGHT

Smaller businesses, start-up companies, and companies going through periods of rapid growth are viewed as risk-intensive. Universally, investors expect the assump-

Include
Don't Include
Research
Research Complete
Draft Written
Final

INVESTMENT CRITERIA

tion of higher risk to offer the opportunity for greater return. Accordingly, investors usually seek current yield (e.g., interest on debt) and/or equity appreciation (e.g., ownership of a portion of the company in anticipation of an increase in the value of the company). The expected annual rate of return can range from several points over the prime rate to 60 percent, depending on the company's stage of development, management's track record, actual and projected sales, actual and projected net income, financial condition, amount and quality of collateral. Generally, an equity investor calculates his or her anticipated rate of return by multiplying projected earnings in year five by the average price/earnings ratio for publicly traded companies in the same industry, multiplying by the percentage of the company that is offered for purchase, and then solving for the internal-rate-of-return based on the total projected investment. For information on how to calculate the internal-rate-of-return, consult any basic corporate finance text.

☐ ☐ ☐ ☐ ☐ ☐   **7**   How and when will equity investors be repaid (e.g., public offering, sale of equity to a larger company, management buyout)?

INSIGHT

An often neglected, but extremely important, part of every equity financing proposal is the exit strategy. Unlike lenders who have a contractual right to return of their principal over a specified period of time, equity investors usually have to wait for someone to purchase their shares. The three most likely purchasers are management, larger companies that are either in the same industry or looking for an entree into the industry, and the public. To support your exit strategy, include information about the sale of other companies in your industry, especially data about the pricing of those companies.

---

8   How many shares of the company's common stock will remain authorized but not issued after this offering?   ❑ ❑ ❑ ❑ ❑ ❑

INSIGHT

The number of shares authorized determines the maximum number that may be issued without further action by the board of directors. The company is not obligated to issue the full number of shares authorized.

---

9   Are the company's shares publicly traded? If so, in the appendix, please include copies of the company's most recent stock offering memorandum and accompanying SEC filings.   ❑ ❑ ❑ ❑ ❑ ❑

INSIGHT

Because publicly traded companies are regulated by the Securities and Exchange Commission, the amount, accuracy, and availability of information is usually superior to that of private companies. The shares of a publicly traded company can also be sold more easily.

☐ ☐ ☐ ☐ ☐ ☐ **10** If the company is seeking bank financing, what rate, term and structure will be requested?

INSIGHT

The borrower should include a term sheet with the amount, rate, purpose, collateral, and repayment schedule for the requested loan.

☐ ☐ ☐ ☐ ☐ ☐ **11** What collateral (include approximate current market values), letters of credit, and personal guarantees are the company and its principals willing to offer? In the appendix, please include copies of personal financial statements for principal stockholders and other individuals who have agreed to personally guarantee loans to the company.

INSIGHT

Lenders look to cash flow as their primary means of repayment. As a secondary means of repayment, collateral offers assurance of repayment regardless of the successful operation of the company. Both investors and lenders look favorably on personal guarantees; they view such guarantees as a performance bond that makes the principals think twice before walking away from the company during difficult times. Personal guarantees are also confirmations of management's total commitment to the company.

Letter of credit *— A guarantee of payment by a third party whose credit is substantially stronger than the credit of the* *party who is directly obligated to make the payment. For example, if a bank is fully collateralized, it may issue a letter of credit on the company's behalf to a supplier who would otherwise ask for cash-on-delivery. In effect, the bank has substituted its own credit for the weaker credit of its customer. The bank customer benefits by not having to borrow funds, at considerable expense, to make immediate payment.*

12 Please list all capital sources (e.g., banks, individuals, institutional investors, suppliers) that have either committed or disbursed credit/funds to the company, and the amounts and terms of their commitments (e.g., pricing, collateral, amortization schedule, restrictive covenants, call provisions, percentage of total equity purchased).

▢ ▢ ▢ ▢ ▢ ▢

INSIGHT

The funding of the company's assets should be carefully structured to assure a proper balance between debt and equity, and a repayment schedule that is comfortably covered by projected cash flow. Accordingly, investors will want to know about the company's obligations to other financing sources before committing its own funds.

Amortization schedule — A schedule used to calculate the amounts and dates of interest and principal payments that must be made to retire a loan over a specified time period. This schedule represents a contractual agreement between the lender and the borrower. Accordingly, the borrower's failure to make a scheduled payment constitutes default and entitles the lender to pursue its legal remedies.

Restrictive covenants — Restrictions on the borrower that are in force during the life of the loan agreement. These restrictions may prevent the company from borrowing additional funds, selling its fixed assets, paying dividends to shareholders, or engaging in any activity that reduces the firm's ability to repay its loan.

Call provisions — A call provision entitles the company to repay all or a portion of its loan before the scheduled maturity date. Naturally, the company would only retire a callable bond that could be refinanced more cheaply (e.g., if market interest rates fall or if the market price for the company's stock increases).

Any gains received by the company through the call provision will be at the expense of the investor, who must reinvest his or her principal at lower market interest rates. Thus, investors find callable bonds to be less attractive and expect them to carry a higher interest rate than standard bonds.

□ □ □ □ □ □   **13**   In the appendix, please include a list of all lenders/investors from which the company has sought but not received financing and associated explanations of why the company's requests were rejected.

INSIGHT

Companies that have shopped the market for funding with little success are viewed negatively by prospective investors. Therefore, the company should acquaint itself with the portfolio requirements of each investor before preparing its prospect list.

7

Marketing Strategy

MARKETING STRATEGY

1   What is the approximate size, in units and dollars, of the ☐ ☐ ☐ ☐ ☐ ☐
target market for each of the company's products/services? In the appendix, please include market surveys, competitive intelligence, media reports, government industry data, SEC filings, trade association reports, transcripts of interviews with industry experts, and other support.

INSIGHT

Investors prefer a large market with both a previous history and future expectations of growth exceeding 20 percent per year. Smaller market growth rates are acceptable if the company is clearly a leader in its industry with a history of increasing market share. The investor will evaluate the market on the basis of several criteria in addition to the size and growth of the market: 1) strength of the competition, 2) number of major competitors, 3) profit margins, 4) barriers to entry (e.g., technical, proprietary, financial), 5) threat of substitute products, 6) bargaining power of customers, 7) bargaining power of suppliers. Investors will then decide whether the company's strengths, weaknesses, and overall strategic plan are complementary to its market. For example, the consumer products industry is dominated by marketing giants such as Proctor & Gamble, Colgate Palmolive, and Lever Brothers. Unless a competitor can afford to match multibillion dollar national advertising budgets (even on a local basis advertising budgets typically run in the millions of dollars), it should consider another industry.

Total market *— A market consists of prospective buyers who are willing and able to purchase a company's products/services. The definition centers around buyers, not products. Thus, if the buyers' needs shift and the company*

MARKETING STRATEGY

finds demand for its products slipping, the company must develop a new product line that better meets the needs of its market. Thus, the firm must always define its market and center its marketing plans around buyers and their anticipated needs.

☐ ☐ ☐ ☐ ☐ ☐   **2**   Please provide management's estimate of the company's market share and associated industry rank for both the last three years (actual) and the next three years (projected).

INSIGHT

Market share — *Represents the percentage of the total market that the company serves on a dollar sales basis or on a unit sales basis. A firm is said to be dominant if it controls the largest market share. The difficulty lies in defining exactly what market the company serves. A hot dog stand and a hamburger stand may both serve the fast food market, yet they also serve autonomous hot dog and hamburger markets. The firms might be dominant in each of their respective markets, while only one firm is dominant in the fast food market.*

Several studies have demonstrated the link between dominant market share and increased profitability. Historically, IBM achieved greater profitability through its economies of scale in production and advertising by spreading the costs of these functions across a larger number of units sold. By devoting its greater resources to research and development, IBM was also able to provide its customers with technology that set the industry standard. Thus, it could demand a premium for its products in the market place and further perpetuate its dominance over the industry.

Market share strategies for new products vary. Management may elect to keep prices relatively low, while building market share to prevent competitors from entering the market. After establishing a dominant market share, the company can afford to compete on superior terms and therefore raise prices.

However, others believe that while a company with a new product has the entire market to itself, it should charge a premium price to recapture its development costs as quickly as possible. This strategy may be appropriate if the company has patent protection or another significant competitive edge.

3 What has been the growth and profitability history of the company's target markets, and what are its future prospects? If the projected growth rate exceeds the historical growth rate, discuss the major factors behind the company's assumptions (e.g., technological breakthroughs, lower production costs that can be passed on to customers).

□ □ □ □ □ □

INSIGHT

Generally, rapidly growing markets are preferred to slowly growing or shrinking markets. However, companies with a dominant market share and/or a significant competitive advantage can generate substantial profits in otherwise unattractive markets.

MARKETING STRATEGY

Technological breakthrough — *A technological innovation that substantially enhances the user benefits of the company's products/services. The hand-held calculator market experienced many technological breakthroughs that led to mass production techniques and resultant lower prices to the consumer. Breakthroughs enable newer firms to compete on a more equal basis with established rivals, thereby offsetting the greater financial resources and broader marketing base of established competitors.*

☐ ☐ ☐ ☐ ☐ ☐ **4**   In which geographic areas are the company's sales concentrated?

INSIGHT

The geographic markets in which the company's products/services are sold will have a direct impact on its marketing plan. For instance, the appropriate marketing mix will differ considerably when its products/services are marketed to rural versus urban areas, or the east coast versus the deep south.

When marketing a new product nationally, great care must be taken to introduce the product in regions of the country where the company's distribution is the strongest, and where advertising dollars can be most effectively spent. Geographic market concentration may be viewed as a liability due to the increased economic volatility of local markets. For example, if a company markets its products exclusively in the midwest, high unemployment in the basic manufacturing industries would have a more severe impact on the company than if it also marketed its

Include	Don't Include	Research	Research Complete	Draft Written	Final

products in the high-tech areas of the sunbelt. However, premature national expansion could eliminate economies of scale and overextend the company's resources.

---

5 Please explain why customers have purchased/will purchase the company's products/services. What benefits do your products/services offer to your customers (e.g., quality, service, price, styling, convenience, improved technology)? What previously unsatisfied customer needs do the company's products/services fulfill?

☐ ☐ ☐ ☐ ☐ ☐

INSIGHT

To serve its market best, the company must constantly update its understanding of why customers purchase its products/services.

Companies that lose touch with their customers expose themselves to loss of market share via increased market penetration by competitors. Instead of thinking about the company in terms of the products/services it sells, all employees should focus on the benefits that the company offers to its customers and the needs that those benefits satisfy.

Underlying customer needs *— Products/services are often purchased for other than functional reasons. Charles Revson, former president of Revlon, once stated that in the factory Revlon makes cosmetics, but in the drug store Revlon sells hope. Expensive cars sometimes sell for the status they represent rather than their superior engineering. Rugged outdoor wear is occasionally purchased for the macho image it projects rather than its durability.*

Include
Don't Include
Research
Research Complete
Draft Written
Final

MARKETING
STRATEGY

Certainly, if the company is aware of the underlying needs and desires that affect customers' purchasing habits, it can more effectively market its products/services.

☐ ☐ ☐ ☐ ☐ ☐   **6**   Please provide evidence that your products/services satisfy unfulfilled market needs (e.g., actual sales, purchase orders, market research, market test results, letters of intent, testimonials, trade show inquiries, interviews with prospective customers). Summarize your data in the body of the business plan. Include detail in the appendix.

INSIGHT

Evidence of market demand will significantly increase the company's chances of raising equity capital, attracting quality salespeople/distributors, recruiting superior management, and earning the confidence of suppliers. The stronger the evidence, the higher the company's probability of success. This component is potentially one of the most persuasive elements of the entire business plan.

☐ ☐ ☐ ☐ ☐ ☐   **7**   What are the social, behavioral, and demographic characteristics of the company's customer base/target market?

INSIGHT

Management's ability to accurately define the characteristics of its market is essential to planning the optimal

MARKETING
STRATEGY

Include
Don't Include
Research
Research Complete
Draft Written
Final

differentiation strategy (please see Insight for question Competitive Analysis 5 (Chapter 8) for more information about differentiation strategies).

Market characteristics — Markets can be divided into different sectors, each possessing a homogeneous set of characteristics affecting purchasing behavior. Marketing strategies can be developed to focus on the customer needs and characteristics of a particular market sector. Markets may be segmented according to geographic area (northeast versus southwest), demographic characteristics (older versus younger, male versus female, single versus married), behavioral attributes (introvert versus extrovert), socioeconomic classification (high income versus low income). Markets can also be segmented according to consumer groups that prefer certain product/service attributes (e.g., status versus economy transportation). The key questions in effective segmentation are: 1) what are the needs of consumers in the target market segment, 2) how well do the user benefits of the company's products/services match customer needs, 3) how well can the company defend the target market segment from the competition?

---

8 How will the company's management both monitor and adjust to significant changes in its current and prospective customers' needs? ☐ ☐ ☐ ☐ ☐ ☐

INSIGHT

Markets are dynamic rather than static. A company that does not monitor and adjust to changes in its customer base will suffer loss of market share. Because the company's survival is directly dependent on its ability to

Include	Don't Include	Research	Research Complete	Draft Written	Final

MARKETING
STRATEGY

satisfy customer needs, employees should strive to continually improve their performance in this area. Accordingly, salespeople, customer service personnel, and other representatives in the field should provide frequent feedback to the company about customers' perceptions of the company's products/services as well as customers' perceptions of competing products/services.

□ □ □ □ □ □   **9**   What significant changes are anticipated by management in the company's customer base/target market over the next three to five years?

INSIGHT

Management should have a familiarity with future trends before they fully develop. The earlier management can make adjustments in its strategic plan, the more effective those adjustments will be.

□ □ □ □ □ □   **10**   What negative customer reactions to the company's products/services have been received/are anticipated by management, and how will they be overcome?

INSIGHT

Negative customer reactions to the company's product/service provide competitors with the opportunity to capture substantial market share at the company's expense. For example, during the early years of the Ford Motor Company, competitors sensed customer dissatis-

MARKETING STRATEGY

*faction with Ford's policy of only offering one color —
black. After capitalizing on this perceived weakness,
competitors were able to capture a significant portion of
Ford's industry-leading market share. The best defense
against losing touch with your market is to actively encourage customer feedback, while developing self-im-
proving internal systems (e.g., certain members of
management should act as a clearing house for all customer feedback, with the responsibility to report both problems and market opportunities). Designated members of
management should also develop, implement, and follow
up on plans for improving the company's products/ser-
vices.*

11 How will the company's products/services be marketed
(i.e., pricing, promotion, advertising, trade show participation, distribution channels/sales organization, private
label arrangements, standard sales terms, customer ser-
vice/warranty program, return privileges, consignment
sales)? Please provide authoritative support for your
choices.

☐ ☐ ☐ ☐ ☐ ☐

INSIGHT

*The company should thoroughly evaluate all the available
methods to market its products/services and explain
clearly why the chosen methods of marketing are most
appropriate. Classically, a company's marketing mix consists of the four P's; Product (user benefits), Price (determined by competitive forces, customer price elasticity,
and/or the company's cost structure), Promotion (advertising, public relations), and Place (channels of distribution). Some of these elements are covered by questions in*

this chapter, in Chapter 8 (Competitive Analysis), and Chapter 9 (Selling Tactics).

Pricing — Pricing decisions are based on the cost to manufacture, purchase, or provide the company's products/services, customer price elasticity (the willingness of customers to purchase a product/service at different price levels), and/or competitive forces.

Promotional methods — Everything from free publicity in local media to a nationally orchestrated coupon program.

Trade show participation — Sometimes provides an effective forum for introduction of the company's products to sales representatives, distributors, retailers, and end users.

Private label arrangements — To minimize marketing expense, a manufacturer may sell its products/services under a retailer's name.

Standard sales terms — Example: 2/10 net 30. Translates to a 2 percent discount off the face amount of an invoice if paid within ten days of issuance. If not paid within ten days, the full balance is due within 30 days. Discounts for prompt payment should reflect short-term interest rates.

Advertising allowance policy — Manufacturers sometimes offer distributors and retailers a rebate, against product purchased, for the purpose of advertising the company's product.

Return privileges/consignment sales — Consignment sales provide for return by retailers and distributors of unsold merchandise. Besides creating a large contingent liability, this arrangement can severely distort interim financial data.

MARKETING STRATEGY

12 In the appendix, please include the company's current price lists, catalogs, brochures, product illustrations, and other promotional materials.

□ □ □ □ □ □

INSIGHT

Promotional materials may give the reader a clearer understanding of both your products/services, and your marketing program.

---

13 If applicable, explain how your products/services can pay for themselves in less than three years by either saving your customers money or increasing their revenues.

□ □ □ □ □ □

INSIGHT

According to Rich and Gumpert, in their book, Business Plans That Win $$$ *(Harper and Row, 1985), products/services that pay for themselves in less than one year essentially are mandatory purchases for many potential customers within a market. If the payback period is less than two years, it's still a probable purchase. If the payback is beyond three years, forget it.*

---

14 What significant changes in the company's products/services, and/or the way they are marketed, are expected to be made over the next three to five years (e.g., technology, styling, pricing, method of distribution)?

□ □ □ □ □ □

Include
Don't Include
Research
Research Complete
Draft Written
Final

MARKETING STRATEGY

INSIGHT

Prospective product/service changes must be planned as early as possible to both prepare the appropriate differentiation strategy and to preempt competitive breakthroughs by other companies who share the same market.

◻ ◻ ◻ ◻ ◻ ◻ **15** If applicable, how will the company's products/services be financed domestically?

INSIGHT

Companies that offer expensive products/services can substantially increase sales by providing their customers with financing. The importance of customer financing programs has been demonstrated by the automobile industry and the numerous below market plans that it makes available to customers.

◻ ◻ ◻ ◻ ◻ ◻ **16** How will the company sell, finance and deliver its products/services to overseas customers?

INSIGHT

Although foreign markets offer explosive growth potential, most small business managers believe that they also involve countless obstacles. Regardless of the size of your company, you must realize that global markets are evolving for most products/services. Even if your company chooses not to compete with foreign products/services

MARKETING STRATEGY

Include
Don't Include
Research
Research Complete
Draft Written
Final

overseas, it will have to contend with the same competitors for domestic market share in the near future. Accordingly, investors prefer a management team that can accurately assess and capitalize on the opportunities that foreign markets offer the company.

8

Competitive Analysis

COMPETITIVE ANALYSIS

1   Please explain the competitive forces that affect your industry and/or market segment (i.e., rivalry among existing firms, threat of new entrants, threat of substitute products, bargaining power of suppliers, bargaining power of customers).

□ □ □ □ □ □

INSIGHT

Michael E. Porter, in his classic book, Competitive Strategy *(Free Press, 1980), states that the goal of competitive strategy is to find a position in the industry where the company can best defend itself against competitive forces or influence them in its favor. Forces that drive industry competition include the following: threat of new entrants (build barriers to entry by differentiating your product/service, creating costs for your customers to switch to another supplier, tying up distributors, developing proprietary technology, tying up favorable locations, gaining industry experience, building sufficient market share and production facilities to benefit from economies of scale, secure hard-to-get government licenses); intensity of rivalry among competitors (the intensity of industry rivalry can be reduced by raising customer's switching costs, increasing product/service differentiation, focusing selling efforts on the fastest growing segments of the industry); pressure from substitute products (pursue similar strategies to those summarized above in threat of new entrants); bargaining power of buyers (reduce adverse influences on the company by differentiating your product/service, increasing switching costs, selecting buyers to whom the company's product does not represent a major cost, selecting buyers to whom the company's products directly affect the quality of their own products/services, selecting buyers who are unlikely to manufacture/provide the company's products/services internally); bargaining power of suppliers (reduce adverse influences on the company by seeking substitute products, eliminating switching costs, increasing your capability to manufacture/provide your supplier's products/services internally).*

☐ ☐ ☐ ☐ ☐ ☐ **2** What are your major competitors' future goals, current strategies, and assumptions about the industry?

INSIGHT

According to Michael Porter, there are four diagnostic components to competitive analysis: future goals, current strategy, assumptions, and capabilities. Knowledge of a competitor's goals will help the company to predict that competitor's reaction to industry events and strategic changes. A competitor's strategy is reflected in its operating policies. Analyzing a competitor's assumptions will reveal blind spots; areas that a competitor will not perceive clearly or correctly. A competitor's strengths and weaknesses will determine its capability to initiate or react to strategic moves and to deal with environmental or industry events that occur (this topic is covered in question Competitive Analysis 3).

☐ ☐ ☐ ☐ ☐ ☐ **3** Please compare the company's strengths and weaknesses with those of its major competitors (e.g., user benefits of its products/services, quality and depth of management, profitability and financial resources, size and strength of parent, production economies, mar-

COMPETITIVE
ANALYSIS

ket share, marketing methods, Unique Selling Proposition (USP)/defensible market niche, sales/distribution).

INSIGHT

Knowledge of a competitor's strengths and weaknesses clarifies its positioning in the industry, illuminates the areas where strategic changes may yield the greatest return, and helps your company to forecast how industry trends will affect that competitor. In their book, Marketing Warfare *(McGraw Hill, 1986), Ries and Trout suggest that the company on the offensive should find a weakness in the leader's strength and attack at that point. Because the weakness is a component of the leader's strength, it will be difficult for the leader to retaliate without attacking itself. For example, knowing that its appeal to children is one of McDonald's strengths, Wendy's was successful in positioning itself as an adult alternative. McDonald's could not easily retaliate without endangering a substantial portion of its customer base.*

Areas of competitor strength and weakness that should be examined include the following: products/services (standing of the company's products/services in the customer's mind, depth and breadth of product/service line), dealer/distribution (channel coverage and quality, strength of channel relationships, ability to service the channels), marketing and selling (skills in each aspect of the marketing mix, skills in market research, training, and skills of the sales force), operations (manufacturing cost position, flexibility of facilities and equipment, quality of suppliers, relationship with suppliers, proprietary advantages, labor force climate), research and engineering (R & D staff skills), overall cost position (shared costs with other business units), financial strength (cash flow, borrowing and new equity capacity), employees (quality of

81

Include
Don't Include
Research
Research Complete
Draft Written
Final

training, clarity of purpose within the organization), management (depth and breadth of management, experience of management).

□ □ □ □ □ □ **4**   Provide an analysis of how the company's management plans to capitalize on competitors' weaknesses and how it will counteract competitors' strengths. Understanding the competitions' strengths and weaknesses, as well as your own, is key to defending your market share, uncovering market opportunities, and developing an effective Unique Selling Proposition.

INSIGHT

By performing an in-depth analysis of its competitors' strengths and weaknesses, as well as its own, your company can better determine how to position itself. For example, your analysis may reveal that your chief competitors, due to production economies, have positioned their products/services as low-cost entries in your market. From your analysis, you may also learn that due to strong local sales/distribution channels, your major competitors' market penetration has yielded industry leading market share in the northeastern and midwestern United States. Based on this competitive information, the fact that your company is too small to enjoy significant production economies, and the fact that your sales/distribution network is very weak east of the Mississippi, you may decide to pursue a higher price, high value-added, differentiation strategy in the western and southwestern United States.

Production economies *— The ability of a company to produce greater volume at a decreasing cost per unit. The*

Include
Don't Include
Research
Research Complete
Draft Written
Final

cost incurred by firms in the production of its products/services consists of both a fixed and a variable component. As volume increases, variable costs also rise, but fixed costs remain relatively constant. Hence, the total cost per unit decreases.

Market penetration — Determines how much market share a company controls. Greater penetration of a market can be achieved by 1) attracting new customers to the industry, 2) attracting existing customers from competitors, 3) increasing the volume of purchases by existing customers.

Sales/distribution channels — Sales/distribution channels link a producer of goods to its buyers and provide the means through which an organization implements its marketing strategy. Please see question Selling Tactics1 (Chapter 9) for more about this subject.

---

5 Please explain how the company differentiates/will differentiate its products/services from the competition's.   ◻ ◻ ◻ ◻ ◻ ◻

INSIGHT

A differentiated product/service is one that is perceived by the buyer as being unique. To be effective, your employees, customers, and suppliers should be able to describe the unique characteristics of your products/services in 25 words or less. The buyer's perception may be based on a number of product/service attributes (user benefits) such as brand image, technology, quality, service, features, and dealer network. Michael Porter stated that differentiation provides insulation against competi-

Include
Don't Include
Research
Research Complete
Draft Written
Final

COMPETITIVE ANALYSIS

tive rivalry by creating customers who are loyal to the company's brand and less sensitive to price. By increasing profit margins, differentiation provides a means for smaller and newer companies to compete with the industry's low-cost-producer. Other marketing terms that are related to the concept of differentiation include the following:

Defensible niche — A small part of a larger market that can be well defended against the competition with the resources and capabilities that a particular company possesses.

Positioning — This strategy requires an analysis of the market to first identify key differences in buyer needs and purchasing behavior. The company then selectively matches its capabilities with customers who seek certain product/service attributes (user benefits). Analysis of the market will highlight areas where the company should confront or avoid the competition.

Market segmentation — The subdivision of a market into homogeneous subsets of customers, each with unique needs and purchasing behaviors, for the purpose of identifying the segment that best matches a company's capabilities.

Unique selling proposition (USP) — In order to establish a brand image, a company may develop a unique selling proposition based on particular attributes (user benefits) of the product/service. For example, Maytag's OLD LONELY (high-quality, low-maintenance), Federal Express' ABSOLUTELY, POSITIVELY, OVERNIGHT (timely service, reliability), and Nordstroms's NO PROBLEM AT NORDSTROMS (high-quality customer service, high-quality products).

COMPETITIVE ANALYSIS

6 Please discuss reasonably foreseeable competitive breakthroughs and how the company's management will protect the market share of its product/services from the continual development and improvement of competitors' products/services.

☐ ☐ ☐ ☐ ☐ ☐

INSIGHT

Competitive breakthroughs may pose a threat to the firm's position in the market and ultimately the firm's survival. Therefore, the company should create formal systems and procedures for monitoring its competition. Once in place, competitive alert systems can warn the company of meaningful changes in the competitive environment. With this information, the company can pre-empt competitive actions (e.g., drop prices before the competition can benefit from the publicity of beating the company to the punch).

Competitive breakthrough *— An enhancement to a competitor's product/service that gives that competitor a significant edge over other companies in its market (e.g., added features (user benefits), lower price, superior distribution, highly effective advertising, new technology). If the company doesn't have the capability to conduct its own research and development, it should consider licensing breakthrough technologies for which there is proven market demand.*

---

7 In what ways is competitor intelligence used in the formulation of your company's marketing plan and strategic plan?

☐ ☐ ☐ ☐ ☐ ☐

85

Include
Don't Include
Research
Research Complete
Draft Written
Final

COMPETITIVE ANALYSIS

INSIGHT

The other companies in your industry, especially the market leaders, define the environment within which your company must operate. Accordingly, your strategic decisions should be made on the basis of your competitive analysis. Even if you believe that you have a new or innovative product/service for which there is no competition, you should analyze the competitive forces affecting companies with similar or substitute products/services.

☐ ☐ ☐ ☐ ☐ ☐   **8**   In the appendix, please list the sources on which you rely for your competitor intelligence.

INSIGHT

Leonard M. Fuld, in his book, Monitoring The Competition *(Wiley, 1988), offers valuable suggestions about gathering competitive intelligence, including the following list of sources: 1) employee interviews, especially with salespeople and suppliers, 2) commercial data bases, 3) trade associations and publications, 4) local newspapers, 5) want ads, 6) published research and industry reports, 7) Wall Street reports, 8) trade shows, 9) filings with regulatory agencies (e.g., SEC, FTC, FDA), 10) advertisements.*

☐ ☐ ☐ ☐ ☐ ☐   **9**   Please describe how your company will monitor the competition on a continual basis.

COMPETITIVE ANALYSIS

Include Don't Include Research Research Complete Draft Written Final

INSIGHT

In order to effectively analyze the competition, you must establish a system that continually monitors your competitors. Industries are dynamic rather than static and therefore require frequent re-evaluation. Accordingly, at least one individual in the company should be appointed as the competitive analysis manager. This individual should act as a clearing house, gathering competitor intelligence and disseminating it to the appropriate people in the organization.

9

Selling Tactics

SELLING TACTICS

1 How will the company sell its products/services (e.g., executive selling, in-house sales force, sales representatives, distributors, direct mail, retailers)? Please provide economic justification for your choice of selling method(s).

□ □ □ □ □ □

INSIGHT

Marketing is strategy and selling is tactics. Salespeople are the foot soldiers who implement the marketing plan. The company's choice of selling methods should be predicated on the economics of the company's products/services. For example, the cost of the average sales call in 1990 was approximately $200. Generally, it takes about five sales calls to complete one sale. On the average, companies spend about 10 percent of total revenues on selling costs. Therefore, to justify an in-house sales force, the company's order size (i.e., unit cost times the average number of units per order) must be at least $10,000 (i.e., 5 X $200 / 0.10 = $10,000). In order to justify the time of a senior executive, the company's order size must be substantially larger. Conversely, a sales representative's expenses and compensation can be adequately covered by a smaller order size than the in-house salesperson's. The sales representative is able to spread his or her costs over a broader base of products which he or she can also expect to sell during the same visit. As a rule of thumb, the following order size ranges should be matched with the following selling methods: 1) executive selling for orders in excess of $100,000, 2) in-house sales force for orders between $10,000 and $100,000, 3) sales representatives for orders between $1,000 and $10,000, 4) distributors, retailers, direct mail, catalogs for orders below $1,000.

SELLING TACTICS

☐ ☐ ☐ ☐ ☐ ☐   **2**   In the appendix, please include a list of the company's sales representatives, distributors, wholesalers, and retailers.

INSIGHT

After choosing the optimal selling method, the company should carefully align itself with the better selling organizations in its industry.

Sometimes, this can be difficult due to existing allegiances between the preferred selling organizations and established industry leaders. Management should utilize the industry contacts of its lawyers, accountants, and board members to open the appropriate doors. To help convince outside organizations to represent your company, you may want to use your business plan as a selling tool.

☐ ☐ ☐ ☐ ☐ ☐   **3**   Relative to the competition, what compensation/margins will be realized on the company's products/services by company salespeople, sales representatives, distributors, and/or retailers? What responsibilities will the above personnel assume (e.g., warranty service, accounts receivable collection, inventory financing, warehousing)?

INSIGHT

The best performing salespeople, sales representatives, and mass distributors are/will be in great demand throughout the industry. Accordingly, if salespeople/distributors are not adequately compensated, they may be motivated to sell competing lines that offer higher mar-

Include
Don't Include
Research
Research Complete
Draft Written
Final

gins. To attract and retain the most capable salespeople/distributors, the company's compensation/margin should be similar to leading competitors'. However, to minimize fixed expenses, the company should tie compensation of its in-house salespeople to performance (e.g., small base salary with large commissions). Smaller businesses may want to offer larger profit margins to distributors in exchange for other expense-reducing services (e.g., warranty service and accounts receivable collection by the distributor in exchange for price concessions from the manufacturer).

Margin — The difference between revenues received and expenses incurred. Gross margin is the difference between sales revenue and the cost of goods sold. It may be expressed as a dollar amount or as a percentage. Net margin is the difference between sales revenues and virtually all costs related to the production of those revenues, such as materials, labor, utilities, interest, administration, and taxes. As with the gross margin, it may be expressed as a percentage or as a total dollar amount.

---

4 Please explain your customer service, customer support, and warranty programs. Include a flow chart in the appendix that depicts the company's warranty and customer service process.

⊓ ⊓ ⊓ ⊓ ⊓ ⊓

INSIGHT

Customer service, support, and warranty programs are all integral parts of the total customer responsiveness philosophy, along with quality.

Include	Don't Include	Research	Research Complete	Draft Written	Final

SELLING TACTICS

Customer service/warranty program — Although essential in many cases, especially for a technical product, a comprehensive service/warranty program can represent a significant contingent liability. If a company's products/services are not of the highest quality, returns, repairs, and repeat jobs may substantially increase expenses, while severely damaging customer goodwill. To reduce risks, some companies insure themselves against excessive warranty claims. The best protection is the continual improvement of quality as discussed in Insight for question Production and Operations 4 (Chapter 11).

□ □ □ □ □ □   **5**   How do competitors' selling methods and selling expenses compare with the company's?

INSIGHT

Analyzing the selling methods chosen by competitors, and the results achieved with those selling methods, may help the company to choose the best approach to selling its products. The company can also better judge if its selling costs are reasonable by comparing competitors' financial statements to its own.

□ □ □ □ □ □   **6**   How will the company gain access to the individuals who make the buying decision? Please include a flow chart in the appendix which illustrates the selling process.

SELLING TACTICS

	Include	Don't Include	Research	Research Complete	Draft Written	Final

---

INSIGHT

Usually, the larger the order, the more difficult it is to gain access to the individual who makes the buying decision. Please see Insight for question Customers and Suppliers 4 (Chapter 10) for more about this topic.

10

Customers and Suppliers

CUSTOMERS AND SUPPLIERS

1   How many active customers does the company have, ☐ ☐ ☐ ☐ ☐ ☐
and how many of those active customers account for
more than 5 percent of the company's total volume?

INSIGHT

High-volume customers can be both an asset and a liability. While the sales volume they generate may represent a major portion of the company's sales, a sudden change in customer loyalty could throw the company into an unprofitable position. Also, high-volume customers sometimes demand preferential treatment (e.g., price concessions, accelerated delivery), which may result in substandard treatment of other customers. Conversely, larger customers provide the company with the opportunity to work more closely with buyers and provide products/services that are more specifically suited to their needs. The higher volume of sales economically justifies the company's more customized approach. Another benefit that may be derived from greater responsiveness to larger customers is an interdependence that strongly encourages loyalty by significantly increasing switching costs.

Switching costs *— The costs that a company incurs, in terms of both time and money, to switch suppliers. The greater the cooperation between customer and supplier, the higher the switching costs (e.g., design work performed jointly by both customer and supplier).*

---

2   If any customers representing more than 5 percent of the ☐ ☐ ☐ ☐ ☐ ☐
company's volume have been lost during the last three
years, please explain why.

Include
Don't Include
Research
Research Complete
Draft Written
Final

CUSTOMERS AND SUPPLIERS

INSIGHT

Readers of your business plan will want to know why major customers were lost. If the loss was management's choice due to your customer's poor credit, or an unrealistically low price schedule that your customer asked you to match, then the decision will be perceived as a positive one. However, if customers leave because your products/services fail to satisfy their needs as well as competitor's products/services, then your company is probably heading in the wrong direction.

□ □ □ □ □ □ **3** Please list the company's five largest customers. Include sales to each customer for both the last three years (actual) and the next three years (projected), percentage of the company's total sales, credit rating, maximum credit extended, terms, a short explanation of why they purchase your products/services, and length of purchasing history with your company.

INSIGHT

Longer customer relationships indicate loyalty and stability, while shorter relationships reflect the opposite. Major customers with marginal credit ratings are perceived as risk intensive because of their questionable ability to survive financial problems and pay their bills to the company in a timely manner, if at all. Buyers with marginal credit ratings should not be permitted to run up large balances that are owed to the company, even if the company must risk losing some if its major customers. A

	Include	Don't Include	Research	Research Complete	Draft Written	Final

customer in a growth industry is a better future prospect than a customer whose total market is shrinking. Also, a customer who perceives the company's product/service to be both unique and essential to its own product/service, is more likely to be a loyal, long-term customer, and less likely to be a highly price sensitive short-term customer. A company is only as strong as its customers.

---

4   How does/will the company identify and contact pro- ☐ ☐ ☐ ☐ ☐ ☐
spective customers?

INSIGHT

Even if the company builds a better mousetrap, nobody will buy it unless the company can identify and reach prospective customers. Accurate analysis and definition of the company's target market is key to locating and contacting buyers. Generally, the more efficiently the company can identify and reach its customers, the more successful its marketing, sales, and advertising will be. Please see Insight for question Market Strategy 7 (Chapter 7) for more about market definition.

---

5   Please list the company's most promising prospective ☐ ☐ ☐ ☐ ☐ ☐
customers. In the appendix, provide names of individual
contacts, firm names, addresses, phone numbers, a short
explanation of why they will buy your products/services,
and estimated annual volume over the next three years
for each prospect.

Include
Don't Include
Research
Research Complete
Draft Written
Final

CUSTOMERS AND SUPPLIERS

INSIGHT

To insure growth, the company must continually build and reevaluate its list of quality prospects. Frequent contact must be maintained with bona fide prospects to communicate the company's unique selling proposition and the superior user benefits of its products/services.

□ □ □ □ □ □   **6**   Please discuss in detail any contracts now in effect with customers/suppliers and any advance payments that have been made. Include copies of contracts and other supporting documentation as an exhibit in the appendix.

INSIGHT

Generally, the company should maximize its flexibility by avoiding supply contracts and advance payments unless cancellation without penalty is provided. However, supply contracts may be necessary to avoid price fluctuations or to assure delivery of scarce components.

□ □ □ □ □ □   **7**   Please list the company's five largest suppliers. Include approximate annual purchases from each supplier, maximum credit extended, and terms.

INSIGHT

Managers who realize how critical strong supplier relationships are to delivering maximum quality and service

CUSTOMERS AND SUPPLIERS

to their customers look for suppliers who can best help them to achieve their company's goals. Suppliers can provide a number of support services including inventory management and financing.

---

8 Please discuss the company's access to key raw materials and the steps that management has taken to protect the company from critical supply shortages.

☐ ☐ ☐ ☐ ☐ ☐

INSIGHT

Generally, management should both diversify its sources of supply and prepare contingency plans for shortages, since the company's production process is directly dependent on its suppliers' ability to deliver.

For example, a company should not rely on a sole, overseas supplier for a particular component because of potential political, economic, and/or transportation problems. Ideally, a multi-national company should have several sources from several parts of the world, including at least one domestic supplier. For a contrary perspective on the diversification of suppliers, please see Insight for question Customers and Suppliers 9.

---

9 Please describe the company's purchasing process. What checks and balances have been put into place to assure that the company is supplied on a timely, efficient, and economic basis? Include a flow chart in the appendix to simplify your explanation.

☐ ☐ ☐ ☐ ☐ ☐

103

Include

Don't Include

Research

Research Complete

Draft Written

Final

CUSTOMERS AND SUPPLIERS

INSIGHT

American businesses generally view their associations with suppliers as interchangeable relationships of convenience. To minimize cost and insure continuity of supply, they tend to work with several suppliers. Japanese businesses view suppliers as valued partners. They believe that numerous suppliers only impair quality due to variations in product and service. Accordingly, prices offered by suppliers should only be evaluated in the context of the quality being purchased.

A company will best serve its interests by developing a long-term relationship of loyalty and trust with a single vendor. Departments from both companies should work together to reduce costs and improve quality. A supplier assured of a long-term contract is more likely to risk being innovative or to modify a production process than a supplier with a short-term contract who can't afford to tailor its products/services to the needs of the buyer. To protect itself from an unexpected interruption of necessary supplies, the single vendor buyer can arrange for emergency supplies from alternate vendors.

☐ ☐ ☐ ☐ ☐ ☐ **10** How often and on what basis are suppliers evaluated by the company (e.g., quality, price, terms, punctuality, reliability)?

INSIGHT

Because of the key role that suppliers play in the production/service delivery process, the quality of the company's suppliers should be evaluated on a continual basis.

11

Production and Operations

PRODUCTION AND OPERATIONS

1 Please describe the production/service delivery process for each of the company's products/services. Illustrate the time frame and relationship of each step to the total production/service delivery cycle with a flow chart. This type of analysis is commonly referred to as the Critical Path Method (CPM). Please include the CPM analysis and other supporting documentation, as an exhibit in the appendix.

☐ ☐ ☐ ☐ ☐ ☐

INSIGHT

A shorter production cycle allows for rapid adjustment of production levels to sudden changes in market demand. Longer cycles create increased vulnerability to delays, fluctuations in customer demand, and the supply of vital materials. Therefore, long production cycles are generally viewed as risk intensive.

Production/service delivery cycle *— The amount of time required for the company to manufacture/provide its product/service. Items such as liquor or livestock have long production cycles, whereas a newspaper has a short production cycle. The length of the cycle is influenced by the nature of the process (e.g., the aging of liquor may take several years), as well as by the availability of component parts, people, and equipment required to complete the process.*

Critical Path Method (CPM) *— This method of planning can help pinpoint critical events to which the company's resources should be committed. For example, if three events are scheduled simultaneously, but only one must be completed before subsequent steps can begin, then that event is a potential bottleneck or critical event. Because production delays result in both lower sales and*

Include
Don't Include
Research
Research Complete
Draft Written
Final

PRODUCTION AND OPERATIONS

the loss of customer goodwill, planning for the allocation of production resources is essential.

☐ ☐ ☐ ☐ ☐ ☐ **2** What steps have been taken and will be taken to continually improve the company's production process?

INSIGHT

In reference to his management philosophy of continual improvement of the production process, Dr. Deming suggests the following: 1) create constancy of purpose among the company's employees for improvement of product and service, 2) improve quality, and both productivity and competitive position will follow, 3) cease dependence on mass inspection; quality comes not from inspection but from improvement of the process, 4) end the practice of awarding business to suppliers on price tag alone, 5) eliminate quotas that take account only of numbers, not quality of method, as they usually guarantee inefficiency and high cost.

☐ ☐ ☐ ☐ ☐ ☐ **3** Please discuss the company's quality control system, the percentage of total units rejected versus units produced and the percentage of total units returned versus units produced for each product line over each of the last three years.

INSIGHT

Although somewhat neglected by American industry

through the 1970s, quality control is now acknowledged to be of major importance. Japan developed into a leading international economic power by making quality control its highest priority. In addition to lost productivity represented by rejects and returns, the company should consider the loss of customer goodwill and the cost of warranty service. The best marketing program and/or the strictest cost controls will not offset poor quality control. Many companies that subscribe to the management methods of W. Edwards Deming, the man who revitalized Japanese industry, have made the continual improvement of quality their corporate religion, (i.e., quality is the most important attribute that the company's products/services offer).

4 What steps have been taken and will be taken to continually improve the company's quality control system?

□ □ □ □ □ □

INSIGHT

There is no such thing as a permanent quality level. Quality requires continuous improvement. Quality is a constantly upward moving target; continuous improvement is an integral part of a quality program, not a separate activity.

If you want to find out about your quality, go out and ask your customers. They are the ones most affected by the quality of your products/services on a daily basis. Quality is not what an engineer, marketer, or plant manager says it is.

PRODUCTION AND OPERATIONS

☐ ☐ ☐ ☐ ☐ ☐   **5**   Does the company fabricate a standard shelf-type product, manufacture to specification, or both? Does the company provide a standard service or a service that is customized to the specific needs of each buyer?

INSIGHT

American industry was built around the philosophy that a standard shelf-type product will offer greater opportunities for automation, will be more widely marketable, and will carry a higher collateral value for financing purposes. However, the Japanese have adopted the philosophy that they can better serve world markets by constructing plants that can economically accommodate differentiation, customization, and continual improvement of their products/services.

☐ ☐ ☐ ☐ ☐ ☐   **6**   What is the present capacity of the company's production facility, in both dollar and unit volume, versus its actual volume over each of the last three years? What percentage of capacity has been utilized for each of the last three years?

INSIGHT

Because expansion of productive capacity can involve major capital expenditures, the availability of additional capacity at minimal cost may provide invaluable flexibility to growing companies. For example, the company may lease part of a plant with an option to lease adjoining space at minimal additional cost.

PRODUCTION AND OPERATIONS

7   How and when will the company acquire additional ☐ ☐ ☐ ☐ ☐ ☐
space and equipment to provide the productive capacity
required by the company's sales projections? If applicable, please describe future expansion needs along with
costs and time estimates.

INSIGHT

*The inability of the company to increase productive ca-
pacity at a reasonable cost within a reasonable time
frame, could severely stifle its growth. As an alternative,
you may want to sub-contract excess volume. Forward
planning is a must.*

8   How do the company's production facilities and produc- ☐ ☐ ☐ ☐ ☐ ☐
tion process compare with the industry's best? If applicable, please describe the proprietary aspects of the
company's manufacturing process.

INSIGHT

*If the efficiency of its manufacturing process provides the
company with a cost and/or quality advantage, the company will have a superior strategic position over its competitors. If, however, the company must reach an
extremely optimistic sales level to pay for its manufacturing facility, it could find itself giving away its profit advantage to attract higher volume.*

111

PRODUCTION AND OPERATIONS

☐ ☐ ☐ ☐ ☐ ☐ **9** Please discuss the company's safety record.

INSIGHT

Management should explain steps that are being taken to maintain or improve its safety performance record to the zero accident level. Accidents reduce productivity, create liability, and damage employee morale. ⌐

☐ ☐ ☐ ☐ ☐ ☐ **10** Please discuss the parts of the production/service delivery process that are outsourced. What criteria does the company's management use to determine whether products/services should be manufactured/performed in-house or purchased from another source?

INSIGHT

Manufacturing in-house affords management the opportunity to better control quality and assure supply. At certain volume levels, in-house manufacturing is also cheaper. However, purchasing from another source reduces fixed overhead and in some cases allows the company to concentrate on what it does most profitably, (e.g., marketing/sales).

Outsource *— To contract out a needed service to a third party. Companies that have strongly embraced this philosophy build their strategies around deep knowledge of a few highly-developed core service skills.*

12

Government Regulation

GOVERNMENT REGULATION

1   Please list all licenses and government approvals (city, county, state, and federal), that the company should obtain or maintain in order to conduct its business. Include copies of licenses, approvals, and other supporting documentation, as an exhibit in the appendix.

□ □ □ □ □ □

INSIGHT

Highly regulated industries are viewed as risk intensive by investors because of the unpredictable nature of political decision makers and their short-term time perspective. For example, the purchase of troubled savings and loans by outside investors was strongly endorsed by the Reagan administration. Accordingly, certain subsidies and tax benefits were offered to purchasers, but were later withdrawn or modified by the Bush administration. Investors who committed funds to savings & loans found themselves in a difficult situation because of the government's change in position.

---

2   To which city, county, state, and federal government regulatory bodies will the company be accountable on a continuing basis (e.g., zoning departments, building departments, health departments, taxing bodies, EPA, EEOC, FDA, FTC, OSHA, SBA, SEC)?

□ □ □ □ □ □

INSIGHT

EPA—Environmental Protection Agency, EEOC—Equal Employment Opportunity Commission, FDA—Food and Drug Administration, FTC—Federal Trade Commission,

Include
Don't Include
Research
Research Complete
Draft Written
Final

GOVERNMENT REGULATION

OSHA— Occupational Safety and Health Administration, SBA—Small Business Administration, SEC—Securities and Exchange Commission.

☐ ☐ ☐ ☐ ☐ ☐ **3** Please discuss the problems that the company has encountered or anticipates encountering while attempting to comply with applicable regulatory bodies.

INSIGHT

If the company becomes the subject of concern to one or more of the regulatory agencies, the repercussions could be extremely serious.

Employees, customers, suppliers, prospective lenders, and investors may prefer to leave or avoid the company while serious regulatory problems persist. Accordingly, a prompt solution to regulatory problems should be sought, but not at the cost of significantly compromising the company's rights.

☐ ☐ ☐ ☐ ☐ ☐ **4** Please discuss proposed changes in the law (city, county, state, and federal) that could adversely affect the company. What steps has management taken to protect itself from unfavorable legislation?

INSIGHT

Smaller companies are very vulnerable to changes in federal, state, and local laws. A contractor whose largest customer is the Department of Defense is vulnerable to

GOVERNMENT REGULATION

changes in procurement legislation. Automobile emission systems manufacturers are vulnerable to EPA changes in anti-pollution standards. A small retailer is vulnerable to changes in the local zoning laws. Unlike larger companies, smaller firms do not have the resources to directly affect the political process. Thus, in addition to researching existing laws and regulations, your company should also gauge the possibilities of and prepare strategic responses to dramatic changes in federal, state, and local laws.

13

Financial Data

FINANCIAL DATA

1   If applicable, please provide historical financial state- ☐ ☐ ☐ ☐ ☐ ☐
ments for the last three years in the appendix.

INSIGHT

Historical financial statements provide a measurment of the company's ability to perform. Informed readers of the business plan will understand that without the growth capital that most companies are seeking, earnings may be understated.

---

2   Please include a copy of the company's interim financial ☐ ☐ ☐ ☐ ☐ ☐
statements, including a summary of recent develop-
ments, in the appendix.

INSIGHT

Ideally, interim financial statements should reflect a continuation or an acceleration of positive trends.

---

3   Please provide projected income statements for the next ☐ ☐ ☐ ☐ ☐ ☐
five years, monthly for the first two years and quarterly
thereafter. Present best case, most likely case, and worst
case scenarios. Summarize your data in the body of the
business plan. Include detail in the appendix.

Include
Don't Include
Research
Research Complete
Draft Written
Final

FINANCIAL DATA

INSIGHT

The most important part of your financial projections is the authoritative substantiation behind your assumptions. The basis for projected sales should be evidence of market demand for your products/services (e.g., actual sales, purchase orders, market research, market test results, letters of intent, trade show inquiries, testimonials, interviews with prospective customers). Competitive analysis and supplier interviews provide support for the validity of your expenses. Without detailed research and evidence that customers prefer your products/services, your projections will have little, if any, credibility.

Best case, most likely case, and worst case scenarios — *By providing the reader with a set of different outcomes, the credibility of the business plan is enhanced and the company's ability to survive difficult situations can be evaluated.*

□ □ □ □ □ □ **4** Please provide cash flow projections, by month, for the next five years. Show the anticipated timing of cash receipts and disbursements. Present best case, most likely case, and worst case scenarios. Summarize your data in the body of the business plan. Include detail in the appendix.

INSIGHT

Net income is a measurement of a company's performance for a given period, but cash flow is the life blood of any business. The company's bills and obligations are paid out of cash flow, not net income. Certain noncash expenses (e.g., depreciation, amortization, deferred taxes)

FINANCIAL DATA

Include	Don't Include	Research	Research Complete	Draft Written	Final

are deducted from revenues to determine net income, but cash flow reflects the internal generation of funds available for payment of expenses, growth, and distribution to investors.

---

5   Please provide annual projected balance sheets for the next five years. Present best case, most likely case, and worst case scenarios. Summarize your data in the body of the business plan. Include detail in the appendix.   ❏ ❏ ❏ ❏ ❏ ❏

INSIGHT

Projected balance sheets forecast the financial condition of the company, its ability to meet its financial obligations, and its capacity to absorb financial setbacks without becoming insolvent.

---

6   If applicable, please provide an analysis of unit sales, dollar sales, gross profit, and gross margin, by product/service line, country, territory, subsidiary, division, and/or branch, for both the last three and the next three years.   ❏ ❏ ❏ ❏ ❏ ❏

INSIGHT

By breaking down the company's profit and loss statement into operating groups, the investor can isolate profitable divisions from losers. If a division has a history of losses,

Include
Don't Include
Research
Research Complete
Draft Written
Final

FINANCIAL DATA

management should consider liquidating or closing it rather than permitting it to bleed the company.

Sales — Virtually all revenues received from customers in exchange for the company's goods and services minus discounts and/or returns. Sales can be measured in dollars or units.

Cost-of-goods-sold (COGS) — Direct costs incurred in the production of the company's goods/services (e.g., materials, manufacturing labor, depreciation of manufacturing machinery and plant, utilities used in the manufacturing process).

Gross profit — Sales minus COGS.

Gross margin — Same as gross profit. Can be expressed in dollars or as a percentage of sales.

□ □ □ □ □ □   **7**   What is the minimum percentage of productive capacity that the company must utilize, the minimum sales volume it must generate, and the minimum market share it must obtain over each of the next three years to break even? Include detail for net income and cash flow break-even analyses, by product/service line, in the appendix.

INSIGHT

Break-even analysis — A method of assessing a firm's profit potential and downside risk. To perform this analysis, the firm's costs should be separated into variable components (e.g., labor, materials, sales commissions) and fixed components (e.g., interest expense, rent, managers' salaries, insurance, utilities). With these costs and the estimated selling price per unit, the company can

FINANCIAL DATA

Include
Don't Include
Research
Research Complete
Draft Written
Final

estimate how many units of production must be sold to cover the costs of operation. At this sales volume, management incurs neither a loss nor a profit. Thus a comparison can be made between projected unit sales and the number of units that must be sold for the company to break even. If the company projects sales of 1,000 units over the first year, but only requires sales of 500 units to break even, then the company has only to attain 50 percent of its projected volume to break even. The break-even point in units (BPIU) and dollars (BPID) is calculated with the following formulas:

BPIU = (Fixed Costs)/(Sales Price Per Unit – Variable Cost Per Unit)

BPID = Break-even Point In Units × Sales Price Per Unit

Fixed costs — Fixed costs are expenses that do not fluctuate with volume. Very large increases in volume would eventually require an addition to productive capacity and associated fixed costs, while a sustained decrease in volume would cause management to liquidate some of its productive capacity. Although total fixed costs remain constant as volume increases, per-unit fixed costs decrease.

Variable costs — Expenses that are uniform per unit of output. Total variable costs fluctuate in direct proportion to volume. They include direct materials, labor used in the production process, and salespeople's commissions.

---

8 What is the company's current sales backlog versus its ending backlog for each of the last three fiscal years?

❏ ❏ ❏ ❏ ❏ ❏

Include
Don't Include
Research
Research Complete
Draft Written
Final

FINANCIAL DATA

INSIGHT

A growing backlog is usually a positive indication of increasing demand for the company's products/services. However, it can also be an indication of inadequate production or distribution.

☐ ☐ ☐ ☐ ☐ ☐ **9** If your business is seasonal, please describe how peaks in sales, production, and employment affect the company. What measures has management taken to offset the negative effects of seasonal fluctuations?

INSIGHT

Seasonal businesses must accumulate extremely large inventories in anticipation of high-volume periods. If inventory is not large enough to meet demand, the company faces lost sales and profits that cannot be recaptured in the off season. If inventory exceeds demand, the company may not generate sufficient cash to pay suppliers and creditors. The company must then absorb inventory carrying costs until surplus merchandise can be sold or disposed of. Because the company's financial performance is dependent on the outcome of the selling season, interim financial reports are distorted and in some cases virtually useless. The best strategy to offset the negative aspects of a seasonal business is to acquire a counterseasonal product line. For example, a lawn mower manufacturer could diversify into the snowmobile business. Diversification would hopefully even out the timing of the company's cash flow.

FINANCIAL DATA

10 What percentage of the company's total annual sales was represented by revenues from overseas sources in each of the last three years (actual), and what will the percentage be in each of the next three years (projected)?

☐ ☐ ☐ ☐ ☐ ☐

INSIGHT

The percentage of overseas sales to total sales indicates the extent to which the company has pursued other markets for its products/services. A high percentage of overseas sales may also expose the company to additional political and credit risks.

---

11 Please discuss the design, installation, and maintenance of the company's cost control system. How often will data be collected and what actions will be taken to continually reduce costs without compromising quality?

☐ ☐ ☐ ☐ ☐ ☐

INSIGHT

Cost control systems allow management to detect variances between carefully calculated cost targets (based on historical and/or projected results) and actual results. Problems causing the variance can then be isolated and solved before losses are permitted to accumulate. For example, if a particular machine has historically produced widgets at a direct cost of 3 cents per item, but cost control systems show a recent cost of 5 cents per item, management is alerted to the problem and can react accordingly. Further research into the problem might indicate a mechanical malfunction, defective raw materials, or improper use of the machine by a new employee.

❑ ❑ ❑ ❑ ❑ ❑ **12** What are the available trade-offs between fixed and variable costs (e.g., hiring part-time versus full-time employees, outsourcing versus manufacturing internally, leasing rather than purchasing a warehouse)? Include projected income statements divided into fixed and variable cost components, for the next three years, in the appendix.

INSIGHT

During periods of prosperity a company may attempt to reduce the overall cost of goods sold by converting variable costs to fixed costs (e.g., a component may be manufactured internally rather than purchased from a supplier).

During economic downturns, a company may follow the opposite strategy (e.g., reduce fixed expense by selling manufacturing capacity and purchasing components that were previously manufactured internally from outside suppliers). Projected income statements, divided between fixed and variable expenses, indicate the potential that a company has to convert fixed costs to variable costs, or vice versa. For a definition of fixed and variable costs, please see Insight for question Financial Data 7.

❑ ❑ ❑ ❑ ❑ ❑ **13** What are the company's most significant costs (e.g., energy, raw materials, freight, packaging, direct labor, interest on borrowed capital)? How volatile are they? How does management propose to minimize their potential for having a negative impact on the company's profitability?

INSIGHT

By pinpointing significant costs, management can closely monitor those costs and prepare alternative strategies for different contingencies. For example, a candy maker may protect itself from a volatile cocoa market by hedging itself against rapid price increases through the commodity futures market. Escalating direct labor costs can be reduced over the long term by automating. Dramatic fluctuations in costs for certain supplies can be reduced through the negotiation of forward contracts and/or diversification of suppliers. Variable interest on borrowed capital can be replaced by a fixed interest charge or a stock offering. Freight costs can be minimized by exploring alternative transportation methods (e.g., rail versus truck).

14 What is the company's cost position relative to the industry, and how well could it withstand prolonged price pressures from competitors? ☐ ☐ ☐ ☐ ☐ ☐

INSIGHT

Various factors reflected in the income statement affect the company's overall cost of delivering its product or service. If the company's cost is significantly higher than its direct competitors', a price war could force the com-

Include
Don't Include
Research
Research Complete
Draft Written
Final

FINANCIAL DATA

pany to price its product below its cost, or lose its customer base. Thus a prolonged period of price competition could deplete the company's capital base and force it into bankruptcy. To protect itself from this situation, the company must differentiate its product. This will hopefully cause the consumer to consider such factors as quality, service, style, and durability, rather than price alone.

☐ ☐ ☐ ☐ ☐ ☐ **15** What were the company's expenditures for capital equipment, research and development, and advertising/promotion during each of the last three years (actual), and what will they be for each of the next three years (projected)?

INSIGHT

These items are viewed as elective expenditures that may divert scarce cash flow from payment of day-to-day operating expenses. However, many financial analysts argue that reduction of expenditures on these elective items will damage that company's long-term growth prospects.

Capital equipment *— Fixed assets used in the production of the company's goods and services (e.g., plant, equipment, machinery).*

☐ ☐ ☐ ☐ ☐ ☐ **16** Please calculate the company's return on assets for both the last three years (actual) and the next three years (projected).

FINANCIAL DATA

INSIGHT

This ratio is used to measure how productively management utilizes its assets. Comparisons are usually made in the following ways: 1) the company's performance for present periods versus previous periods, 2) the company's projected performance versus present performance, 3) the company's performance versus competitors' performance, 4) the company's performance versus the industry median or average.

Return on assets = Year end net income/year end total assets.

---

17 Please calculate the company's net income and cash flow returns on investment for both the last three years (actual) and the next three years (projected). ❏ ❏ ❏ ❏ ❏ ❏

INSIGHT

Because investors are risking their capital in exchange for the promise of a substantial return, this figure is a very important indicator of what specific returns the investor can expect. If the company's return on investment doesn't significantly exceed the riskless rate of return (i.e., the interest rate offered by U.S. Treasuries), then investors will not believe they are receiving a return that is commensurate with the underlying risk.

Net income return on investment = year end net income/year end net worth.

131

FINANCIAL DATA

Include
Don't Include
Research
Research Complete
Draft Written
Final

Cash flow return on investment = year end cash flow/year end net worth.

Net worth — *Also referred to as net book value, invested capital, and owner's equity, net worth is equal to total assets minus total liabilities.*

□ □ □ □ □ □ **18** If applicable, please list customer accounts that represent more than 10 percent of the company's total accounts receivable.

INSIGHT

Diversification is preferred over concentration. Should one of the company's major customers not be able to pay amounts owed to the company, the loss could be devastating. To reduce risk, exposure to any one customer should not exceed 10 percent of total receivables. However, if the company regularly receives financial statements or other assurances of its customer's financial strength, management may decide to deviate from this policy. The company also has the option of insuring larger or questionable accounts receivable through a third-party insurer. Of course, the costs of this practice should be weighed against the benefits.

□ □ □ □ □ □ **19** If applicable, please list in the appendix uncollectible notes/accounts receivable which have NOT been charged off.

FINANCIAL DATA

INSIGHT

Unless uncollectible accounts receivable are charged off, the company's assets will be overstated and management's credibility will be questioned.

Charge-off *— When an account or loan receivable is deemed to be uncollectible, it is either charged against a reserve for bad debts or directly to net income.*

Reserve for bad debts *— An account that should be gradually accumulated to provide a cushion against anticipated charge-offs.*

---

20 How much has the company charged off and/or reserved for bad debts over the last three years?

❑ ❑ ❑ ❑ ❑ ❑

INSIGHT

Although charge-offs should be held to a minimum, their absence may indicate a credit policy that is overly strict and therefore a deterrent to potential customers that buy from competitors with more lenient credit policies.

---

21 If applicable, please list in the appendix the company's collectable accounts receivable that are more than 90 days old. Please explain why each account has not been collected, and include management's estimate of the amount for each account that will be collected.

❑ ❑ ❑ ❑ ❑ ❑

133

Include
Don't Include
Research
Research Complete
Draft Written
Final

FINANCIAL DATA

INSIGHT

Usually the probability of collecting an account receivable decreases with age. In most industries, after 90 days, the collectibility of an account becomes questionable unless special terms have been extended by the company.

☐ ☐ ☐ ☐ ☐ ☐ **22** Please calculate the number of days it has taken for the company's accounts receivable to turn in each of the last three years (actual), and the number of days it will take in each of the next three years (projected). Please include an accounts receivable aging in the appendix.

INSIGHT

The Day's Receivable Outstanding formula is used to measure both the efficiency of the company's accounts receivable collection methods and the quality of its accounts receivable portfolio. Generally, days receivables outstanding should not exceed 30 to 45, although certain industries will deviate from this guideline.

Accounts receivable aging *— As of a given date, a classification of accounts receivable in categories of 0 to 30 days, 31 to 60 days, 61 to 90 days, 91 to 120 days, greater than 120 days.*

Days receivables outstanding = (year end receivables/year end sales) × 365.

134

23 What credit analysis procedures has the company fol-
lowed/will the company follow both to screen and to
monitor noncash customers?

□ □ □ □ □ □

INSIGHT

*Well thought out credit control and analysis procedures
are essential to holding accounts receivable write-offs to
a minimum. Credit services and trade associations provide support to internal credit departments. The
company's bank can also offer valuable credit information. Credit managers must be sufficiently disciplined to
confront salespeople who would like to deviate from
credit control procedures for the purpose of enticing or
retaining important customers.*

---

24 How many days has it taken for the company's inventory
to turn in each of the last three years (actual), and how
many days will it take in each of the next three years
(projected)?

□ □ □ □ □ □

INSIGHT

*This figure is used to evaluate how effectively the com-
pany is managing its inventory. Robert Morris Associates
figures can be used to establish an industry range. A low
figure relative to the industry reflects efficient inventory
management and minimal carrying costs. However, a low*

figure could also reflect frequent product shortages. A high figure may indicate inefficient inventory management, the retention of obsolete inventory that should be written off, excessive carrying costs, or the maintenance of a large inventory to better serve customers.

Days inventory on hand = (year end inventory/year end cost of goods sold) × 365.

☐ ☐ ☐ ☐ ☐ ☐ **25** In both dollars and percentage, please list the amount of the company's inventories that fall into each of the following categories: 0 to 30 days old, 31 to 60 days old, 61 to 90 days old, 91 to 120 days old, more than 120 days old.

INSIGHT

Readers can gauge the marketability of the company's inventory by examining how long the inventory has been on hand. Older inventory is more likely to be obsolete or slow moving.

☐ ☐ ☐ ☐ ☐ ☐ **26** Please describe the company's inventory control system (e.g., manual or computerized, frequency of physical inventories, method of inventory valuation).

INSIGHT

A quality inventory control system is essential to prevent inventory mismanagement, obsolescence, and theft. The cost of carrying surplus inventory during periods of high interest rates can severely deplete the company's financial resources.

---

27 If applicable, how does the company account for slow moving/obsolete inventory (e.g., write-down, charge-off, carry at full cost)?

☐ ☐ ☐ ☐ ☐ ☐

INSIGHT

The conservative approach should be taken. Marginal inventory should be written off.

---

28 If applicable, please discuss details of all major inventory adjustments made during the last three years (i.e., inventory write-ups or write-downs).

☐ ☐ ☐ ☐ ☐ ☐

INSIGHT

Inventory adjustments can dramatically reverse the company's profit position. They also indicate poor inventory control systems.

---

29 In the appendix, please describe all real property owned or occupied by the company (e.g., plants, warehouses, offices, retail space). For each location, provide the following: if owned, amount, type, and date of last

137

appraisal; condition, total square feet, and age; method of financing (e.g., lease, mortgage, cash purchase).

INSIGHT

These data may be used to establish the current value of the company's real property and the potential borrowing power that its real estate holdings represent.

Mortgage/lien — A claim against an asset pledged as collateral for a loan.

☐ ☐ ☐ ☐ ☐ ☐ **30** Excluding real property, please list in the appendix major fixed assets owned by the company. For each item, provide the following: amount, type and date of last appraisal; description, age, condition, and location; method of acquisition (e.g., financing lease, bank loan, cash purchase).

INSIGHT

These data are required to establish the current value of the company's fixed assets, other than real property, and an inventory of its productive capacity.

Fixed assets — Assets with a useful life that generally exceeds one year.

☐ ☐ ☐ ☐ ☐ ☐ **31** If applicable, please discuss the original amount and current valuation of advances to or investments in affiliates.

FINANCIAL DATA

INSIGHT

To facilitate the evaluation of the company's investment in affiliates, provide detailed financial information about each affiliate.

32 Please discuss any "hidden assets" that do not appear on the company's balance sheet (e.g., LIFO reserve, understated fixed assets, patents, bargain leases, mailing lists, trade names).

❏ ❏ ❏ ❏ ❏ ❏

INSIGHT

Certain intangible assets can be sold for substantial amounts that are not reflected on the company's balance sheet (e.g., a long-term lease on a very desirable property at 50 percent of market value). Management should include an estimate of the value of all intangible assets.

LIFO — Last-In, First-Out, is an inventory costing method that assumes the last units purchased are the first units to be sold. The cost of goods sold consists primarily of the most recently added unit. Ending inventory consists of older layers of inventory. During periods of inflation, when prices are rising, LIFO leads to higher reported expenses and lower reported earnings. Also, the company's balance sheet will reflect a lower inventory account than valuation under the FIFO method (see below). This difference is referred to as LIFO reserve. As a result of lower income recognition for tax purposes, LIFO provides a method of cash flow conservation during inflationary periods.

Include
Don't Include
Research
Research Complete
Draft Written
Final

FIFO — First In, First Out, is an inventory costing method that assumes the first units purchased are the first units to be sold. The cost of goods sold consists primarily of older units, and the ending inventory consists of newer layers of inventory. During inflationary times, FIFO relative to LIFO results in lower inventory expense and higher net income. While the balance sheet more accurately reflects true inventory value, the company recognizes greater income, pays higher taxes, and therefore suffers a reduction in cash flow.

❏ ❏ ❏ ❏ ❏ ❏   **33**   How many days has it taken for the company's accounts payable to turn in each of the last three years (actual), and how many days will it take in each of the next three years (projected)? Please include an accounts payable aging in the appendix.

INSIGHT

If the company is carrying accounts payable that are more than 90 days old, other than disputed accounts and/or accounts which have been granted special terms by suppliers, it is likely that the company is financing a working capital shortage at its suppliers' expense. Suppliers usually respond by demanding cash on delivery for new orders, compromising service, and/or cutting the company off completely.

❏ ❏ ❏ ❏ ❏ ❏   **34**   If applicable, please list the company's past due accounts payable, delinquent notes payable, and other delinquent obligations.

FINANCIAL DATA

INSIGHT

Generally, the further behind a company falls in meeting its obligations, the closer that company comes to insolvency.

---

35 If applicable, please list dates and amounts of delinquent taxes and associated tax liens. ❑ ❑ ❑ ❑ ❑ ❑

INSIGHT

Because the government is likely to pursue delinquent taxpayers vigorously, tax delinquencies should be avoided at all costs. Tax delinquency is an indication of the company's inability to handle its obligations.

---

36 In the appendix, please include copies of the company's real estate and equipment leases. ❑ ❑ ❑ ❑ ❑ ❑

INSIGHT

Readers of your business plan may want to examine your leases to determine how long you are contractually bound, what your renewal options are, what your continuing costs will be, and what purchase options you have.

FINANCIAL DATA

☐ ☐ ☐ ☐ ☐ ☐ **37** Please describe the company's contingent liabilities (e.g., unfunded pension obligations, guarantees, off balance sheet leases, warranties, conditional sales, return privileges, license agreements, tax returns open for audit). For each item, estimate the company's maximum liability and discuss action taken by management to limit exposure.

INSIGHT

All of the company's current and potential liabilities should be fully disclosed. Contingent liabilities can dramatically change the company's financial position. If investors, or others evaluating the business plan, feel that management has attempted to hide any contingent liabilities, the company will be immediately eliminated from further consideration.

__Unfunded pension and profit-sharing commitments__ — Although not always reflected on the balance sheet, the company is fully liable for all future benefits promised to employees.

__Off balance sheet leases__ — Although the company must honor certain lease obligations (e.g., short-term operating leases), the liability may not be included on the company's balance sheet.

__Guarantee__ — An undertaking of responsibility to pay the financial obligations of another entity, if that entity is not able to pay the obligation itself. For example, in order to procure bank financing for a subsidiary, the parent company may guarantee the subsidiary's bank debt.

__Conditional sales/return privileges__ — Similar to consignment sales, under certain circumstances, buyers may be entitled to return the company's products for a full refund of their money. Obviously, this type of arrangement can wreak havoc with the production planning, inventory control, and the accuracy of the company's financial reports.

---

38 Please explain unusual items not clearly identified in the company's financial statements.

❏ ❏ ❏ ❏ ❏ ❏

INSIGHT

Regardless of the quality of a company's financial statements, certain issues are not discussed in adequate detail (e.g., pending litigation, operating leases, major agreements). Parties interested in the company prefer full disclosure of all relevant information.

---

39 Please include copies of all appraisals for company-owned assets in the appendix.

❏ ❏ ❏ ❏ ❏ ❏

INSIGHT

Before investing in the company, capital sources will want to determine the value of the company. There are several ways to calculate a company's value (e.g., a multiple of current or future earnings, the present value of future cash flow, a multiple of net worth, the net liquidation value of the company's assets). This last figure, which usually establishes the company's minimum value, represents the anticipated proceeds that the company's stockholders

Include
Don't Include
Research
Research Complete
Draft Written
Final

FINANCIAL DATA

would receive by selling the company's assets on an orderly basis to interested buyers over a six-month period, after all liabilities have been paid.

The net liquidation value of the company's assets will also give the investor a good indication of the company's collateral value and therefore its borrowing capacity. To calculate this figure, financial analysts will subtract questionable assets, such as past due accounts receivable and obsolete inventory, from figures stated in the company's financial statements. The investor will also request a credible appraisal for the company's fixed assets.

Orderly liquidation value — Estimated amount for which an asset will sell over a six-month period.

☐ ☐ ☐ ☐ ☐ ☐ **40** Please include copies of all loan documents, security agreements, and mortgages in the appendix.

INSIGHT

Readers of your business plan may want to review your loan documents to better understand the terms of your obligations to lenders.

☐ ☐ ☐ ☐ ☐ ☐ **41** Please include copies of the last five years of tax returns in the appendix.

FINANCIAL DATA

INSIGHT

Because privately held companies can usually adjust their financial statements to overstate earnings, especially if they are not audited, tax returns are generally regarded as a more conservative and accurately stated alternative.

14

Strategic Planning

STRATEGIC PLANNING

1   What is the company's overall strategic plan? In the context of the functional sections summarized above (e.g., Sales, Marketing, and Finance), please describe the company's goals and how management proposes to achieve its objectives over the next three to five years.

    □ □ □ □ □ □

INSIGHT

The strategic plan should bring together and coordinate all subject matter reviewed in the business plan. It should explain how the different functional areas of the company will coordinate efforts to execute the strategic plan. For example, if a manufacturing company chose to establish itself as the industry leader (i.e., control the largest market share), it could begin to implement its strategic plan by raising capital through its finance department to purchase the most efficient plant and equipment available. The company could then utilize its new productive capacity and employee training program to achieve lower per-unit cost and improved quality.

With its operational superiority, the company would be in the position to increase market penetration by lowering prices and/or emphasizing quality. As the company grew, it could recruit quality management personnel with stock options and a competitive compensation package. Incremental cash flow would provide funding to increase its advertising effort and attendant sales volume. Higher revenues would permit the company to penetrate new geographic markets and establish new distribution channels leading to even greater economies of scale. As profits grew, the company could repay expansion debt, attract investor interest and eventually go public, yielding impressive returns to the original investors.

Include
Don't Include
Research
Research Complete
Draft Written
Final

STRATEGIC
PLANNING

Strategic plan — Large-scale, future oriented plan for establishing sustainable competitive advantages. Clearly identifies future goals and objectives (such as market share, return on investment, and growth, both in units sold and in dollar revenues) and explains how the company will achieve those goals and objectives.

□ □ □ □ □ □   **2**   Please compare key elements of your company's strategic plan with those of your competitors.

INSIGHT

Please see Insight for question Competitive Analysis 3 (Chapter 8) for more about this topic.

□ □ □ □ □ □   **3**   Please prepare a flow chart that shows the timing and interdependence of major events necessary for the company to realize its objectives (e.g., completion of prototypes, organization of sales/distribution network, receipt of first orders, first sales and deliveries, first positive monthly cash flow, final payment to investors).

INSIGHT

Please see Insight for question Production and Operations 1 (Chapter 11) for information on using CPM to plan timely completion of important events.

	Include	Don't Include	Research	Research Complete	Draft Written	Final

4   Please discuss the critical risks, problems, and obstacles associated with the company, and how management plans to minimize the impact of unfavorable developments in each critical area (e.g., management inexperience, competitive price cutting, cost overruns, lower than projected sales, supply shortages or delays, capital shortages).

    ☐   ☐   ☐   ☐   ☐   ☐

INSIGHT

Identifying and preparing for potential problems is the most effective way to manage risk. Because most managers avoid the time consuming process of planning, preferring instead to confront problems as they occur, these problems often prove fatal to the firm. However, if managers anticipate problems and prepare effective contingency plans, the severity of those problems may be reduced. In some cases, certain problems can be prevented altogether. For example, the company can compensate for management inexperience by hiring consultants and electing directors with extensive industry experience. The threat of price cutting, and lower than projected sales, can be partially offset by converting some fixed expenses to variable expenses (e.g., part of your personnel needs can be filled by part-time staff rather than full-time employees). Inadequate research and development programs can be supplemented with licensed technologies. Raw material shortages can be avoided by diversifying sources.

It should be noted that many problems do not have simple or painless solutions. For example, the tripling of oil prices by the OPEC nations created monumental problems that few corporate planners anticipated. Reducing expenses,

in response to lower sales, by laying off full-time employ-ees and cutting advertising expenditures can have very negative long-term consequences. Similar to other as-pects of business management, strategic planning is more of an art than a science.

☐ ☐ ☐ ☐ ☐ ☐ **5** Please discuss the activities that are likely to cause a substantial delay in the company's development. What preventive steps will management take to avoid or to minimize the impact of serious delays?

INSIGHT

Delays in the company's development may damage customer and supplier goodwill, and give competitors valuable time with which to capture strategically impor-tant market share. Because of the time value of money, delays also decrease investors' rate of return. Accordingly, management must prepare in-depth contingency plans for potential problems that may cause critical delays.

☐ ☐ ☐ ☐ ☐ ☐ **6** What steps will management take to sustain the company's growth? Please describe the company's pro-gram for researching, developing, analyzing, and ex-ploiting new market opportunities.

INSIGHT

The company that stops growing usually dies. One of the most compelling arguments for sound strategic planning

STRATEGIC PLANNING

Include

Don't Include

Research

Research Complete

Draft Written

Final

is the possibility of identifying new growth opportunities for the firm. This is accomplished by recognizing unfulfilled customer needs to which the firm can apply its specialized skills, thereby gaining a competitive edge. Often, the firm must look outside the narrow market segment with which it is familiar, and identify the broader market need being served by the product/service. If this process is followed, the firm avoids the danger of being supplanted by another firm that more expeditiously perceives and reacts to a market opportunity through the application of a newer technology. For example, it would be a strategic blunder to build a new plant for the purpose of manufacturing buggy whips at the same time that the automobile was achieving universal consumer acceptance.

Railroads were supplanted by air transportation companies because railroad management ignored the full potential of a promising new technology. Railroad executives limited their market definition to the railroad business rather than the transportation business. Thus, effective strategic planning is essential to the long-term prosperity of the firm.

---

7 What procedures will management implement to facilitate the company's continual improvement?

□ □ □ □ □ □

INSIGHT

Please see Insight for questions Management 10, Employees 13, and Production and Operations 2, for a review of W. Edwards Deming's management philosophy of continual improvement.

Include
Don't Include
Research
Research Complete
Draft Written
Final

STRATEGIC PLANNING

☐ ☐ ☐ ☐ ☐ ☐ **8** How does management expect the local, U.S., and world economies to perform over the next three to five years (e.g., recession/depression, real growth, interest rates, unemployment, inflation)?

INSIGHT

Due to the volatility of local, U.S., and world economies, management should prepare strategies for different economic scenarios.

☐ ☐ ☐ ☐ ☐ ☐ **9** How vulnerable is the company's profitability to cyclical fluctuations in the local, U.S., and world economies (e.g., changes in the rates of real growth, interest, inflation)? How will management protect the company from the negative consequences of economic volatility?

INSIGHT

Investors prefer a management team that both understands and prepares for the frequent economic fluctuations that have characterized local, U.S., and world economies over the last twenty years. Management can structure the company for maximum economic flexibility by emphasizing variable expenses over fixed expenses during the company's formative years. For example, the company may decide to subcontract part of its manufacturing process during the early stages of its development. After a certain threshold level of revenues is achieved, the company can reconsider investment in additional plant and equipment or a continuation of its subcontracting arrangement.

STRATEGIC PLANNING

Include   Don't Include   Research   Research Complete   Draft Written   Final

Changes in the state of the economy at the local, national, and world levels are usually explained in terms of cyclical downturns (weakening) or cyclical upturns (strengthening). Basically, most economies present numerous variations of the same boom and bust cycle. Since each stage is associated with certain economic characteristics, it is in management's best interests to prepare a variety of economic strategies. For example, near the top of the economic cycle, interest rates climb and demand starts dropping. Accordingly, management should reduce inventories in an effort to minimize interest expense and carrying charges. Near the bottom of the economic cycle, interest rates continue to drop and demand begins to climb. In this case, the opposite strategy applies.

Appendix

Documentation

APPENDIX

The inclusion of authoritative support for the business plan is essential. Because the reader will not want to rely solely on the author's plan, the appendix should contain detailed documentation that helps to substantiate statements made or positions taken.

APPENDIX

☐ ☐ ☐ ☐ ☐ ☐ **MANAGEMENT 8**

Organizations and individuals providing counsel to the company

☐ ☐ ☐ ☐ ☐ ☐ **MANAGEMENT 13**

Copies of employment agreements, covenants not to compete, and non-disclosure agreements

☐ ☐ ☐ ☐ ☐ ☐ **OWNERSHIP 1**

Ownership

☐ ☐ ☐ ☐ ☐ ☐ **OWNERSHIP 2**

Prospective owners of the company's common and preferred stock, and the number of shares available under warrants, conversion privileges, and employee stock bonus/option agreements

☐ ☐ ☐ ☐ ☐ ☐ **OWNERSHIP 5**

Shareholder buy/sell agreements

☐ ☐ ☐ ☐ ☐ ☐ **OWNERSHIP 7**

If applicable, a copy of the ESOP/ESOT agreement

☐ ☐ ☐ ☐ ☐ ☐ **EMPLOYEES 11**

Copies of the company's pension, profit sharing, and stock bonus plans

☐ ☐ ☐ ☐ ☐ ☐ **INVESTMENT CRITERIA 9**

If applicable, the company's most recent public stock offering memorandum and SEC filings

APPENDIX

INVESTMENT CRITERIA 11

If applicable, personal financial statements of principal stockholders and guarantors

☐ ☐ ☐ ☐ ☐ ☐

INVESTMENT CRITERIA 13

Prospective sources from which the company has sought but not received financing

☐ ☐ ☐ ☐ ☐ ☐

MARKETING STRATEGY 1

Market data including market research, market test results, focus group data, competitive intelligence, media reports, government industry data, SEC filings, trade association reports, and transcripts of interviews with industry experts

☐ ☐ ☐ ☐ ☐ ☐

MARKETING STRATEGY 6

Evidence of market acceptance including actual sales, purchase orders, market research, market test results, letters of intent, testimonials, trade show inquiries, and transcripts of interviews with prospective customers

☐ ☐ ☐ ☐ ☐ ☐

MARKETING STRATEGY 12

The company's current price lists, catalogs, brochures, product illustrations, and other promotional materials

☐ ☐ ☐ ☐ ☐ ☐

COMPETITIVE ANALYSIS 8

Sources used by the company for competitive intelligence

☐ ☐ ☐ ☐ ☐ ☐

Include
Don't Include
Research
Research Complete
Draft Written
Final

APPENDIX

◻ ◻ ◻ ◻ ◻ ◻ **SELLING TACTICS 2**
If applicable, a list of the company's sales representatives, distributors, wholesalers, and retailers

◻ ◻ ◻ ◻ ◻ ◻ **SELLING TACTICS 4**
A flow chart depicting the company's warranty and customer service process

◻ ◻ ◻ ◻ ◻ ◻ **CUSTOMERS AND SUPPLIERS 5**
Most promising prospective customers

◻ ◻ ◻ ◻ ◻ ◻ **CUSTOMERS AND SUPPLIERS 6**
Contracts with customers and suppliers

◻ ◻ ◻ ◻ ◻ ◻ **CUSTOMERS AND SUPPLIERS 9**
A flow chart depicting the company's purchasing process

◻ ◻ ◻ ◻ ◻ ◻ **PRODUCTION AND OPERATIONS 1**
A flow chart depicting the company's production or service delivery process

◻ ◻ ◻ ◻ ◻ ◻ **GOVERNMENT REGULATION 1**
Government licenses and approvals

◻ ◻ ◻ ◻ ◻ ◻ **FINANCIAL DATA 1**
The company's most recent three years of historical financial statements

APPENDIX

FINANCIAL DATA 2   ☐ ☐ ☐ ☐ ☐ ☐

The company's interim financial statements, including a summary of recent developments

FINANCIAL DATA 3   ☐ ☐ ☐ ☐ ☐ ☐

Detail for projected income statements, including sales, cost of goods sold, gross margin, operating expenses, operating income (loss), interest income (expense), extraordinary items, taxes, and net income (loss)

FINANCIAL DATA 4   ☐ ☐ ☐ ☐ ☐ ☐

Detail for projected cash flow forecast, including proceeds from collection of accounts receivable, interest income, dividends, total receipts, payment of accounts payable, payment of other expenses, income tax payments, total disbursements, total from operations, proceeds from the sale of stock, capital expenditures, loan proceeds (payments)

FINANCIAL DATA 5   ☐ ☐ ☐ ☐ ☐ ☐

Detail for projected balance sheets, including cash, investments, accounts receivable, inventory, total current assets, fixed assets, short-term debt, accounts payable, taxes payable, accruals, total current liabilities, long-term debt, deferred taxes, preferred stock, common stock, retained earnings (deficit), total stockholders' equity

FINANCIAL DATA 7   ☐ ☐ ☐ ☐ ☐ ☐

Net income and cash flow break-even analyses by product/service line.

APPENDIX

APPENDIX

	Include	Don't Include	Research	Research Complete	Draft Written	Final

FINANCIAL DATA 40
Loan documents, security agreements, and mortgages

☐ ☐ ☐ ☐ ☐ ☐

FINANCIAL DATA 41
The company's tax returns for the last five years

☐ ☐ ☐ ☐ ☐ ☐

PART II

Transforming Your Answers into a Business Plan

These sample business plans were prepared by graduate students. Although the information contained herein was carefully researched, some of the data presented may no longer be valid. The sample plans are presented here as illustrative material, and are not intended for any other purpose.

INTRODUCTION

As mentioned in the introduction to this book, it would be unwise to simply submit to readers of your business plan a series of questions and answers based on the format of this book. Although the questions provided in *Creating a Winning Business Plan* address all the pertinent issues, answering the questions alone will not give the reader what he or she really needs to evaluate a business, namely, a synthesis and analysis of the material that the workbook section of this book helps to generate.

What follows are two business plans that were developed using the question and answer format provided in *Creating a Winning Business Plan.* These plans are the culmination of the efforts of two very capable groups from a graduate level business planning course which the author teaches at the Keller Graduate School of Management. They are included to both illustrate the concepts discussed in this book and to give the user a more concrete idea of how to transform the workbook portion of the text into a readable and effective business plan.

You will notice that both business plans do not follow the exact order of the workbook itself. This is intentional. The workbook portion of the text is meant as a guide for you to generate material to write your business plan. You should not feel compelled to follow the exact order of the questions in the workbook. Indeed, you may find it essential to put certain sections before others due to their relative importance to your specific business plan.

Synthesis and analysis are important here. Because most readers are inundated with business proposals, you must put the most important information about your venture at the beginning of your business plan.

What are the significant facts and ideas about a business? Obviously, this depends upon the business. There are no hard and fast rules you can apply. What seems eminently appropriate as an organizational principle for one venture's business plan may be inappropriate for another's.

In the process of reworking the material from the questionnaire to the final written business plan, you will probably reevaluate your answers. This reevaluation may lead you to add significant material you may have left out. You may entirely reword certain sections to explain more clearly what your business is and how it operates. In some cases, you may even eliminate material that you decide is superfluous or redundant.

There is more involved in producing the final version than merely reassembling the answers to the workbook questions. The process of coming to the final versions of the two business plans presented here was a dynamic one. Questions answered cursorily were explored in greater detail. As the authors worked through the business-planning process, they generated more factual support and more specifics.

No matter what tactical approach you take, the workbook portion of *Creating a Winning Business Plan* is designed to make you think thoroughly about all the essential issues affecting your business. And the process of transforming the workbook answers into a prose version should make you think even harder about your business. If this happens when you produce your business plan, you have derived all the benefits that this book can offer.

The author would like to thank Mark S. Antman, Nancy L. Toyama, Myron M. Warshaw, Bob L. Goin, Sharon M. Kaczmarek, Judith Lukas and Wayne L. Wiest for their invaluable contributions to this book.

Sample Business Plan A
Quality Health Care Temporaries

TABLE OF CONTENTS

EXECUTIVE SUMMARY

QUALITY HEALTH CARE TEMPORARIES (QHC) is a start-up venture that will provide temporary professional health care services to hospitals and nursing homes. The customer uses these supplemental nurses and nursing assistants to fill vacancies caused by chronic personnel shortages, vacations, sick leave, and fluctuations in demand. The current nursing shortages have exacerbated the need for this staffing relief. Without such services, hospitals and nursing homes would have to turn patients away, cancel elective surgeries, and eventually downsize. All of these alternative options would reduce revenue and profitability. Appropriate use of agency nurses in these situations can annually save an institution up to $30,000 per position.

The principals of QHC — Bob Smith, Jane Jones and John Anderson — comprise a management team with a broad knowledge of the health care industry and with excellent preparation for the management of a temporary nursing agency. Individually, they have extensive experience in nursing, personnel management, temporary staffing, hospital administration, and small business management. Collectively, they are fully committed to combining and applying their various talents toward this company's success.

Median projections show the first profitable month to be the eighth. The projected net income before taxes at the end of year five is $921,000 or 10.9 percent of a net sales of $8,452,000, representing an earnings growth of 273 percent from year two to year five. Net earnings of $603,000 represents an increase of 300 percent from year two to five.

This venture will require $325,000 to provide for start-up expenses, initial operating expenses, and cash flow. The founders will contribute $125,000 in exchange for 125,000 shares of common stock ($1.00 par value). The remaining $200,000 will be raised using conventional debt. The projected value of QHC at the end of year five is $4.5 million, or $36 per share. At the beginning of year five, the principals will reevaluate their continued ownership.

There are 100 hospitals and 230 nursing homes employing an estimated 30,000 RN & LPN full-time equivalents, and 13,000 CNA full-time equivalents in metropolitan Chicago. Approximately 3 percent of this employment represents supplemental staffing valued at $100 million annually. The Chicago market contains an estimated 65,000 RNs, 12,000 LPNs, and 20,000 CNAs. The market for all types of health care temporaries is difficult to predict at this time. Estimates of its growth range between 3 to 5 percent annually.

Over 200 agency offices, representing 127 different nursing temporary agencies, provide a variety of temporary nursing services to hospitals, nursing homes, and the home care needs of metropolitan Chicago. Approximately 105 of these agency offices specifically serve hospital and nursing home clients. Hospitals are another source of competition. Many have their own internal agency with compensation packages intermediate between that of an agency and a staff position.

The success and profitability of a temporary placement agency is completely dependent on its ability to recruit and retain a willing, satisfied and competent pool of nurses. It must compete with other agencies as well as its client institutions for a limited supply of nurses. As suppliers to the agencies, the nurses possess significant bargaining power. The nurse evaluates the agencies according to wage, benefits, convenience, scheduling ease, bonuses, working conditions, and location of the client hospital.

A successful agency must have competitive pricing and wages. It must meet its customers' needs with prompt, dependable, quality service. Promptness and dependability are achieved by consistently filling orders with qualified personnel within one hour. The quality of its service depends on the experience and qualifications of its personnel, and the excellence of its operations. QHC's management plan will economically achieve these basic industry fundamentals.

Our surveys demonstrate that the nurses are not being treated fairly and professionally. Agencies as a rule have poor orientation programs and a lack of understanding of the stressful working environment of its nursing personnel. The design and philosophy of our management programs will meet these important needs. The response to our survey gives us every indication that nurses will be strongly attracted to working with QHC. Most of the hospital schedulers who are responsible for choosing the agencies have told us that they would be very interested in an agency with our credentials and would try QHC.

Our objective is to capture a significant portion of the institutional placement market and begin entering the growing home care market by the beginning of our third year of operations.

COMPANY

BACKGROUND

- Start up is planned for May 1991, targeting hospitals and nursing homes.

- Agencies help their customers avoid losses and can save them considerable staffing costs.

- QHC's successful recruitment of quality personnel provides a strong competitive edge in obtaining a lucrative customer base.

- As an independent agency, QHC has a competitive advantage and will reach profitable sales levels within the first year.

QUALITY HEALTH CARE TEMPORARIES, QHC, plans to start its operations by supplying experienced temporary nursing staff to Chicago-area hospitals and nursing homes May 1, 1991. Hospitals are currently the primary users of registered nurses (RNs) for supplemental (temporary relief) staffing, although recent developments and trends suggest that the smaller need for nursing homes will increase. Certified nursing assistant (CNA) temporaries are more often requested by nursing homes. Licensed practical nurses (LPNs) are an intermediate category of nurse that is becoming obsolete as the technology of medical care rapidly increases. Both nursing homes and hospitals currently request temporary LPNs.

Hospitals and nursing homes use these temporaries to fill unexpected as well as expected vacancies for required positions. Sudden vacancies occur when the staffing requirements exceed the institutions' staffing resources. These situations occur when there is either a sudden increase in the patient population (census) or increase in the level and intensity of illness (acuity). The more ill patients require more nursing care. Management estimates that a hospital, for example, can annually save as much as $30,000 per position (full-time equivalent or FTE) by using a temporary RN rather than budgeting a permanent position to handle fluctuations (see "Customer's Economic Justification" in Appendix).

Temporary institutional staffing agencies have been in existence for more than forty years. Originally, they primarily provided private duty nurses to hospitals, nursing homes, and residences. Recent increases in shortages (both in the 70s and 80s) of all types of nursing care personnel has increased the demand for temporary staffing.

Currently these agencies serve institutions, clinics, physician's offices, and patients in their homes. The size of the national hospital market segment alone is estimated to be four billion dollars per year.

Agencies receive personnel requests from their institutional clients on both an urgent basis (eight- to 24-hour notice) and as part of a planned schedule (ranging from weekly to occasionally as far in advance as monthly). The client can cancel the order without penalty on as little as a two-hour notice, causing the agency to cancel the scheduled nurse. The nurse accepts this inconvenience in exchange for substantially higher compensation than she could obtain from a permanent position. The client is billed weekly for the positions used. Payroll is generated weekly as well.

A temporary placement agency's success in serving the needs of its customers is completely dependent on its ability to recruit and retain a willing, qualified, experienced, and satisfied pool of nurses and aides. The temporary placement agencies compete for a limited supply of nurses and aides not only with other agencies but with the institutional customers they are attempting to serve. A hospital may have a registry (i.e., its own "internal agency") as well.

The nurses and aides are unique suppliers, more like quasi-customers. As such, they must be attracted via a thoughtful marketing strategy. The user benefits that agencies typically offer are high pay, choice of schedule and working location, and various types of bonuses and benefits. These professionals have significant bargaining power. They have made a significant trade-off between the above-mentioned benefits and the possibility of sudden cancellation or lack of available positions.

Approximately half of the agency professionals work exclusively as temporaries. Many full-time and part-time hospital and nursing home employees also seek additional employment with agencies. However, a majority are unwilling to accept the uncertainties and stress, and prefer the security of a permanent position.

In 1981, The Robert Wood Johnson Foundation conducted a national survey of temporary agencies for the HHS, which was published in *Medical Care*. The results show that an agency office had a median customer base size of six institutions, and placed 70 shifts per week. Based on the above study and on our competitive analysis, it is reasonable to expect to achieve the median size by the end of the first year. At current prices for RNs, an office of this size can expect annual revenues of $1.4 million.

The survey indicated a very wide distribution of customer base and unit sales, however. It appears that the biggest offices surveyed could have over $12 million in annual revenues. The study also showed that the independent agency performed significantly better than a typical office belonging to a large corporate chain. Our investigations confirm that this is also true of the Chicago market.

QHC will recruit its professional staff from the entire Chicago metropolitan area. Our office will be centrally and conveniently located near the Cook County border of a western or northwestern suburb. Our initial target hospitals and nursing homes will be selected according to size, location, and opportunity, particularly based on the interest expressed in our surveys. A roster of 50 to 100 active, reliable personnel will be required.

In preparation for this business plan, we surveyed nurses, nurse recruiters, and schedulers, interviewed agency owners and directors, and reviewed many articles. We concluded that a successful agency will best serve its customers by doing the following:

1. Offering competitive prices with volume discounting;

2. Promptly and consistently providing nurses as requested, by having an adequate-sized roster;

3. Attracting and retaining the most motivated, competent, experienced, and technically qualified personnel; and

4. Insisting that workers always arrive on time.

MISSION STATEMENT: *QUALITY HEALTH CARE TEMPORARIES* is dedicated to profitably providing the highest quality health care placement services for its customers. We are sensitive to the ever-changing needs of our industry, customers, suppliers, and employees, and will provide the necessary support, training, and continuing education in order to be superior in our industry.

MANAGEMENT

- Management has extensive experience in nursing, temporary staffing, hospital administration, and small business management.

- Management's proven teamwork capabilities will enable them to meet both expected and unexpected challenges.

Members

Dr. Bob Smith	President & Director of Marketing
Ms. Jane Jones	Vice President and Director of Operations/ Nursing Supervisor
Dr. John Anderson	Vice President and Chief Financial Officer

(A complete Organization Chart of the company is in the Appendix.)

Bob Smith, 51, is the President & Director of Marketing of QHC. He earned his Ph.D. in chemistry from the University of California at Berkeley, after which he served as an Assistant Professor of Chemistry at New York University for six years. Upon his relocation to Chicago, Dr. Smith accepted a position as a chemist in the Department of Pathology of Northwest Community Hospital, advancing within three years to Associate Director of the Chemistry Department. After receiving his M.B.A. from Keller Graduate School of Management, Dr. Smith accepted the Caremark Division directorship at Baxter International, the post he subsequently held for 11 years. Caremark is a pharmaceutical services and nurse staffing agency serving the home care market. In his capacity as Division Director, Dr. Smith developed considerable expertise as an administrator and in the recruitment and management of nursing and pharmacy personnel. As President & Director of Marketing of QHC, Dr. Smith will be responsible for planning and managing the implementation of company strategies, locating and securing new sales opportunities, and guiding the gradual diversification of the company's range of services.

Jane Jones, 30, is Vice President and Director of Operations. As an Illinois-licensed Registered Nurse (RN), Ms. Jones also serves as Nursing Supervisor, in compliance with a requirement of the Illinois Nurse Agency Act (see "Government Regulations"). Ms. Jones received her Bachelor of Science in Nursing from the University of Illinois and her Master of Science in Adult Education from National College of Education. She was employed for nine years at Weiss Memorial Hospital in Chicago, as a staff RN for the first six years and subsequently as a nursing supervisor and a part-time member of the nursing faculty. Ms. Jones is highly experienced in the management and education of nurses. Having worked closely with both agency and non-agency nursing personnel, she is also well-acquainted with the advantages and disadvantages of temporary staffing. She has also recently completed her M.B.A. at Keller Graduate School of Management. As Vice President and Director of Operations, Ms. Jones will oversee all nurse recruitment and scheduling activities and will manage the company's training and continuing education program.

John Anderson, 36, is Vice President and Chief Financial Officer. He received his D.D.S. degree from the University of Illinois and practiced general dentistry in the Chicago area for five years. Like the other members of the management team, Dr. Anderson also holds an M.B.A. from Keller Graduate School of Management. After leaving clinical practice, Dr. Anderson co-founded Chicago D.D.S., Ltd. and served as that company's President and Chief Financial Officer for three years. Chicago D.D.S. (Dental Directory and Staffing) is a dental information and temporary staffing service, providing its customers with information on the availability of licensed dentists for temporary clinical assignments and contracting for their placement in those vacancies. Under Dr. Anderson's guidance, Chicago D.D.S. survived early losses to ultimately record a 35 percent return on investment. As Vice President and Chief Financial Officer of QHC, Dr. Anderson will be responsible for all financial planning and reporting, as well as all day-to-day accounting activities.

As the company expands and its pool of nursing personnel grows along with the demand for its services, management anticipates the need to add to the management team. Accordingly, in its fourth year of operations the company plans to recruit and hire a nursing coordinator (sooner if warranted by growth). The nursing coordinator will assume responsibility for managing and enhancing the efficiency of nurse scheduling, allowing Ms. Jones to concentrate more on recruitment and retention of personnel and other operational activities.

Ms. Jones and Drs. Smith and Anderson each receive a base compensation of $40,000 and share in the profits or losses of the company, in proportion to their fractional ownership of the company's stock. This is in accordance with the features of Sub-chapter S corporation status. All present and future members of the management team are required to sign a restrictive covenant protecting the company from the threat of competition from any individual who might leave QHC and develop or seek employment with a competing agency.

Board of Directors

In addition to the members of the management team, the board of directors of QHC will also consist of several individuals whose professional expertise is desirable to enhance the prospects for the company's success. Candidates for directors are currently being interviewed and selected by management, with terms of directors' compensation and future election procedures yet to be determined. The board will consist of one representative of each of the following professional categories:

- Critical-care RN, presently a hospital staff member

- Medical-surgical RN, presently a hospital staff member

- Hospital administrator

- Nursing home administrator

- Accountant, experienced in accounting for personnel services

- An attorney, specializing in health care-related legal issues

- Physician with hospital and/or nursing home affiliation

■ An official of either the Joint Commission on Accreditation of Healthcare Organizations (JCAHO) or the American Hospital Association (AHA), well-versed in hospital and nursing home regulatory issues

■ A middle to upper-level official of either the Illinois or the Chicago Department of Public Health

Various other professional associates and acquaintances have counseled management in the development of this business plan and may be contacted as references. Their names, phone numbers, professional affiliations, etc., will be made available on request.

Goals of Management

Each member of the management team is fully committed to working toward the success of QHC, and will devote one hundred percent of his or her working time to those efforts. This commitment is made with the understanding that, in a start-up company, each individual in management may frequently be called upon to fill multiple roles. Management is dedicated to tailoring and managing the company's services to best serve the needs of both the nursing personnel who provide those services, and the institutions and individuals who utilize them. Management further intends to be continually responsive to changes in the nursing industry, altering the company's strategies and services as necessary to remain competitive in the market.

Management intends to achieve profitability for the company within its first year of operations. It then intends to attain sufficient market penetration and market share to support steady growth, at a rate which meets the requirements of all individuals with a financial interest in the company.

The specific strategies and tactics by which management intends to attain these goals will be detailed in subsequent sections of this Business Plan.

Strengths and Weaknesses of Management

Each of the three principals of the company contributes a distinct area of knowledge and expertise to the management team. Dr. Smith's many years as an administrator have given him extensive experience in the management of a large staff of health care professionals. His experience related to nurse staffing and home care services will be of obvious value to QHC. Additionally, his 14 years of professional work within the health care industry have enabled him to develop a vast network of professional contacts in local hospital management, as well as many contacts in the management of hospital-affiliated nursing homes. This will be very much to the company's advantage as Dr. Smith seeks to market the company's services to local health care institutions.

Ms. Jones' thorough first-hand familiarity with every aspect of the nursing industry is one of the company's greatest strengths. With the recent completion of her M.B.A., she has added to the broad base of knowledge and expertise she acquired in many years of nursing and nursing supervision. She also brings to the management team a distinct advantage over the company's competitors through her academic credentials and professional experience as a nurse educator.

Dr. Anderson contributes to the management team the knowledge and experience gained in his recent success in small business management. He also gained from that business experience a thorough understanding of the considerations and procedures unique to the management of a staff of temporary health care service professionals.

The principal weakness of the management team is that no individual member possesses experience in *all* critical areas of the management of a temporary nursing agency. Lacking first-hand experience in nursing, both Dr. Anderson and Dr. Smith will need to draw heavily on Ms. Jones' knowledge and insights. Similarly, although she has worked *with* agency nurses, Ms. Jones has not personally managed temporary staff members; she will thus need to draw upon Dr. Anderson's experience in that area. Finally, Dr. Anderson's unfamiliarity with the environment of medical institutions will make him dependent upon the experience of both of the other management team members. All three individuals, however, have demonstrated in their previous professional work their ability to work successfully in a team. With the application of such teamwork to this management team, the abilities of each individual will complement those of the others in addressing all aspects of the company's management.

STRATEGIC PLAN

- QHC plans to concentrate on the institutional staffing segment for the first three years of business. In the fourth year we will enter the home health care industry.

- The major critical risk is the competition from hospital internal agencies.

QHC plans to have six hospitals and six nursing homes as customers by the end of the first year of operations. The goal for year two is to achieve positive cash flow and to enhance profitability through the continued growth of our business. This will be achieved through an increase in both the number of hospital and nursing homes and the number of orders.

Our expectations for these first two years were based upon reasonable estimates from general industry data ("Market Estimations and Calculations" in Appendix) and competitor performance (see "Competitor Summary Sheets" in Appendix). During the second year we will begin market research, and planning our entrance into the home health care segment.

In year three, as long as market conditions are optimal, we will expand into the home health care business, a growth opportunity industry (see "Marketing"). A major portion of our growth in year four and five comes from expansion of the home health segment.

Our company strategy is to competitively meet the industry standards for salaries, benefits, service, and pricing. Beyond meeting these standards, our uniqueness will be achieved by offering our customers more experienced nursing personnel, staffing advisory services, and a sophisticated skills-matching and scheduling computer system. For example, by using computer software, we can skill match the right employee to the right job and locate the employee to fill the assignment so that dependability of service is enhanced and efficiency maintained.

Critical Risks. Increased formation of hospital registries represents a significant threat to the institutional staffing segment of the business. QHC will respond by offering to manage hospital temporary staffing needs. In addition, QHC will focus on those hospitals that do not have internal registries, and will increase its emphasis in the home health care segment.

Economic downturns have a generally negative effect on the temporary placement industry. Because the health care industry is usually more insulated from economic downturns, we would expect the effect on temporary agencies to be less severe. In response, QHC would reduce costs by streamlining operations.

If the nursing shortage decreases, the demand for nursing temporaries at an agency would be reduced. In order to replace lost revenues, QHC would explore other allied health disciplines having temporary staffing needs.

There is a potential risk of reduction in demand for RN temporaries because of job substitution with LPNs and CNAs. If this were to occur, we would see the demand for LPNs and CNAs increasing, and would focus our recruiting efforts on these individuals.

LEGAL

Quality Health Care Temporaries is incorporated in the state of Illinois with Sub-chapter S corporation status. No legal actions have been filed against the company or its principals. As a business involved in the delivery of health care services, however, the company is subject to the possibility of professional liability claims. Appropriate professional and general liability insurance coverage has been purchased, as detailed in the "Employees" section of this Business Plan.

Flow of Service and Communications

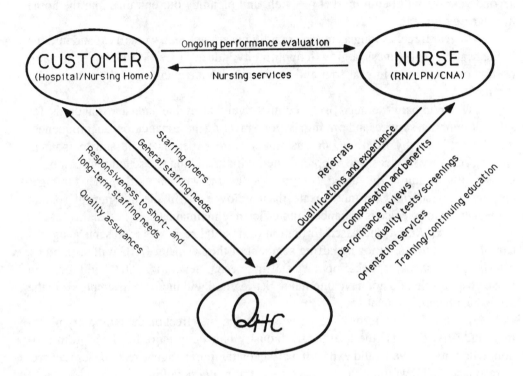

MARKETING AND COMPETITION

MARKETING

- The total nursing temporaries market for the Chicago area is estimated to be $100 million.

- Agencies provide customers with high-quality professionals and reliable service at competitive prices.

- Agencies provide suppliers with flexible scheduling and supplemental income.

- QHC's market strategy is to choose a niche by uniquely catering to clients requiring highly skilled nurses with experience and motivation.

PRESENT MARKET

Temporary nursing personnel agencies supply hospitals, nursing homes, and home health care organizations with nurses and nursing aides.

NATIONAL MARKET FOR HEALTH CARE

	Totals	Temporaries
Hospitals	$230 billion	$4 billion
Nursing Homes	$35 billion	$800 million
Home Health	—	$9 billion

These groups make up the total market. Below are two charts representing the total market for hospitals and nursing homes in Chicago, and the North, Northwest, West, South, and Southwest suburbs.

We have estimated the total nursing temporaries market for the Chicago metropolitan area to be about $100 million. This is broken down as $85 million for hospital staffing and $15 million for nursing home staffing. The support for this estimate is given in "Market Estimations and Calculations" in the Appendix.

CHICAGO HOSPITAL MARKET
(Excerpted from "HOSPITAL MARKET" in Appendix)

	Hospitals	Total Beds	Percent Occupied	Occupied Beds	Patient Days
Totals	98	31,474		22,079	8,058,877
Average		321	68	225	82,233

CHICAGO NURSING HOME MARKET
(excerpted from "NURSING HOMES IN CHICAGO" in the Appendix)

	Nursing Homes	Skilled Nursing Facility Beds	Intermediate Care Facility Beds
Totals	238	24,802	15,421

COMPETITION

- QHC will be differentiated significantly by its policy of attentiveness to the needs and professionalism of the nurses.

- The increased formation of internal agencies in hospitals is a major competitive and industry factor.

- The major industry weaknesses are its maturity and slowing growth.

- QHC will exploit the industry's inability to explain its cost benefits to the user.

Over 200 nursing agency offices provide a broad range of temporary nursing services to hospitals, nursing homes, and homes in Chicago and its immediate suburban collar counties. (A full listing of Hospital Temporary Agencies in Chicago Service Area is given in the Appendix.) Of these, approximately 100 serve hospital or nursing home clients, and 170 serve the home care market — 35 exclusively. Six offices have only hospital and nursing home clients.

The distinction is important. For although many of the institutional providers also serve the home care segment, it requires different systems, policies, employee attitudes and preferences, billing, marketing strategies, and selling tactics. A start-up agency would have major difficulty targeting both segments simultaneously.

There are three major types of agencies. The independent agency has one local, or at most two, offices. The subsidiary agency of a large national or regional temporary placement firm can have from three to ten or more offices scattered throughout the metropolitan area. These offices can be franchise owner operated, corporate operated, or a combination. The third is a hospital registry operated as a temporary agency for internal use only. We do not know of a hospital that markets its internal agency business to other hospitals or nursing homes. Moreover, this would be unlikely because of the intense competition that exists among hospitals. A significant number of the Chicago area hospitals operate home care services.

Structural analysis of the relief staffing segment of the industry (see inset) suggests a few major industry strengths and weaknesses as well as opportunities for QHC.

Strengths

- The health care temporaries industry fulfills a major need. Nursing temporaries clearly help hospitals and nursing homes handle their ever-fluctuating staffing requirements. It can do this cost effectively. Supplemental staffing provides a desired job alternative to a significant number of health care personnel. The elderly, handicapped, and convalescent patients heavily rely on home care services of all kinds. This segment will continue growing as the elderly population grows, as families look for assistance and alternatives to nursing homes, and as hospitals continue to release patients sooner.

- The existence of a nursing personnel shortage is a major factor affecting the size and strength of the industry. The future size of this shortage is difficult to predict. On the one hand, the number of nursing graduates is increasing. On the other hand, the amount of nursing care each patient receives is increasing, due to increasing acuity and technology. Also, nursing homes are seeking more RNs to fulfill an increased need for skilled nursing care.

  Surveys published by the American Hospital Association and Illinois Hospital Association suggest the shortage has stopped increasing.

  This is based on a leveling of the vacancy rate. According to the Health and Human Services' *Secretary's Commission on Nursing,* at current conditions the increase in supply will just balance the increase in demand.

- Supplemental staffing positions will continue to be a highly desirable alternative for the nurse, especially as the two-income family continues to grow and as more workers trade full-time jobs for more leisure time.

RELIEF STAFFING INDUSTRY ANALYSIS

I. Threat of New Entrants

- Relatively low capital requirements.
- Owner or manager needs nursing experience.
- Economies of scale are small since variable cost is more than 85% of total cost.
- Market is highly differentiated, with over 127 different agencies in 210 offices.
- Government regulations are minimal and not yet policed or enforced.

II. Threat of Substitution

- Hospitals may increase their use of non-nursing personnel in order to relieve the RN to concentrate on patient care duties, thereby reducing RN demand and cost.
- Many hospitals will be reluctant to substitute as the patient acuity and the technological requirements increase.

III. Bargaining Power of Suppliers

- Nurses, etc., often jump from one agency to the next as they hear of new incentives, increased salaries, or better locations and treatment.
- RNs, LPNs and CNAs are currently in short supply and may remain so. The future is difficult to predict. On the one hand, the number of nursing graduates is increasing. On the other hand, the amount of nursing care each patient receives is increasing, due to increasing acuity and technology.
- These professionals are unique, and from an agency's point of view there are no substitutes.
- Agencies are not the most important user; hospitals and nursing homes are.
- The agency cannot develop its own independent supply of health care workers.

IV. Bargaining Power of Buyers

- Large hospital agency users are demanding contracts with negotiated prices.
- Hospital and nursing home groups are obtaining group contracts.
- Threat of backward integration: hospitals have or are developing their own in-house agencies, called registries. Two agencies have noted that registries have cut into their business.
- With few exceptions, nursing personnel are relatively undifferentiated between agencies.

V. Agency Rivalry

- Very few published industry facts; few agencies advertise their unique selling proposition.
- Many agencies appear similar and indistinguishable to the institutions they are serving. For example, most agencies ask for a minimum of one year experience. Very few require more.
- Mature industry with low or little growth.
- Lack of significant differentiation among each type of worker forces intense price and service competition.
- In order to adequately meet their customers' needs, all agencies must significantly possess the following: competitive pricing; consistent, prompt filling of orders; high-quality professionals who are experienced, competent, technically qualified, mature, and motivated; dependable service without sudden cancellations or no shows.

Weaknesses

■ The industry is mature. Little or no growth in the institutional segment is expected in the near term. There is very moderate growth predicted in the home care segment. The resulting increased competition has contracted operating margins. This has been very significant for some firms. An Allstate securities analysis reports that Lifetime, the parent company of Kimberly Quality Care, plans to de-emphasize institutional staffing (currently 12 percent of sales) and concentrate on home health (currently 65 percent of sales). By 1995, Lifetime expects the institutional division to be only 4 percent, and the home health division to be up to 77 percent of sales.

■ The barriers to entry are minor. Thirty additional office listings were noted in the just published phone directory, compared to the previous year. We estimate that a significant proportion represents newly opened offices. This increased competition puts strong pressure on operating margins.

■ The newly instituted Illinois Nurse Agency Licensing Department lacks the resources to police and enforce the regulations. Some agencies operate below standards, enabling them to offer cut-rate pricing to those institutions knowingly or unknowingly willing to accept the substandard service.

■ The industry has been generally unable to convince hospital and nursing administrators that planned and controlled use of temporaries is cost effective. They see the discrepancy between the wages they pay and the agency's hourly charge as very inflated and not cost effective for them. The comparison which they make is inappropriate. Rather, agency prices should be compared to the institution's actual total hourly costs. Yet many, but not all, feel they are being over-charged. This strongly felt opinion is difficult to change. Accordingly, there is a strong desire to eliminate the need for agency supplied staffing. Hospitals are continually attempting to start internal agencies. Additionally, they are attempting to increase nurse retention with costly incentive and bonus packages.

Opportunities for QHC

■ A significantly large market (greater than $100 million) is present in the Chicago metropolitan area. The market appears stable but could grow, on average, 1 to 3 percent per year over the next five years.

■ There are only four different agencies with a total of six offices which exclusively serve institutional clients. Three of these agencies would most likely be direct competitors. They are independent. This niche appears relatively empty and, therefore, is our niche of choice.

- Careful differentiation choices are necessary and will be made in order to capture the attention of clients and to recruit health care professionals. We plan to differentiate both our service and our personnel.

- A significant degree of quality can be guaranteed by having a highly experienced nursing pool. We plan to require a minimum experience of two years for medical/surgical RNs and three years for critical care RNs.

- A number of sources (our surveys, interviews with nurses management, and some articles) reveal a need for fairer, more professional treatment of the nursing personnel. These sources also disclose that temporary agencies especially lack proper attention to this subject. QHC will seize this distinguishing opportunity to significantly differentiate its programs, policies, and philosophy.

- Since many agency users and most non-users are not convinced that a planned, carefully budgeted use of supplemental staffing is cost effective, we plan to provide a consulting and advisory program to help our clients effectively utilize our staffing services. We also note that hospitals with their own internal agencies use external agencies as well.

- The nursing professionals are the essence of an agency. Many agencies use various financial incentives almost exclusively. We plan to make every effort to not only competitively meet their salary needs but to direct our attention to their needs for recognition, growth, motivation, and professionalism.

COMPETITIVE ANALYSIS

Nine agencies stood out as significant and representative as a result of our surveys and research. We concentrated our investigations on these nine. Our findings are condensed in the Competitor Summary Sheets presented in the Appendix. This information is summarized in the accompanying table by rating their strengths and weaknesses along with those expected for QHC.

Although this type of analysis is not very accurate and has significant limitations, it does allow one to focus on the distinctive elements of each competing agency. This is especially valid when we also take into account all the specific information

Analysis of Competitor Strength and Weakness
Staffing Relief Industry

AGENCY NAME:	Alpha Chris-tian	Health-Staf	Kimber-ly Qual-ity Care	Medical Person-nel Pool	Myers-cough	Norrell	Nurse-Finder	Pro-Nurse	QHC Temps	Reliable Nursing Service
CORE CAPABILITY										
SERVICES	3	3		2	3	2	3	3	3	3
CUSTOMER BASE		3	1	2	3	3	3	2	1	3
MARKETING/SELLING	2	3	2	1	3	2	2	3	3	3
RECRUITING		2	2	2	3	3	3	3	3	3
OPERATIONS		3		1	2	2	1	3	3	3
MANAGERIAL ABILITIES		2			3		2	3	3	3
SALARIES		3	2		2	2	2		2	2
ORGANIZATION	2	2	2	2	2	3	3	3	2	2
PRICING	2	3			2	2	1		3	3
EMPLOYEE POLICY		3			3	3	1	3	3	3
Items Rated **Sub Average**	4 2.25	10 2.70	5 1.80	6 1.67	10 2.60	9 2.44	10 2.10	8 2.88	10 2.60	10 2.80
ABILITY TO GROW										
LOCAL		2	1	2	2	2	1		3	3
REGIONAL/NATIONAL	2		1	2		3	3			
Items Rated **Sub Average**	1 2.00	1 2.00	2 1.00	2 2.00	1 2.00	2 2.50	2 2.00		1 3.00	1 3.00
ADAPTABILITY and **RESPONSE to CHANGE**										
NEW SERVICES						3			2	2
EXPANSION					2				2	2
Items Rated **Sub Average**					1 2	1 3			2 2	2 2
ITEMS RATED **OVERALL AVERAGE**	5 2.20	11 2.64	7 1.57	8 1.75	12 2.50	12 2.50	12 2.08	8 2.88	13 2.54	13 2.69

Ratings are based on role in the staff relief market only. 3 = good; 2 = average; 1= poor. Items were left unrated when data was either unavailable or insufficient. This analysis is limited by both sufficiency and depth of the information either because it was unavailable or we were refused.

gathered in the competitor summaries. The ratings for QHC appear generous but well within our expectations and capabilities.

The three top-rated agencies are ProNurse, HealthStaf, and Reliable Nursing Service. These agencies are all independents. All are young, having started in business within the last three years. Our plan is to use these top-rated agencies as models. We will further distinguish ourselves with more experienced nurses, staffing advisory services, and a sophisticated computerized scheduling system.

CUSTOMER BENEFITS

A temporary agency has been well established as a method to help hospitals and nursing homes provide supplemental staffing to meet unexpected as well as expected staffing needs. The customer uses supplemental nurses and nursing assistants to fill vacancies caused by chronic personnel shortages, vacations, sick leave, and fluctuations in demand. The employee arrives at the institution and completes the job assignment, and the institution wants the employee to return again for another shift.

Hospitals insist on quality care in order to satisfy their patient needs. There is a direct relationship between a hospital's care quality and its economic viability. The quality of nursing temporaries must match the quality demanded of the hospital's regular nursing staff. Agencies can assume this quality by requiring their nursing staff to have extensive experience and to meet strict screening criteria.

We plan to provide the customer with advisory services on how to use our staffing effectively. This need is not now being served. In addition, QHC significantly differentiates its services by providing management and programs that treat nurses more professionally.

Agencies have an available supply of nurses, especially in the critical care and medical/surgical area. Based on our "Nursing Department Survey" (in the Appendix) and surveys conducted by the AHA and IHA, the two specialties in greatest demand are critical care and medical/surgical nurses. This demand will increase as a result of improved technology and increasing acuity of patient illnesses.

Customer will be offered discounts as incentives for initial as well as repeat orders. This is factored into our financial projections.

Nurse User Benefits

Agencies allow nurses to be in a variety of settings and a number of different hospitals, so they are not tied down to one unit or place. For nurses who are returning to active practice, the environment is more conducive to their temporary lifestyle before they decide to commit to a full-time work schedule. Temporary nurses are free to choose a varied work schedule, the hospital location, and the type of nursing unit they wish to work in. This flexibility is extremely attractive.

Agencies allow nurses to keep their patient care experience current. If they are currently in a management or administrative role, they have more paperwork to prepare rather than directly dealing with patients.

Nurses can conveniently supplement their income by working for agencies. They can easily shift to inactive status as their personal needs change. They are also free to work for more than one agency at a time.

In-service education programs are welcomed by the nursing professionals. They recognize that it will increase their overall effectiveness in service to customers as well as fulfill a personal need.

Market, Near Term

There are approximately 98 hospitals and 238 nursing homes in the target market area. The number of hospitals has been decreasing in the past five years due to financial failures and consolidations. The competition from internal hospital agencies has already begun to affect the temporary agencies. Medical Personnel Pool and Nursefinders have stated that internal registries have begun to make cuts in their profits.

Market, Long Term

The temporary agency industry is beginning to shift from servicing slower growth hospital staffing needs to the growing home health care needs. We already noted that Kimberly Quality has been de-emphasizing hospital staffing. Medical Personnel Pool has also been attempting to shift their sales toward home care. Currently their sales are distributed 70 percent home care and 30 percent hospital staffing. The elderly, handicapped and convalescent patients heavily rely on home care services of all kinds. This segment will continue growing as the elderly populations grow, as families look for assistance and alternatives to nursing homes, and as hospitals continue to release patients sooner. Growth in the elderly population will also result in an increased demand for nursing personnel in nursing homes. QHC will begin entry into this segment in our third year.

Market Share

There is no data to ascertain specific market shares. Based on our estimation of the market for hospital nurse temporaries for the Chicago area, the market is about $2 million per week (see Appendix for "Market Estimations and Calculations"). The best estimate was the weekly per agency calculation based on 105 agencies.

Industry Growth

Kimberly Quality Care has noted a 10.5 percent compounded annual real growth in the home health industry. We estimate the institutional staffing to be growing at about 3 to 5 percent per year.

Specific Target Markets

Our initial target hospitals and nursing homes will be in the city of Chicago and the north, northwest, and west suburbs. The agency office is looking to start the year with one hospital and one nursing home, and to expand to six hospitals and six nursing homes in year one.

Projected Sales

We project QHC to experience sales as follows:

Year One	$1.1 million
Year Two	$3.4 million
Year Three	$4.9 million
Year Four	$6.5 million
Year Five	$8.4 million

Increased revenues in the second year are due to the addition of two nursing home clients and two hospital clients. By the third year, we will increase to nine nursing homes and nine hospitals, and will have entered the home health care business.

In Year Four, it is difficult to predict sales increases for the institutional staffing portion of the business. Therefore only minimal increases in institutional customers are projected for Years Four and Five. However, our expansion to home health care will result in a substantial increase in revenues. In Year Five, we will have increased our sales of home health care to 18 percent of sales (see Appendix "Shift in Customer Base").

Market Strategy

Even though they have vacancies, some institutions do not use agencies but allow current staff to work overtime, reduce admissions, or go unstaffed. The addressed market includes those who are currently using temporary agencies. Based on our market research, over 81 percent responded that they use agencies.

Our market strategy is to position ourselves as a high-quality, responsive agency at a competitive price. This will place us in a niche similar to that occupied by a few successful independent agencies, such as HealthStaf, ProNurse, and Reliable Nursing Service. In order to further differentiate our image, we plan the following:

- Provide an advisory program as mentioned above in "User Benefits."

- Treat our nursing personnel more fairly and more professionally than other agencies do. Our orientations and orientation materials will be directed at lessening the stress and anxiety of working in unfamiliar surroundings. These needs were strongly expressed in our surveys and in our conversations with nursing temporaries.

- Our nurses are required to have, depending on qualifications, two to three years of experience, and are carefully screened and tested for skill levels. Our potential customers feel this is a crucial requirement.

- We offer nurses flexible scheduling as well as attractive compensation and benefits in order to retain their services. We will continually be responsive to both our customers' and suppliers' needs.

- It is more difficult to directly enter the home care market than it is to enter the institutional market. Once a nursing pool is established and hospital and physician contacts are made, expansion into this segment becomes more feasible. QHC will develop its home care business in Year Three.

Market Research and Competitive Intelligence

Management recognizes the need to seek and analyze information regarding competitors on an on-going basis using our already established competitive intelligence system. On-going surveys of our nurses regarding contacts with personnel representing other agencies will be an important part of this system.

EMPLOYEES

The nurses and aides represent over 95 percent of the employees and 75 percent of the operational costs. Below is a table representing the number of employees presently employed and forecasted to be employed over the next five years.

	1991*	1992	1993	1994	1995
Management	3	3	3	4	4
Full-Time Support Staff	3	4	4	4	4
Part-Time Support Staff	0	0	1	1	1
RN	50	75	100	110	120
LPN	15	22	29	32	35
CNA	35	53	71	78	85
Totals:	106	157	208	229	249

*According to the previously mentioned article appearing in *Medical Care*, the average nursing roster size was 95. It is realistic to project a roster of 50 RNs at the end of the first year. LPNs and CNAs were scaled accordingly.

Management will oversee operations, sales, and financial issues. The initial support staff will consist of a computer operator, a payroll scheduler, and a receptionist. The functions of these support staff are critical to smooth operations. Their roles include receiving orders, scheduling, billing, and payroll processing.

QHC intends to offer its health care employees above-average compensation in order to recruit and retain skilled and excellent talent. Health care personnel who work evenings, nights and weekends, or holidays customarily receive higher pay. Holiday pay is one-and-a-half times the corresponding posted rate. Nurses and LPNs are skilled workers registered and licensed by the Illinois Department of Professional Regulations. CNAs are certified by the Illinois Department of Public Health. For simplicity, we have used an average hourly rate (see Appendix) in order to easily generate the pro forma statements. We also assumed that the filled orders would be evenly distributed.

Average Hourly Rates Used for Calculations

RN rate	$27.30
CNA rate	$10.32
LPN rate	$17.68

The counties of Cook, Lake, and DuPage contain more than 90 percent of the Chicago-area nursing personnel. The majority of the hospitals we plan to target are also in these three counties.

The Distribution of Nursing Personnel

County	No. of RNs	No. of LPNs
Cook	44,628	9,919
Lake	4,426	543
DuPage	9,839	781
McHenry	1,708	187
Kankakee	957	370
Will	3,515	699
Grundy	330	74
Totals	65,403	12,573

Employee recruitment and retention is critical to QHC's success. The strategy QHC will use to accomplish this goal has the following elements:

■ Competitive salary levels are carefully chosen so they are very close to our major competitors. For example, the maximum wage offered for a specialty RN by HealthStaf is $35.25/hour. QHC is offering $35.35/hour.

■ Our orientation and training programs will be not only directed toward technical improvement, but also toward professional and personal development. For example, personnel will be given the opportunity to teach classes and receive career guidance and counseling. The nurse survey clearly demonstrated this need. Few, if any, other agencies approach this need as well as we intend to.

■ Temporary staff crave fair and understanding treatment. QHC will provide the nurse with easy-to-use orientation manuals about the institution's location, floor plans of the nursing unit, unique policies and procedures, and the names of the staff they will be working with. This is just as important for regular attendance as for the first assignment. The competitive intelligence which we have gathered thus far suggests that this approach will not only fill an important need but will also set us apart and make us unique.

■ Continual feedback will be sought from our health care personnel. Our programs will be upgraded on a regular basis. We will make full use of our sophisticated computer system to accomplish this.

The planned benefits are outlined below. This package was designed by considering a large number of factors. Two of the most important considerations in constructing this package were the competition's offerings and the preferences expressed in our Nursing Survey (see Appendix). For example, strong interest was expressed in both training and self-improvement seminars.

Itemized Benefit Costs

The benefits are available through payroll deduction. Nursing employees must complete a minimum of 12 shifts/month to be eligible for these benefits. Management and support staff are also eligible for these benefits.

Health Care offered through HMO; Employee pays the full cost. Rates are established by carrier yearly. The current monthly premium costs are single - $112.88; family - $290.52	$ 0
Dental Care offered through First Commonwealth. Employee pays full cost. Single - $6.00; Family - $12.00	$ 0
Life Insurance offered through Hartford Life. The benefit maximum is $15,000; Employee pays full cost. Rates are based on age.	$ 0
Training Budget based on a maximum of 5.5 training hours/employee /calendar year (100 employees)($18.18 avg. rate) (5.5 hours)	$10,000

Cash Bonus
Maximum of $50/month to be paid $15,000
(50%)(50 RNs)($50)(12 months)

Education Seminars
Maximum of $100 to be reimbursed $ 5,000
per year
(50%)(100 RNs, LPNs, CNAs)

TOTAL COST: $ 30,000

In the first year of operations, QHC will emphasize the $100 sign-on bonus to RNs who agree to work 12 shifts per month from May through December 1991. Gradually, as QHC gains visibility and recognition through its clients and nurses, we may phase out this sign-on bonus in year two. The effectiveness of this program will be reviewed after year one.

The referral bonus will apply if a QHC nurse refers another nurse. The referring nurse receives $50/referral as long as both are actively working three shifts per week.

Nurse Recruitment Costs

Referral Bonus
Assume one-third of 50, or 17,
nurses refer two nurses.
Nurse receives referral fee of
$100 for two nurses.
(17)($100) = $1,700 × 12 months = $20,400
Deferred payment for six months $10,200
Year Two will be $20,400

Sign-on Bonus
Employee receives "instant"
payment for hire. Assume
20% referees, 20% new hires
(50 RNs)(40%)($100) $ 2,000

TOTAL RECRUITMENT COST $12,200

Workers' compensation, general and professional and auto liability will be purchased for health-care staff. QHC pays these rates quarterly. These rates are based upon the number of hours of work exposure and upon the number of individuals covered (see Appendix). Professional liability coverage is $1,000,000 per incident and up to $3,000,000 aggregate. We strive for RN safety by stressing these issues in the orientation as well as in the nursing brochure. The incentive for complying with these principles is the nurses' need to maintain their own health and well being.

Orientation is an ongoing process of familiarizing the temporaries with the customers' procedures, policies, and environment. Orientation programs will be held at QHC. Hospitals will be able to contribute information to the orientation program if they request.

Retention of nurses will occur by developing career opportunities for RNs, CNAs, and LPNs. Nurses can work in a variety of units in order to determine which one she or he would like to continue in. Management will encourage continuing education and will present seminars on nursing legal issues and health care trends. Temporary agency nurses will also have the opportunity to teach classes at QHC for additional compensation. QHC will try to reduce turnover by encouraging nurses to change from active status to inactive status on the roster list rather than terminate employment. This will allow us to keep in better contact and help reduce costs of recruitment, reapplication, and administration.

Client reviews will occur after the agency personnel completes the shift. The performance results are based on a QHC checklist that is sent to the customer. Results of the checklist are fed into the computer and tracked. Each employee will also receive yearly performance appraisals based on the customer results.

Our temporary work force is based on variable costs. In periods of low demand, no variable salary costs are paid to nurses, and we would not have to initiate any re-scheduling/reduction in staff of RNs, CNAs, or LPNs.

SELLING

- Nurse recruitment through "word-of-mouth" will be promoted by maintaining a positive agency image.

- Nurses will also be contacted through selective advertising and direct mail.

- Executive selling will be used for contacting institutional customers.

Due to the particular nature of our business, "selling" for QHC Temps encompasses tactics employed in identifying and contacting prospective "suppliers," the nursing personnel, as well as prospective customers. These two groups of prospects require very different sets of selling tactics.

With the ongoing nursing shortage and the consequent intense competition to acquire the services of nursing personnel, competing employers advertise heavily in the local print media. Specifically, the overwhelming majority of nursing recruitment ads are placed in the Illinois Edition of *The Nursing Spectrum* and the classified job listings in the Sunday edition of *The Chicago Tribune*. *The Nursing Spectrum* is a biweekly publication with a circulation of over 106,000 Illinois-registered RNs, over 44,000 of whom reside in Cook County alone. Job listings in the *Tribune* target all nursing personnel in the entire midwest area of circulation.

It is notable that only a relatively few agencies advertise for RNs. With 127 or more different agencies in the Chicago area, no more than 10 to 20 ads appear per edition of the Sunday *Tribune*. Many smaller agencies opt for other recruiting methods or advertise only sporadically.

The ads in the two publications mentioned above tend to emphasize pay rates, "flexibility," and incentives and vary greatly in size and style. In order to be competitive, the content of ads placed by QHC Temps must to some extent be consistent with those placed by other nursing agencies. However, some emphasis will also be placed upon the company's quality orientation, efficient scheduling capabilities, and responsiveness to the nurses' needs.

In keeping with our relatively small advertising budget, these objectives must be accomplished with ads that will be large enough to be noticeable but much smaller than those of many of our larger competitors who are better able to purchase costly display ads. Within these guidelines, an effort will be made to ensure that our ads convey our recruitment message boldly and persuasively, but in a manner consistent with and representative of the company's integrity. It is evident that this is more important than the size of the ad.

The results of our survey of nurses confirm the importance of reaching them via the print media. Survey responses indicated, however, that "word-of-mouth" among nursing personnel, their friends, and their other professional contacts is of even greater importance: over 50 percent of survey respondents listed personal contacts as the most often used source of employment information. Therefore, it is critical that a positive image of QHC Temps be projected and communicated by the nursing personnel on our staff. Ensuring that our nurses always feel well-served by the company will be the key to attracting *more* nurses to our employ — a contented staff of employees can be our best advertisement.

Concurrent with our initial ad placements, one month prior to our beginning of operations, we will also begin a direct mail campaign targeting RNs in metropolitan Chicago. Such a campaign represents an additional, less costly, means of communicating with a large number of prospective employees. However, according to marketing experts, direct mail tends to generate relatively few responses per mailing and will therefore be employed as inexpensively as possible, utilizing postcards and/or bulk rates where possible. After an initial large-volume mailing, direct mail will periodically be used on a smaller, more-directed scale and will be discontinued if the response rate is found to be particularly low.

Conventional marketing wisdom states that executive selling should be employed only in targeting prospective customers whose orders might generate revenues in excess of $100,000. The sales and revenue projections contained in the Appendix of this Business Plan demonstrate that this condition is indeed likely to apply to many of the institutional customers of QHC. In fact, depending upon the degree of utilization of our nursing personnel, a single hospital or nursing home can generate revenues in the range of $100,000 to $450,000. Executive selling will therefore be our method of choice for contacting our prospective institutional customers. As indicated previously, executive selling will primarily be the responsibility of Dr. Smith, capitalizing upon his extensive network of professional contacts in local hospital and nursing home management.

Our third-year expansion into the home care market will call for the use of new sales methods. We expect to identify potential customers primarily through contacting hospital discharge planners and physicians' groups with large geriatric practices.

OPERATIONS

- The major pre-operations planning functions are the commitment of first sales from customers and recruitment of temporary staffing personnel.

- Important operations functions include scheduling of nursing temporaries, billing to customers, payroll processing, and monitoring quality of temporary staff.

PRE-OPERATIONS PLANNING

Below is a chart representing the necessary activities and target dates that need to be achieved. QHC will open on May 1, 1991.

PRE OPENING MILESTONES

```
                           Jan        Feb        March       April       May
raise capital           — — — — — — — —  ongoing  — — — — — — — — — — — — — — — — —-
find location      begin search — — — — — — — —-move in — — — — — — — — — — — — — —-
recruitment of RNs — — — — —  start  — — — — — — — — — —  ongoing  — — — — — — —
system purchase    —- order  — receive  —  implement  — — — — — —·— — — — — — —-
distribute customer brochure  —- start  — — — — — — — —-  ongoing  — — — — — — — — —
hire temporaries  — — — — — — — — — —·  start  — — — — — — — —-  ongoing  — — — —
commitment of first sale(s)  —-·— — — — — —-  start  — —-  ongoing  — — — — — — —-
collection of first of A/R   — — — — — — — — — — — — — — — — — — — — — — — —-  achieved
advertising/marketing  — — —  1st mailing  — — — — —  2nd mailing  —  ongoing  — —-·—-
```

OTHER MILESTONES TO COMPLETE IN FIRST TWO YEARS

Issue	Month Achieved
first positive monthly cash flow	March, 1992
first profitable month of operation	December, 1991

LOCATION

Our office is located in Itasca, Illinois. It is approximately 800 square feet with a parking lot. Monthly rent is $800. The location is easily accessible for employees to pick up their checks. There is also adjoining office space available if QHC expands.

RECRUITMENT

In April, we plan to start a direct mail campaign for recruiting nursing personnel. We are looking for nurses with a minimum of three years of specialty experience and two years of medical/surgical experience. CNAs and LPNs are required to have one year of current experience.

HIRING PROCESS

To ensure that quality control of supply is maintained and enhanced, employees are carefully screened and tested. Health care workers must come in to fill out an application, interview, and then take an exam. A score of at least 80 percent on the exam in the applied or specialty area is acceptable. Strict adherence to this policy is necessary to meet our customers' needs for highly competent staff. We request license information and TB skin results to be presented, as required by the Illinois Nurse Agency Act. A brochure of QHC policy and procedures is given to each nurse in the hiring process, and the information is reviewed with the employee by management staff. Orienting the employee to the customer's environment is done by giving the nurse a data sheet of extensive hospital information so that staff can easily adapt in the new environment.

ORDER PLACEMENT

Customers call requesting orders for staffing. Matching of the request to personnel qualifications is achieved through the use of our computer system. The order is then filled through a sequence of contacting eligible personnel and the customer as shown in the Operations Flowchart. Turnaround time for an order is less than one hour between a client call to confirmation of the order. The types of order are: a) Routine-short-term fill of more than four hours and less than two weeks, b) Long-term orders with block scheduling of more than two weeks in advance, c) Emergency orders to be filled within

Operations Flowchart

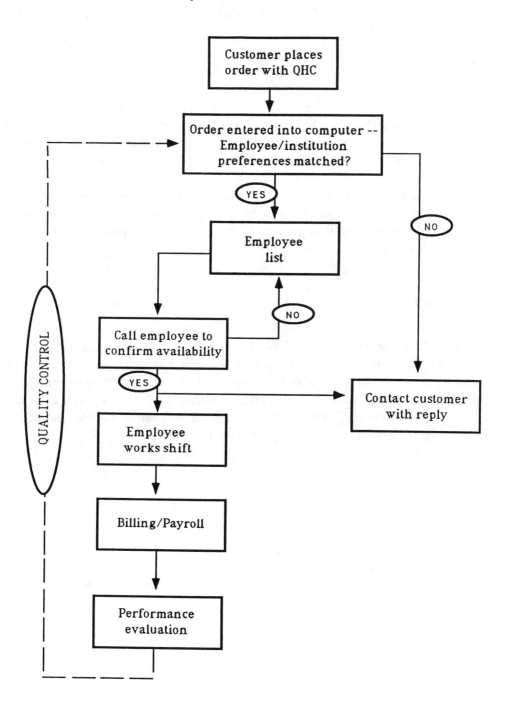

four hours. If orders are not confirmed quickly, business will flow to other agencies. A Supplemental Staffing Agreement is signed between the customer and QHC.

BILLING

In addition to the skill-matching function and accurate scheduling lists, the computer system generates invoices weekly. Billing terms are a 2 percent discount if paid within ten days, net 20 days. If hospital orders are slow in coming, we will offer more trade discount incentives to increase sales. Trade discounts will be given at a maximum of 3 percent for initial business or volume orders. Some hospitals may request special/extended billing terms. The CFO will check their credit rating before approving special terms. QHC requests that institutions contact the agency not less than two hours before canceling the scheduled shift. If this is not done, there is a minimum billing rate to the customer of two hours.

PAYROLL

Payroll will be processed weekly. The payroll week ends on the Sunday night shift. Checks are available the following Thursday of each week worked, as long as time slips have been accurately completed and turned in by Monday morning before 10 a.m. Deductions for state, federal, and FICA will be withheld from each paycheck as well as any benefit deductions. Overtime is based on hours worked over 40 in one pay period. The overtime and holiday rate is 1 1/2 times the hourly rate.

QUALITY MANAGEMENT

The customer evaluates staff performance after the assignment is completed based on a QHC checklist. If the employee requires improvement due to below quality performance, then the employee is re-oriented. One example of quality improvement is done by having the employee attend a specialized training session. Temporary personnel view videotapes of situations that may be encountered while on assignment.

OWNERSHIP/INVESTMENT STRUCTURE

- The principals of QHC will invest $125,000 in company stock.

- No ownership is offered to investors.

- $200,000 is sought in debt financing.

QHC will initially be capitalized with 125,000 shares of common stock ($1.00 par value), divided as follows: Dr. Smith will invest $45,000 in exchange for 36 percent (45,000 shares) of the stock. Dr. Anderson will also invest $45,000 in exchange for 36 percent (45,000 shares) of stock. Ms. Jones will invest $35,000 in exchange for 28 percent (35,000 shares) of stock.

The $325,000 of financing required by QHC, including the investments of the principals, will be used to fund start-up costs and general working capital needs until an adequate cash flow has been generated.

It is the choice of the principals of QHC to retain full ownership of the company for at least the next five years. Equity financing will therefore not be sought. QHC is instead seeking to obtain financing through bank debt. Based upon the financial projections contained in this Business Plan, the company will require $200,000 of debt financing. Recent conversations with commercial loan officers have indicated that the following terms for a $200,000 loan can reasonably be expected: payment on a 15- to 20-year amortization schedule with a balloon payment due after the fifth year, interest at approximately 11.5 to 12 percent, with the full amount of the loan personally collateralized by the principals. (The balloon remaining after the fifth year would be eligible for refinancing.) The principals are fully prepared to offer as collateral their personal real estate holdings and other equity totaling substantially in excess of $200,000. After business operations commence, accounts receivable will be included in the collateral package.

Management recognizes that the cash flow information does not require that we obtain all of the loan funds up front. We plan to initially borrow $100,000 against a $200,000 line of credit. However in the interest of a conservative projection, we have assumed the full $200,000 amount of debt at the outset.

FINANCIAL PROFILE

ASSUMPTIONS BEHIND SALES AND REVENUE PROJECTIONS

Sales Units (Shifts/Week) Per Customer

The market survey conducted for this Business Plan (see Appendix) indicated that 31 percent of the hospitals surveyed utilize temporary nursing services for RN staffing at a rate of one to five shifts per week; 69 percent utilize six or more shifts per week. For the purpose of our first-year projections, a utilization rate of five shifts per week per hospital customer is therefore taken as a reasonable minimum ("worst case"). The "median" projection of 15 shifts per week is based upon the calculations performed using data contained in the 1986 Ernst & Whinney survey, as found in the Appendix ("Calculation of an Estimated Market for Hospital Temporaries"). This projection was further supported by our own survey: the weighted average of responses to the shifts/week utilization question was also 15. Median projections for LPNs and CNAs (three and two, respectively) were also based upon the Ernst & Whinney analysis.

Initial projections for shifts/week utilization by nursing homes are based upon similar calculations performed upon available nursing home data (see Appendix). In the absence of reliable data, home care utilization projections were made conservatively, assuming equal demand for RNs and CNAs, lesser demand for LPNs.

Projections for increased hospital utilization of RNs in the second year of operations are based upon available competitor data: after 21 months of operations, Reliable Nursing Service attained an average of 250 total shift placements per month. As the best example of success (within two years) found in our industry research, this information was used as foundation for our "best case" projection for the second year (seven hospitals × 35 shifts/wk. = 245); the "worst" and "median" projections were scaled down accordingly, assuming at least the minimum utilization projected for the first year. Without any similar data with which to project further growth in hospital utilization of RNs, the projected utilization of hospital RNs was kept constant for years two through five. Growth was projected by conservatively adding one additional hospital customer in years three through five (see next section below). Utilization in nursing homes and home care as well as for all LPN and CNA utilization were kept constant at the initial projections.

Average Number of Customers

Available competitor information regarding the number of institutional customers per agency, including the 1984 study of the temporary nursing service industry (previously cited), led to the following expectations for QHC: six hospital and six nursing home customers by the end of the first year, increasing to eight each by the end of the second year. Assuming steady growth from zero to six in the first year and from six to eight in the second year, the "average number of customers" is assumed to be three and seven, respectively. Minimum expectations of growth and the presence of over twice as many nursing homes as hospitals in the market area chosen led to the customer volume projections for years three through five.

Other available competitor information (regarding Nursefinders and other agencies) supported a projection of 15 to 20 percent of total sales for QHC to be in the home care segment by the end of the fifth year of operations. Customer volume projections were chosen and scaled back to Year Three accordingly.

Sales Price (Average Billing Rate/Hour)

Our market survey indicated that the greatest market need for RNs is for staffing weekday evenings and nights, med./surg. and critical care.

Competitor billing data ($/hr.) available (for October, 1990):

	Nursefinders	Pro-Nurse	Myerscough
Med.-Surg.			
Weekday P.M.	38.95	35.75	36.00
Weekday Night	40.95	37.75	37.70
Critical Care			
Weekday P.M.	41.95	41.75	41.40
Weekday Night	42.95	42.75	42.40

We can enact our market strategy, as previously indicated, billing slightly *below* the market, by initially setting our average (P.M. & night) RN med./surg. billing rate at $36.50 and our average critical care billing rate at $41.50. *Average sales price is thus (36.50 + 41.50)/2 = $39.00.* Average LPN and CNA billing rates were determined by similar analyses of competitor billing data.

Industry data indicates that RN billing rates are expected to increase an average of 8 percent/year over the next several years; LPN rates and CNA rates are expected to increase 7 percent/year and 6 percent/year, respectively. QHC billing rates are projected accordingly for years two through five.

ASSUMPTIONS BEHIND FINANCIAL STATEMENTS

Income Statement and Cash Flow Statement Items

1) **Wages:** Data available from Nursefinders from January, 1990 indicates that their nurses' pay rates range from approximately *59 to 62 percent* as a percentage of the corresponding billing rates. Again, to be consistent with our market strategy, QHC seeks to *exceed* that range. Other data compiled from competitors' current ads and the October, 1990 billing data referred to above indicates this pay rate/billing rate ratio to be approximately 69 percent for Myerscough, 70 percent for Favorite, and 71 to 73 percent for Nurse Care. We can thus be consistent with the market and pay our nurses at rates *higher* than that of two of our principal competitors, Nursefinders and Myerscough, by setting an average pay rate of *70 percent of the average billing rate.* For example, pay rate for RNs: (39.00)(.7) = $27.30. All nurses' wages are therefore computed at 70 percent of billings (gross revenues).

2) **Worker's Compensation and Payroll Taxes** are based upon the following industry averages:

	% of wages
Worker's Compensation	3.5
FICA	7.65
Unemployment Insurance	3.1
Total	14.25

3) **Insurance:** Professional and general liability and non-owned automobile liability are both based upon total hours of exposure.

4) **Benefits:** Total cost of benefits package increases in Years Two through Five in proportion to increases in temporary staff (see "Employees" section).

5) **Advertising, Mailings, Selling Expenses, and Supplies:** Initial projections are based on competitor data and vendor quotes. These expenses double in the second year and, thereafter, increase in proportion to sales.

6) Depreciation is based upon a ten-year, straight-line schedule (see "Depreciation Schedule" in the Appendix).

7) Interest Income: A 7 percent interest rate is assumed on the following minimum cash balances:

1st year	$ 75,000
2nd year	$ 75,000
3rd year	$100,000
4th year	$150,000
5th year	$200,000

8) Interest Expense and Long-Term Debt Service: A 12 percent interest rate with a 15-year term is assumed (see "Loan Amortization Schedule" in the Appendix).

9) Pre-Opening Expenses:

Incorporation Costs	
Attorney's fees	$1,000
Supplies	150
Equipment	
Computer hardware/software	15,000
(based on a quote from Farnsworth)	
Furniture and Fixtures	6,000
(based on estimates in Nursefinders franchises' documents)	
Licensing	250
Advertising (see "Selling")	2,000
Direct Mail (see "Selling")	3,200

10) Collection of Receivables: For cash-flow projections, cash receipts are assumed to lag an average of two weeks after billings. This is based on limited information available about competitors' collection periods.

11) Total Financing Requirements: This amount was based upon the month in the first two years in which the cumulative net cash flow "bottoms out" at ($224,875) in May, 1992. Additional funds are needed to provide a reserve in that month to cover at least two weeks of payroll ($95,000). Thus the total estimated need is $325,000.

Balance Sheet Items

1) Accounts receivable and payable are projected beyond the first year in proportion to sales.

2) Other Current Assets: Marketable securities or other short-term investments: No interest is assumed for these amounts due to the wide variety of investment options available to management, including possible withdrawal of some funds from the company.

3) Current Portion, Long-Term Debt: Balance remaining after the last fifth-year loan payment is presumed to become current as a balloon payment due. This balance will be repaid with current funds. If adequate funds are unavailable, refinancing will be sought using receivables as collateral.

FINANCIAL STATEMENTS

The following pro forma statements are found in this section:

> Income Statements, yearly
> Cash Flow Statements, monthly for the first two years
> Balance Sheets, yearly

Additional statements and supporting schedules are contained in the Appendix:

> Sales Projections
> Revenue Projections
> Insurance Projections
> Depreciation Schedule
> Loan Amortization Schedule
> Income Statements, monthly for the first two years
> Break-Even Analysis

Sample Business Plan A

QHC TEMPS
INCOME STATEMENT
FOR THE FISCAL YEAR MAY 1, 1991 - APRIL 30, 1992
(1st YEAR OF OPERATIONS)

"WORST CASE" PROJECTION

Service Revenue
Sales
Hospital revenues	243,360
Nurs. home revenues	92,040
Home care revenues	0
Gross Service Revenue	$335,400
Sales discounts (@ 3%)	$10,062
Net Service Revenue	$325,338

Cost of Goods Sold
Wages
(@70% of Gross Rev.)	234,780
Worker's Comp. &	
Payroll Taxes	33,456
Insurance	2,654
Benefits	30,000
Cost of Goods Sold	$300,890
Gross Margin	$24,448

Operating Expenses
Selling
Advertising	24,000
Mailings/other	
selling expenses	6,200
General & Admin.	
Licensing	500
Incorporation costs	1,150
Mgmnt. compensation	120,000
Employee comp.	48,000
Rent	9,600
Utilities	1,800
Recruitment costs	12,200
Supplies	2,400
Depreciation	2,100
Total Operating Expense	$227,950

Net Operating
Income (Loss)	($203,502)
Interest Income	5,200
Interest Expense	24,000

Net Income (Loss)
Before Taxes	($222,302)
Income Tax	
Net Income	($222,302)

MEDIAN PROJECTION

Service Revenue
Sales
Hospital revenues	861,432
Nurs. home revenues	295,776
Home care revenues	0
Gross Service Revenue	$1,157,208
Sales discounts (@ 3%)	$34,716
Net Service Revenue	$1,122,492

Cost of Goods Sold
Wages
(@70% of Gross Rev.)	810,046
Worker's Comp. &	
Payroll Taxes	115,431
Insurance	5,883
Benefits	30,000
Cost of Goods Sold	$961,360
Gross Margin	$161,132

Operating Expenses
Selling
Advertising	24,000
Mailings/other	
selling expenses	6,200
General & Admin.	
Licensing	500
Incorporation costs	1,150
Mgmnt. compensation	120,000
Employee comp.	48,000
Rent	9,600
Utilities	1,800
Recruitment costs	12,200
Supplies	2,400
Depreciation	2,100
Total Operating Expense	$227,950

Net Operating
Income (Loss)	($66,818)
Interest Income	5,200
Interest Expense	24,000

Net Income (Loss)
Before Taxes	($85,618)
Income Tax	
Net Income	($85,618)

"BEST CASE" PROJECTION

Service Revenue
Sales
Hospital revenues	1,479,504
Nurs. home revenues	499,512
Home care revenues	0
Gross Service Revenue	$1,979,016
Sales discounts (@ 3%)	$59,370
Net Service Revenue	$1,919,646

Cost of Goods Sold
Wages
(@70% of Gross Rev.)	1,385,311
Worker's Comp. &	
Payroll Taxes	197,407
Insurance	9,112
Benefits	30,000
Cost of Goods Sold	$1,621,830
Gross Margin	$297,815

Operating Expenses
Selling
Advertising	24,000
Mailings/other	
selling expenses	6,200
General & Admin.	
Licensing	500
Incorporation costs	1,150
Mgmnt. compensation	120,000
Employee comp.	48,000
Rent	9,600
Utilities	1,800
Recruitment costs	12,200
Supplies	2,400
Depreciation	2,100
Total Operating Expense	$227,950

Net Operating
Income (Loss)	$69,865
Interest Income	5,200
Interest Expense	24,000

Net Income (Loss)
Before Taxes	$51,065
Income Tax (@34%)	17,362
Net Income	$33,703

213

Sample Business Plan A

"WORST CASE" PROJECTION

Service Revenue	
Sales	
Hospital revenues	613,267
Nurs. home revenues	227,646
Home care revenues	0
Gross Service Revenue	$840,913
Sales discounts (@ 3%)	$25,227
Net Service Revenue	$815,686
Cost of Goods Sold	
Wages	
(@70% of Gross Rev.)	588,639
Worker's Comp. &	
Payroll Taxes	83,881
Insurance	4,751
Benefits	45,000
Cost of Goods Sold	$722,271
Gross Margin	$93,414
Operating Expenses	
Selling	
Advertising	48,000
Mailings/other	
selling expenses	12,400
General & Admin.	
Licensing	250
Mgmnt. compensation	126,120
Employee comp.	64,296
Rent	10,080
Utilities	1,890
Recruitment costs	22,400
Supplies	4,800
Depreciation	2,100
Total Operating Expense	$292,336
Net Operating	
Income (Loss)	($198,922)
Interest Income	5,250
Interest Expense	23,356
Net Income (Loss)	
Before Taxes	($217,028)
Income Tax	
Net Income	($217,028)

MEDIAN PROJECTION

Service Revenue	
Sales	
Hospital revenues	2,780,152
Nurs. home revenues	735,295
Home care revenues	0
Gross Service Revenue	$3,515,447
Sales discounts (@ 3%)	$105,463
Net Service Revenue	$3,409,984
Cost of Goods Sold	
Wages	
(@70% of Gross Rev.)	2,460,813
Worker's Comp. &	
Payroll Taxes	350,666
Insurance	13,924
Benefits	45,000
Cost of Goods Sold	$2,870,403
Gross Margin	$539,581
Operating Expenses	
Selling	
Advertising	48,000
Mailings/other	
selling expenses	12,400
General & Admin.	
Licensing	250
Mgmnt. compensation	126,120
Employee comp.	64,296
Rent	10,080
Utilities	1,890
Recruitment costs	22,400
Supplies	4,800
Depreciation	2,100
Total Operating Expense	$292,336
Net Operating	
Income (Loss)	$247,245
Interest Income	5,250
Interest Expense	23,356
Net Income (Loss)	
Before Taxes	$229,139
Income Tax (@34%)	77,907
Net Income	$151,232

"BEST CASE" PROJECTION

Service Revenue	
Sales	
Hospital revenues	4,947,037
Nurs. home revenues	1,242,944
Home care revenues	0
Gross Service Revenue	$6,189,981
Sales discounts (@ 3%)	$185,699
Net Service Revenue	$6,004,282
Cost of Goods Sold	
Wages	
(@70% of Gross Rev.)	4,332,987
Worker's Comp. &	
Payroll Taxes	617,451
Insurance	23,097
Benefits	45,000
Cost of Goods Sold	$5,018,534
Gross Margin	$985,747
Operating Expenses	
Selling	
Advertising	48,000
Mailings/other	
selling expenses	12,400
General & Admin.	
Licensing	250
Mgmnt. compensation	126,120
Employee comp.	64,296
Rent	10,080
Utilities	1,890
Recruitment costs	22,400
Supplies	4,800
Depreciation	2,100
Total Operating Expense	$292,336
Net Operating	
Income (Loss)	$693,411
Interest Income	5,250
Interest Expense	23,356
Net Income (Loss)	
Before Taxes	$675,305
Income Tax (@34%)	229,604
Net Income	$445,701

Sample Business Plan A

MAY 1, 1993 - APRIL 30, 1994

Service Revenue	
Sales	
Hospital revenues	3,855,063
Nurs. home revenues	1,007,278
Home care revenues	228,800
Gross Service Revenue	$5,091,141
Sales discounts (@ 3%)	$152,734
Net Service Revenue	$4,938,407
Cost of Goods Sold	
Wages	
(@70% of Gross Rev.)	3,563,799
Worker's Comp. &	
Payroll Taxes	507,841
Insurance	18,178
Benefits	60,000
Cost of Goods Sold	$4,149,818
Gross Margin	$788,589
Operating Expenses	
Selling	
Advertising	69,138
Mailings/other	
selling expenses	19,754
General & Admin.	
Licensing	250
Mgmnt. compensation	132,552
Employee comp.	72,581
Rent	10,584
Utilities	1,985
Recruitment costs	24,640
Supplies	6,914
Depreciation	2,100
Total Operating Expense	$340,497
Net Operating	
Income (Loss)	$448,092
Interest Income	7,000
Interest Expense	22,635
Net Income (Loss)	
Before Taxes	$432,457
Income Tax (@34%)	147,035
Net Income	$285,422

MAY 1, 1994 - APRIL 30, 1995

Service Revenue	
Sales	
Hospital revenues	4,619,711
Nurs. home revenues	1,311,794
Home care revenues	736,632
Gross Service Revenue	$6,668,137
Sales discounts (@ 3%)	$200,044
Net Service Revenue	$6,468,093
Cost of Goods Sold	
Wages	
(@70% of Gross Rev.)	4,667,696
Worker's Comp. &	
Payroll Taxes	665,147
Insurance	21,960
Benefits	66,000
Cost of Goods Sold	$5,420,803
Gross Margin	$1,047,290
Operating Expenses	
Selling	
Advertising	90,553
Mailings/other	
selling expenses	25,872
General & Admin.	
Licensing	250
Mgmnt. compensation	171,312
Employee comp.	75,997
Rent	11,113
Utilities	2,084
Recruitment costs	24,640
Supplies	9,055
Depreciation	2,100
Total Operating Expense	$412,977
Net Operating	
Income (Loss)	$634,313
Interest Income	10,500
Interest Expense	21,828
Net Income (Loss)	
Before Taxes	$622,985
Income Tax (@34%)	211,815
Net Income	$411,170

MAY 1, 1995 - APRIL 30, 1996

Service Revenue	
Sales	
Hospital revenues	5,480,754
Nurs. home revenues	1,651,980
Home care revenues	1,581,172
Gross Service Revenue	$8,713,906
Sales discounts (@ 3%)	$261,417
Net Service Revenue	$8,452,489
Cost of Goods Sold	
Wages	
(@70% of Gross Rev.)	6,099,734
Worker's Comp. &	
Payroll Taxes	869,212
Insurance	26,102
Benefits	71,940
Cost of Goods Sold	$7,066,988
Gross Margin	$1,385,500
Operating Expenses	
Selling	
Advertising	118,335
Mailings/other	
selling expenses	33,810
General & Admin.	
Licensing	250
Mgmnt. compensation	180,049
Employee comp.	79,574
Rent	11,669
Utilities	2,188
Recruitment costs	24,640
Supplies	11,833
Depreciation	2,100
Total Operating Expense	$464,448
Net Operating	
Income (Loss)	$921,052
Interest Income	14,000
Interest Expense	20,923
Net Income (Loss)	
Before Taxes	$914,129
Income Tax (@34%)	310,804
Net Income	$603,325

215

Sample Business Plan A

OHC TEMPS
NET CASH FLOW STATEMENT
MEDIAN PROJECTION FOR THE 1st YEAR OF OPERATIONS, BY MONTH
MAY 1, 1991 - APRIL 30, 1992

	Pre-Opening	1	2	3	4	5	6	7	8	9	10	11	12
Uses of Cash													
Incorporation costs	1,150	0	0	0	0	0	0	0	0	0	0	0	0
Equipment	15,000	0	0	0	0	0	0	0	0	0	0	0	0
Furniture and fixtures	6,000	0	0	0	0	0	0	0	0	0	0	0	0
Licensing	250	0	0	0	0	0	0	0	0	250	0	0	0
Advertising	2,000	2,000	2,000	2,000	2,000	2,000	2,000	1,000	1,000	2,000	2,000	2,000	2,000
Mailings/other selling expenses	3,200	250	250	250	250	250	250	250	250	250	250	250	250
Nursing staff wages	0	0	22,501	22,501	45,003	45,003	67,504	67,504	90,005	90,005	112,506	112,506	135,008
Worker's Comp. & payroll taxes	0	0	3,206	3,206	6,413	6,413	9,619	9,619	12,826	12,826	16,032	16,032	19,239
Insurance	0	1,471	0	0	1,471	0	0	1,471	0	0	1,470	0	0
Benefits	0	2,500	2,500	2,500	2,500	2,500	2,500	2,500	2,500	2,500	2,500	2,500	2,500
Mgmnt. compensation	0	10,000	10,000	10,000	10,000	10,000	10,000	10,000	10,000	10,000	10,000	10,000	10,000
Employee comp.	0	4,000	4,000	4,000	4,000	4,000	4,000	4,000	4,000	4,000	4,000	4,000	4,000
Rent	0	800	800	800	800	800	800	800	800	800	800	800	800
Utilities	0	150	150	150	150	150	150	150	150	150	150	150	150
Recruitment costs	0	600	400	100	100	100	100	1,800	1,800	1,800	1,800	1,800	1,800
Supplies	0	200	200	200	200	200	200	200	200	200	200	200	200
Long-term debt service	0	2,447	2,447	2,447	2,447	2,447	2,447	2,447	2,447	2,447	2,447	2,447	2,448
Income tax	0	0	0	0	0	0	0	0	0	0	0	0	0
Total Uses of Cash	$27,600	$24,418	$48,454	$48,154	$75,334	$73,863	$99,570	$101,741	$125,978	$127,228	$154,155	$152,685	$178,395
Sources of Cash													
Collection of receivables	0	0	15590	31,180	46,771	62,361	77,951	93,541	109,131	124,721	140,311	155,902	171,492
Interest income	0	437	438	437	438	437	438	437	438	437	438	437	438
Total Sources of Cash	$0	$437	$16,028	$31,617	$47,209	$62,798	$78,389	$93,978	$109,569	$125,158	$140,749	$156,339	$171,930
Net Cash Flow Before Financing	($27,600)	($23,981)	($32,426)	($16,537)	($28,125)	($11,065)	($21,181)	($7,763)	($16,409)	($2,070)	($13,406)	$3,654	($6,465)
Cumulative Net Cash Flow	($27,600)	($51,581)	($84,007)	($100,544)	($128,669)	($139,734)	($160,915)	($168,678)	($185,087)	($187,157)	($200,563)	($196,909)	($203,374)
Financing Acquired	$325,000												
Cumulative Net Cash Flow After Financing	$297,400	$273,419	$240,993	$224,456	$196,331	$185,266	$164,085	$156,322	$139,913	$137,843	$124,437	$128,091	$121,626

QHC TEMPS
NET CASH FLOW STATEMENT
MEDIAN PROJECTION FOR THE 2nd YEAR OF OPERATIONS, BY MONTH
MAY 1, 1992 - APRIL 30, 1993

	1	2	3	4	5	6	7	8	9	10	11	12
Uses of Cash												
Incorporation costs	0	0	0	0	0	0	0	0	0	0	0	0
Equipment	0	0	0	0	0	0	0	0	0	0	0	0
Furniture and fixtures	0	0	0	0	0	0	0	0	0	0	0	0
Licensing	0	0	0	0	0	0	0	0	250	0	0	0
Advertising	4,000	4,000	4,000	4,000	4,000	4,000	4,000	4,000	4,000	4,000	4,000	4,000
Mailings/other selling expenses	3,700	3,700	500	500	500	500	500	500	500	500	500	500
Nursing staff wages	175,772	175,772	175,772	175,772	205,068	205,068	205,068	205,068	234,363	234,363	234,363	234,363
Worker's Comp. & payroll taxes	25,048	25,048	25,048	25,048	29,222	29,222	29,222	29,222	33,397	33,397	33,397	33,397
Insurance	3,481	0	0	3,481	0	0	3,481	0	0	3,481	0	0
Benefits	3,750	3,750	3,750	3,750	3,750	3,750	3,750	3,750	3,750	3,750	3,750	3,750
Mgmt. compensation	10,510	10,510	10,510	10,510	10,510	10,510	10,510	10,510	10,510	10,510	10,510	10,510
Employee comp.	5,358	5,358	5,358	5,358	5,358	5,358	5,358	5,358	5,358	5,358	5,358	5,358
Rent	840	840	840	840	840	840	840	840	840	840	840	840
Utilities	158	158	158	158	158	158	158	158	158	158	158	158
Recruitment costs	1,800	1,800	1,800	1,800	1,900	1,900	1,900	1,900	1,900	1,900	1,900	1,900
Supplies	400	400	400	400	400	400	400	400	400	400	400	400
Long-term debt service	2,447	2,447	2,447	2,447	2,447	2,447	2,447	2,447	2,447	2,447	2,447	2,448
Income tax	0	0	19,476	0	0	19,477	0	0	19,477	0	0	19,477
Total Uses of Cash	$237,264	$233,783	$250,059	$234,064	$264,153	$283,630	$267,634	$264,153	$317,350	$301,104	$297,623	$317,101
Sources of Cash												
Collection of receivables	215,326	243,570	243,570	243,570	263,868	284,165	284,165	284,165	304,463	324,760	324,760	324,760
Interest income	437	438	437	438	437	438	437	438	437	438	437	438
Total Sources of Cash	$215,763	$244,008	$244,007	$244,008	$264,305	$284,603	$284,602	$284,603	$304,900	$325,198	$325,197	$325,198
Net Cash Flow Before Financing	($21,501)	$10,225	($6,052)	$9,944	$152	$973	$16,968	$20,450	($12,450)	$24,094	$27,574	$8,097
Cumulative Net Cash Flow	($224,875) *	($214,650)	($220,702)	($210,758)	($210,606)	($209,633)	($192,665)	($172,215)	($184,665)	($160,571)	($132,997)	($124,900)
Financing Acquired												
Cumulative Net Cash Flow After Financing	$100,125 *	$110,350	$104,298	$114,242	$114,394	$115,367	$132,335	$152,785	$140,335	$164,429	$192,003	$200,100

* Includes balance from end of 1st year

217

OHC TEMPS
PRO FORMA BALANCE SHEET
YEARLY, ENDING APRIL 30, 1996
1st-5th YEARS OF OPERATIONS

	APRIL 30, 1992	APRIL 30, 1993	APRIL 30, 1994	APRIL 30, 1995	APRIL 30, 1996
ASSETS					
Current Assets					
Cash	151,576	169,411	200,000	300,000	400,000
Accounts Receivable	93,541	284,165	411,534	539,008	704,374
Other Current Assets	0	0	163,683	382,825	767,477
Total Current Assets	$245,117	$453,576	$775,217	$1,221,833	$1,871,851
Fixed Assets					
Equipment	15,000	15,000	15,000	15,000	15,000
Furniture & Fixtures	6,000	6,000	6,000	6,000	6,000
Less Accumulated Depreciation	2,100	4,200	6,300	8,400	10,500
Total Fixed Assets	18,900	16,800	14,700	12,600	10,500
TOTAL ASSETS	$264,017	$470,376	$789,917	$1,234,433	$1,882,351
LIABILITIES					
Current Liabilities					
Accounts Payable	30,000	91,136	131,985	172,868	225,903
Current Portion, L-T Debt	6,009	6,730	7,537	8,442	165,917
Total Current Liabilities	$36,009	$97,866	$139,522	$181,310	$391,820
Long-Term Liabilities					
Long-Term Debt	188,626	181,896	174,359	165,917	0
SHAREHOLDERS' EQUITY					
Capital Stock	$125,000	$125,000	$125,000	$125,000	$125,000
Retained Earnings	($85,618)	$85,614	$351,036	$762,206	$1,365,531
Total Equity	$39,382	$190,614	$476,036	$887,206	$1,490,531
TOTAL LIABILITIES AND SHAREHOLDERS' EQUITY	$264,017	$470,376	$789,917	$1,234,433	$1,882,351

GOVERNMENT REGULATIONS

- The regulations provide minimum, but acceptable, standards for personnel, operations, and insurance.

- Currently the Nurse Agency Licensing Division is not sufficiently staffed to inspect or enforce its regulations.

- No problem is anticipated in meeting the regulatory requirements.

The Illinois Nurse Agency Act requires all temporary nursing agencies that assign nurses within Illinois to be licensed, effective July 23, 1990. It is administered by the Director of the Illinois Department of Labor. The application is for one year only, with a fee of $250.00. Annual renewal is required at least 90 days prior to expiration.

Every agency must apply using the form provided. All information contained in the application and submitted with the application is protected from public disclosure by being exempted from the freedom of information statutes. A certificate of insurance must accompany the application. A separate statement detailing the experience and qualifications of the licensee to operate a nurse agency is also required. If the agency is a corporation, it must submit copies of its articles of incorporation and current bylaws along with the application.

The regulations require the following:

- A registered nurse must serve as the manager or supervisor of all nurses and certified nurses aides.

- The licensee must conduct in-person applicant interviews performed or supervised by a nurse.

- The stated registration or certification of each applicant must be verified with the appropriate state agency.

- Every licensee must check and verify at least two recent references and dates of employment listed on the application and keep written records of such for a minimum of two years.

- Requires professional liability coverage of at least $500,000 per incident and $1,000,000 in aggregate. Many agencies choose more expanded coverage of

$1,000,000/$3,000,000. QHC's insurance carrier, Maginnis & Associates, Inc. of Chicago has recommended the larger coverage.

■ Maintain yearly TB testing and CPR certification with the corresponding records.

■ Evaluate each nurse and aide annually and keep records for at least two years.

■ The licensee must receive a clinical skills description from the health care facility before assignment.

A number of Illinois regulatory agencies interface with agency operations.

■ Department of Public Health regulates and inspects nursing homes. It is also responsible for certification of certified nursing assistants. Agencies are required to verify the license of every applicant in writing.

■ Department of Professional Regulation Regulates and licenses RNs and LPNs. Agencies are required to verify the license of every applicant in writing.

QHC is concerned that the Nurse Agency Licensing Division is not yet sufficiently staffed to enforce its requirements. There is a significant number of agencies which "cut corners," obtaining a possible competitive advantage by avoiding costs required to comply with the regulations. We agree with a number of reputable agencies that these substandard agencies obtain customers unfairly and tarnish the industry's reputation. Effective inspection and enforcement programs would weed out some of these substandard agencies. A quality agency like QHC should benefit from increased enforcement.

With good standard operating procedures linked to our computerized record-keeping, no problems working with the regulatory agencies are anticipated. Compliance will be the responsibility of the nursing supervisor. When the operation expands to home care, it will also come under the jurisdiction of the Department of Public Health.

Sample Business Plan A: Appendix

The inclusion of authoritative support for the business plan in essential. Because the reader will not want to rely solely on the author's plan, the appendix should contain detailed documentation that helps to substantiate statements made or positions taken. Due to space limitations, this plan uses only a representative sample of the types of support documents that should be included.

Sample Business Plan A: Appendix

TOTAL HOSPITAL MARKET
WITH ADDITIONS TO HOSP MKT 1/13/91

HOSP. NAME	TOTALS	OCCUPANCY	STAFFED	LOCATION
Alcholism Treatment Center of Cent. DuP.	52	59.6	31	north suburbs
Shriners Hospital for Crippled Children	60	71.7	43	west
La Rabida Children's	65	70.8	46	south
Schwab Rehabilitation Center	70	82.9	58	south west
American International	87	69	60	north suburbs
Parkside Lutheran	88	78.4	69	NW suburbs
Belmont Community	97	57.7	56	north west
Hartgrove	99	70.7	70	west
Marianjoy Rehabilitation Center	100	88.4	88	west suburbs
Lincoln West	105	38.3	40	north
Lakeside Community	106	50.9	54	near south
HCA Chicago Lakeshore	110	68.2	75	north
Glenoaks Medical Center	120	62.5	75	west suburbs
Suburban Hosp. & Sanitarium of Cook Cty	122	33.6	41	SW suburbs
Charter Barclay	123	87.8	108	north
CPC Old Orchard	123	70.7	97	north suburbs
Saint Anthony	142	67.9	96	west
Roseland Community	154	64.9	100	south west
Condell	155	61.7	96	north suburbs
Edward	155	67.7	105	west suburbs
Edgewater	156	69.9	109	north
Delnor Community	160	53.1	85	west suburbs
Good Sheppard	162	61.1	99	NW suburbs
South Shore Hospital	170	52.4	89	south
Thorek	170	47.6	81	north
Martha Washington	175	53.7	94	north
Hyde Park	176	58	102	south
Loretto	184	77.2	142	west
Illinois State Psychiatric Institute	197	91.4	180	loop
St. Cabrini	200	61.8	124	near west
Swedish Covenant	200	96.5	193	north
Methodist Hospital of Chicago	201	44.8	90	north
Copley Memorial	201	56.2	113	SW suburbs
HCA Riveredge	210	79.5	167	west suburbs
South Suburban	211	70.2	148	south suburbs
Bethany	212	70.3	149	west
Oak Park	215	52.3	112	west suburbs
St. Bernard	217	81.6	177	south west
Humana	226	57.5	130	NW suburbs
Norwegian-American	230	50	115	west
La Grange Memorial	236	68.9	163	SW suburbs
Lake Forest	242	78.9	191	north suburbs
Louis A. Weiss Memorial	243	79.6	193	north
St. Elizabeth's	243	67.9	165	near west
Chicago Osteopathic	245	67.8	166	south
Holy Family	246	53.3	131	NW suburbs
Children's Memorial	254	74	188	near north
Saint Mary of Nazareth	255	81.6	208	west
Rush North Shore Medical Center	260	60.4	157	north suburbs
Jackson Park	265	55.5	147	south
Gottlieb Memorial	275	63.6	175	west suburbs
Saint Joseph-Elgin	280	49.6	139	NW suburbs
Highland Park	288	58.6	169	north suburbs
Our Lady of Resurrection	288	58.3	168	northwest

TOTAL HOSPITAL MARKET
WITH ADDITIONS TO HOSP MKT 1/13/91

HOSP. NAME	TOTALS	OCCUPANCY	STAFFED	LOCATION
Westlake Community	288	67	193	west suburbs
St. Francis- Blue Island	294	70.6	208	south suburbs
Mercy Center for Health Care Services	295	63.1	186	SW suburbs
Grant	302	69.3	209	near north
Saint Therese Medical Center	310	54.8	170	north suburbs
Columbus	311	67.2	209	near north
Good Samaritan	311	71.1	221	west suburbs
Ravenswood	316	78.7	249	north
St. James	330	59.8	197	south suburbs
Sherman	331	61	202	NW suburbs
Little Company of Mary	332	71.8	238	SW suburbs
Victory Memorial	333	53.7	179	north suburbs
Holy Cross	337	77.3	261	south
Central DuPage	338	67.2	227	west suburbs
Lakeside VA	354	61.6	218	loop
Mount Sinai	356	78.4	279	west
University of Illinois	358	72.1	258	loop
Palos Community	361	74.2	268	SW suburbs
West Suburban	370	43.5	161	west suburbs
South Chicago Community	385	59.2	228	south
Elmhurst	392	73.8	289	west suburbs
Alexian Brothers	395	66.3	262	NW suburbs
Northwest Community	407	80.6	328	NW suburbs
MacNeal	427	55.5	237	SW suburbs
Hinsdale	435	64.8	282	SW suburbs
St. Francis	446	68.2	304	north suburbs
Mercy	477	69.5	332	near south
West side VA	484	68.6	332	loop
St. Joseph	511	50.1	256	near north
Evanston	545	80.1	437	north suburbs
University of Chicago Hospitals	560	81.3	455	south
Foster G. Mcgaw (Loyola)	567	81.5	462	west suburbs
Ingalls Memorial	579	69.8	404	south suburbs
Chicago-Read Mental Health Center	607	100	607	north west
Michael Reese	652	71.8	468	near south
Northwestern Memorial	708	76.3	540	loop
Illinois Masonic	722	80.9	584	north
Resurrection	749	74.9	561	far northwest
Christ Community	824	71.4	588	SW suburbs
Elgin Mental Health Center	824	97.7	805	NW suburbs
Lutheran General	880	72.6	639	NW suburbs
Cook County	951	67.8	645	loop
Rush-Presbyterian-St. Lukes	983	77.1	758	loop
Hines VA	1111	79.7	885	west

		TOTALS			STAFFED
COUNT 98		31474			22079
	AVERAGES	321	67.6		225

NURSING HOMES IN CHICAGO

CITY\TOWN	NURSING HOMES	SNF BEDS	ICF BEDS	TOTAL BEDS
ARLINGTON HEIGHTS	5	703	142	845
BARRINGTON	1	68	67	135
BENSENVILLE	1	90	142	232
BERWYN	1	160	...	160
BLOOMINGDALE	3	494	...	494
BLUE ISLAND	1	...	30	30
BRIDGEVIEW	2	505	51	556
BROOKFIELD	1	46	26	72
BURBANK	1	165	78	243
BURNHAM	1	103	206	309
BURR RIDGE	1	35	83	118
CAROL STREAM	1	60	...	60
CHICAGO	88	8987	6896	15883
CHICAGO HEIGHTS	3	151	419	570
CHICAGO RIDGE	1	231	...	231
CICERO	1	76	409	485
CRESTWOOD	1	...	126	126
CRETE	1	110	...	110
CRYSTAL LAKE	1	83	...	83
DEERFIELD	1	170	...	170
DESPLAINES	5	977	260	1237
DOLTON	2	125	139	264
DOWNERS GROVE	2	40	211	251
ELGIN	4	386	30	416
ELK GROVE VILLAGE	1	60	60	120
ELMHURST	2	237	63	300
ELMWOOD PARK	1	245	...	245
EVANSTON	12	677	1095	1772
EVERGREEN PARK	2	491	...	491
FOREST PARK	1	99	...	99
FRANKFORT	1	...	120	120
FRANKLIN PARK	1	129	25	154
GLENVIEW	2	335	105	440
GLENWOOD	1	92	92	184
HARVEY	2	212	...	212
HAZELCREST	1	204	...	204
HICKORY HILLS	1	...	74	74
HIGHLAND PARK	2	...	188	188
HIGHWOOD	1	82	13	95
HILLSIDE	1	58	15	73
HINSDALE	1	200	...	200
HOFFMAN ESTATES	1	154	63	217
HOMEWOOD	1	256	...	256
INDIAN HILLS PARK	1	88	157	245
ISLAND LAKE	1	...	70	70
ITASCA	1	...	80	80

NURSING HOMES IN CHICAGO

CITY\TOWN	NURSING HOMES	SNF BEDS	ICF BEDS	TOTAL BEDS
JUSTICE	1	...	18	18
LAGRANGE	1	96	107	203
LAGRANGE PARK	2	155	76	231
LAKE BLUFF	2	255	...	255
LAKE FOREST	2	48	139	187
LEMONT	2	60	150	210
LIBERTYVILLE	3	479	174	653
LISLE	1	51	...	51
LOMBARD	2	220	40	260
LONG GROVE	1	61	93	154
MATTESON	1	105	...	105
MAYWOOD	1	...	69	69
MIDLOTHIAN	3	108	434	542
MORTON GROVE	1	103	160	263
NAPERVILLE	3	472	...	472
NILES	5	752	501	1253
NORRIDGE	1	...	118	118
NORTHBROOK	3	356	180	536
NORTHLAKE	1	120	82	202
OAKBROOK	1	110	28	138
OAKLAWN	4	489	129	618
OAKPARK	2	242	28	270
PALATINE	2	53	113	166
PALOS HEIGHTS	3	188	217	405
PALOS HILLS	1	83	120	203
PARK RIDGE	3	428	102	530
PLAINFIELD	1	50	...	50
RICHTON PARK	1	142	152	294
RIVERWOODS	1	248	...	248
ROLLING MEADOWS	1	155	...	155
SCHAUMBURG	1	180	...	180
SKOKIE	5	512	162	674
TINLEY PARK	1	59	42	101
WESTMONT	3	369	212	581
WHEATON	3	549	137	686
WHEELING	1	20	60	80
WILLOWBROOK	1	100	43	143
TOTALS 83	238	24802	15421	40223

HOSPITAL TEMPORARY AGENCIES IN CHICAGO SERVICE AREA

AGENCY	SPECIALTY	LOCATION	CODE	COMMENT
A BETTER NURSING SERVICE	RN,LPN,NA,LIVE,COMP	NCHICAGO	H	
A-1 HEALTHCARE RESOURCE ASSOC	RN,LPN,CNA,COMP,HSK	SCHICAGO	H	RN: TOP PAY, FLEX HRS
A-ABIDING CARE INC	RN,LPN,NA,COMP,LIVE,HOSPICE	PARK RIDGE	H	SPECIALISTS IN QUALITY HOME HEALTH CARE
ABBARD RN REGISTRY		NCHICAGO	B	ESTABLISHED IN 1934
ABC HOME HEALTH of ILLINOIS	RN	SCHICAGO	H	RN: JOIN BY JAN, RECEIVE FREE CAR PHONE; OVER 40 FACILITIES
ABC HOME HEALTH of ILLINOIS	RN	NCHICAGO	H	
ABC HOME HEALTH of ILLINOIS	RN	OAK PARK	H	
ABLE HEALTH CARE AGENCY		NCHICAGO	B	
ACCESS NURSING	RN,LPN	NAPERVILLE	B	
ACCESS NURSING	RN,LPN	GLENDALE HT	B	RN: OFFERS TOP PAY, BONUS PLAN, FLEXIBILITY
AETNA NURSES REGISTRY	RN,LPN,CNA	NCHICAGO	B	OPEN SINCE 1948
ALEDA NURSING SERVICE	RN,LPN,LIVE,COMP,CNA	SCHICAGO	B	
ALICE TOCH NURSES REGISTRY		EVANSTON	B	
ALL BETTER CARE INC	RN,AIDE,HOME	NCHICAGO	H	
ALL HELP HEALTH SERVICES	RN,AIDE,HOME,LIVE	NCHICAGO	H	
ALL-AMERICA NURSE	OCCRN,HH	SCHICAGO	H	CASE MGMT, INSUR CONSULTATION, FIRST AID MOVIES
ALL-WAYS CARING SERVICES	RN,LPN,AIDE,MHOME,HSKP,COMP	NCHICAGO	H	
ALLCARE HEALTH SERVICES	RN	SUBURBS	H	EXPANDING HOME HEALTH AGENCY
ALPHA CHRISTIAN REGISTRY	RN,LPN,CNA,HH	CHAMPAIGN	X	
ALPHA CHRISTIAN REGISTRY	RN,LPN,CNA,HH	CHICAGO HTS	B	
ALPHA CHRISTIAN REGISTRY	RN,LPN,CNA,HH	GLEN ELLYN	B	
ALPHA CHRISTIAN REGISTRY	RN,LPN,CNA,HH	ACHICAGO	B	
ALPHA CHRISTIAN REGISTRY	RN,LPN,CNA,HH	ARLINGTON HTS	B	
ALPHA CHRISTIAN REGISTRY	RN,LPN,CNA,HH	ELGIN	B	
ALPHA CHRISTIAN REGISTRY	RN,LPN,CNA,HH	DEKALB	X	
ALPHA CHRISTIAN REGISTRY	RN,LPN,CNA,HH	ROCKFORD	X	
ALPHA CHRISTIAN REGISTRY	RN,LPN,CNA,HH	BLOOMINGTON	X	
ALPHA CHRISTIAN REGISTRY	RN,LPN,CNA,HH	EVANSTON	B	
ALPHA CHRISTIAN REGISTRY	RN,LPN,CNA,HH	AURORA	X	FREE PATIENT ASSESSMENT FOR PRIV NURS CARE
ALTRU NURSES REGISTRY		WILMETTE	B	PROFESSIONAL/NON-PROFESSIONAL CARE OF ELDERLY
ALVERNA HOME NURSING CENTER		SCHICAGO	H	
AM SERV		FAIRVIEW HTS	X	
AMERICAN HOME CARE		NCHICAGO	H	

Legend to CODE: H = home care only; I = institutional staff relief only; B = both home care and institutional staff relief; X = in fringe locality or specialty

HOSPITAL TEMPORARY AGENCIES IN CHICAGO SERVICE AREA

AGENCY	SPECIALTY	LOCATION	CODE	COMMENT
AMERICAN REG FOR NURSES &	PED,BABYSIT,VAC HELP	NCHICAGO	H	
AMERICANURSE LTD	HOMECARE	SCHICAGO	H	
BONUS NEIMES NURSING SERVICE		SCHICAGO	B	
CARE AT HOME COOP		CHICAGO	H	
CAREER-PRO	RN	ARLINGTON HTS	B	
CAREER-PRO	RN	PALATINE	B	
CAREER-PRO	RN	ROCKFORD	X	
CARING TOUCH	RN,CNA,COMP',LIVE	ACHICAGO	H	RN: WORK ONLY 1 WEEKEND/MONTH; PERSONAL CARE AND
CEMCO MEDICAL	RN	OAKBROOK	X	SEARCH FIRM
CHGO CHAP NAT BLACK NURSES		SCHICAGO	X	1991 ADD'N
CHICAGO REGISTRY CORP		CHICAGO	B	1991 ADD'N
CHICAGO ST.RITA'S REGISTRY		PALOS HILLS	B	
CIRCLE TEMP NURSING SER		SCHICAGO	B	
CITY WIDE NURSING SERV		SCHICAGO	B	
CM HEALTHCARE RESOURCES INC	PED REG, HH	ARLINGTON HTS	X	LOOKING FOR SPANISH SPEAKING IN HH
CONCERNED CARE		HOMEWOOD	H	EXPANDED FROM 3 TO 4 LOCATIONS,1991 ADD'N
CONCERNED CARE INC	RN,LPN,AIDE, HOME,LIVE	SKOKIE	H	COMPREHENSIVE SERVICES
CONCERNED CARE INC	RN,LPN,AIDE, HOME,LIVE	ST. CHARLES	H	
CONCERNED CARE INC	RN,LPN,AIDE, HOME,LIVE	DES PLAINES	H	
CONTINUAL HH AGENCY		SCHICAGO	H	
CRITICAL CONNECTION	RN	MI	X	OBTAIN WORK ASSIGNMENTS AS INDEPENDENT CONTRACTORS
CROSS COUNTRY HC PERSONNEL	TRAVEL RN	FL	X	
DEPENDABLE NIGHTENGALES	PRIVATE DUTY RN	NCHICAGO	H	1991 ADD'N
DUNCAN REGISTRY	RN,LPN,NA, HOME	EVERGREEN PARK	B	
ELDORADO HH CARE SERVICE		NCHICAGO	H	
EVA'S NURSING SERVICE		NCHICAGO	B	
EXCELLCARE	RN,LPN,CNA,PT,ST,OT	ACHICAGO	B	STAFFING HOMECARE, 1991 ADD'N
EXCELLCARE	RN,LPN,CNA,PT,ST,OT	OAKLAWN	B	1991 ADD'N
EXTENDED HEALTH SERVICES		SKOKIE	B	
FAVORITE NURSES	RN,LPN,UNIT CLERK	KS	X	
FIVE HOSPITAL ELDERLY HOME		NCHICAGO	H	FULL SERVICE HH CARE AGENCY
FRANCISCAN HH INC		SCHICAGO	H	
FROELICH & ASSOC	RN	DES PLAINES	B	

Legend to CODE: H = home care only; I = institutional staff relief only; B = both home care and institutional staff relief; X = in fringe locality or specialty

HOSPITAL TEMPORARY AGENCIES IN CHICAGO SERVICE AREA

AGENCY	SPECIALTY	LOCATION	CODE	COMMENT
HAMILTON AGENCY		DCHICAGO	B	
HARDY HH INC		SCHICAGO	H	
HARRIET HLOMES HC SERVICE		EVERGREEN PARK	H	HH CARE SERVICE
HEALTH CARE INC	RN,LPN,AIDE	FRANKFORT	X	
HEALTH CONNECTIONS	RN,HHAIDE,THER,LIVE,PED	DCHICAGO	H	
HEALTH CONNECTIONS	RN,HHAIDE,THER,LIVE,PED	SKOKIE	H	
HEALTH EXCHANGE	RN	MI	X	RN: 100%DAILY PAY,SIGN UP BONUS $200, PAID INSURANCE
HEALTHCARE PERSONNEL INC		SCHICAGO	B	1991 ADD'N
HEALTHCO NURSING SERVICE	RN,AIDE,COMP,	ALSIP	H	
HEALTHSTAF NURSING SERVICES	RN	OAKBROOK	I	INSTANT PAY, VACATION BONUS, 40+ HOSPITALS
HEALTHSTAF NURSING SERVICES	RN	ACHICAGO	I	RN:OFFERS COMPUTER SKILLS/TRAINING
HELP AT HOME	COMPLETE HOME NURSING SERVICES	CHICAGO	H	
HELPING CARE, INC	RN,LPN,AIDE	CHICAGO	H	CARE FOR DISABLED AGES 18-59
HELPING CARE, INC	RN,LPN,AIDE	PROSPECT HEIGHTS	H	CARE FOR DISABLED AGES 18-59
HELPING CARE, INC	RN,LPN,AIDE	MOKENA	H	CARE FOR DISABLED AGES 18-59
HELPING CARE SERVICES	IV THERAPY	DCHICAGO	H	SPECIALISTS IN HOME CARE
HMSS		SUBURBS	X	
HOME CARE PLUS	RN,LPN,HH,LIVE,COMP,THER	NWCHICAGO	H	FREE HOME CONSULT
HOME CARE SERVICE	RN,ST,SW,PT OT,HHA, HOME	ALSIP	H	HOME CARE FOR MEDICARE/MEDICAID
HOME HEALTH CARE	RN,LPN,CNA,PT,OT,SW,MSW,HOME	SCHICAGO	H	
HOME HEALTH PLUS	RN,LLPN,THERAP,HHA,LIVE,HOME,COMP	NCHICAGO	H	SPECIALIZING IN HHCARE; SUBSIDIARY OF HOME HEALTH INC 1991
HOME HEALTH SERVICE OF		NCHICAGO	H	
HOMECARE & NURSING SERV		DCHICAGO	H	
HOMECORPS		CHICAGO	H	COMPREHESIVE HOME SERV, 1991 ADD'N
HOSPICE CARE INC		LINCOLNWOOD	X	
IL MASONIC MC	NURSE MIDWIFERY	CHICAGO	X	
IN HOME HC SERV OF SUB		MORTON GROVE	H	
INDEPENDENT HEALTH SERVICES		SCHICAGO	B	
INTENSICARE INC	NURSING ALTERNATIVES	CHICAGO	B	
JMK NURSING RESOURCES		SCHICAGO	B	1991 ADD'N
KIMBERLY QUALITY CARE	RN,LPN,HH,HOMEMAK,CONMP,LIVE	DCHICAGO	B	5 ADD'L IN AREA,CO DID WELL IN 80'S BY SHIFTING USE TO RN
KIMBERLY QUALITY CARE	RN,LPN,HH,HOMEMAK,CONMP,LIVE	NCHICAGO	B	EXPANDED, 1991 ADD'N,CORPORATE: KANSAS CITY
KIMBERLY QUALITY CARE	RN,LPN,HH,HOMEMAK,CONMP,LIVE	OAKLAWN	B	PRIMARILY HC

Legend to CODE: H = home care only; I = institutional staff relief only; B = both home care and institutional staff relief; X = in fringe locality or specialty

229

HOSPITAL TEMPORARY AGENCIES IN CHICAGO SERVICE AREA

AGENCY	SPECIALTY	LOCATION	CODE	COMMENT
KIMBERLY QUALITY CARE	RN,LPN,HH,HOMEMAK,CONMP,LIVE	SKOKIE	B	
KIMBERLY QUALITY CARE	RN,LPN,IHH,HOMEMAK,CONMP,LIVE	ELGIN	B	
KIMBERLY QUALITY CARE	RN,LPN,HH,HOMEMAK,CONMP,LIVE	DOWNERS GROVE	B	
LITTLE COMPANY OF MARY AT	HOMEHEALTH	EVERGREEN PARK	H	
MANPOWER HC		LAKE BLUFF	B	1991 ADD'N
MATERNITY&HOMEMAKING SERVICE	RN ASST IN CONV,GERIA,INFANT	CHICAGO	H	
MEDICAL PERSONNEL POOL	TRAVEL RN	FL	X	
MEDICAL PERSONNEL POOL	RN,LIVE, AIDE,HOMEMAKER	OAK PARK	B	300 OFFICES INCL CANADA; CORPORATE IN FT LAUDERDALE
MEDICAL PERSONNEL POOL	RN,LIVE, AIDE,HOMEMAKER	AURORA	X	
MEDICAL PERSONNEL POOL	RN,LIVE, AIDE,HOMEMAKER	OAK LAWN	B	
MEDICAL PERSONNEL POOL	RN,LIVE, AIDE,HOMEMAKER	SCHAUMBURG	B	
MEDICAL PERSONNEL POOL	RN,LIVE, AIDE,HOMEMAKER	EVANSTON	B	
MEDICAL PERSONNEL POOL	RN,LIVE, AIDE,HOMEMAKER	ST CHARLES	B	
MEDICAL PERSONNEL POOL	RN,LIVE, AIDE,HOMEMAKER	NAPERVILLE	B	
MEDICAL PERSONNEL POOL	RN,LIVE, AIDE,HOMEMAKER	LIBERTYVILLE	B	
MEDICAL PERSONNEL POOL	RN,LIVE, AIDE,HOMEMAKER	JOLIET	B	
MOST UNIQUE NURSING SER	RN,LIVE, AIDE,HOMEMAKER	EVANSTON	B	
MYERSCOUGH	RN	ACHICAGO	I	RN:HIGH RATES, FLEX HOURS, BENEFIT PACKAGE; SERVICES
MYERSCOUGH MEDICAL STAFFING	RN,LPN,CNA,RT,RADTECH,MEDTECH	NAPERVILLE	I	WE ARE HERE FOR YOU"
NIGHTINGALE HC SERV INC		SCHICAGO	B	1991 ADD'N
NIGHTINGALE REGISTRY		SCHICAGO	B	1991 ADD'N
NIGHTINGALE REGISTRY		ARLINGTON HTS	B	1991 ADD'N
NORRELL HEALTH CARE	RN,HH,LPN	HOMEWOOD	B	RN: MONTHLY INSERVICES, CPR CLASS,
NORRELL HEALTH CARE	RN,HH,LPN	DCHICAGO	B	RN: MONTHLY INSERVICES, CPR CLASS,
NORRELL HEALTH CARE	RN,HH,LPN	DEERFIELD	B	BUSS. OFF., CORPORATE: ATLANTA, NATIONWIDE OVER 100
NORRELL HEALTH CARE	RN,HH,LPN	OAKPARK	B	DOES MOST OF HC BOOKINGS, RN:INSERVICES, CPR CLASS,
NSI SERVICES		JOLIET	X	
NSI SERVICES		DUPAGE COUNTY	B	
NSI SERVICES		SURBURBS	B	
NSI SERVICES		DCHICAGO	B	
NURSE AMERICA	TRAVEL RN	KS	X	RN:COMPETITVE PAY
NURSE CARE	RN,LPN,CNA	CHICAGO	B	RN:CONTINUING ED CLASSES
NURSE CARE	RN,LPN,CNA	SKOKIE	B	

Legend to CODE: H = home care only; I = institutional staff relief only; B = both home care and institutional staff relief; X = in fringe locality or specialty

HOSPITAL TEMPORARY AGENCIES IN CHICAGO SERVICE AREA

AGENCY	SPECIALTY	LOCATION	CODE	COMMENT
NURSE PRN		DCHICAGO	B	1991 ADD'N
NURSE PROVIDERS	RN,,LPN,CNA	CHICAGO HEIGHTS	B	MAIN OFF., FULL SERVICE, HH AGENCY, SISTER COMPANY:CLAIM SERVICE
NURSE PROVIDERS		SCHICAGO	B	BRANCH OFF.
NURSE STAFFERS, INC	RN,LPN,CNA	DCHICAGO	B	RN:OFFERS TOP PAY, FLEX HOURS, INCENTIVES, FT,PT,8-10-12 HR
NURSEFINDERS	RN,LPN,HHA,LIVE,PT,HOMEMAK,OT,CNA	MERRILLVILLE IN	X	FREE EVALUATION AT YOUR HOME
NURSEFINDERS	RN,LPN,HHA,LIVE,PT,HOMEMAK,OT,CNA	ROCKFORD	X	
NURSEFINDERS	RN,LPN,HHA,LIVE,PT,HOMEMAK,OT,CNA	DCHICAGO	B	
NURSEFINDERS	RN,LPN,HHA,LIVE,PT,HOMEMAK,OT,CNA	NCHICAGO	B	
NURSEFINDERS	RN,LPN,HHA,LIVE,PT,HOMEMAK,OT,CNA	JOLIET	X	
NURSEFINDERS	RN,LPN,HHA,LIVE,PT,HOMEMAK,OT,CNA	WILL	X	
NURSEFINDERS	RN,LPN,HHA,LIVE,PT,HOMEMAK,OT,CNA	ACHICAGO	B	RN: TOP PAY, CHOICE, FLEX HRS INSTANT PAY, INCENTIVES
NURSEFINDERS	RN,LPN,HHA,LIVE,PT,HOMEMAK,OT,CNA	MCHENRY	X	
NURSEFINDERS	RN,LPN,HHA,LIVE,PT,HOMEMAK,OT,CNA	SUBURBS N, NW S	B	
NURSEFINDERS	RN,LPN,HHA,LIVE,PT,HOMEMAK,OT,CNA	DUPAGE	B	USP - COMPLETE NURSING SERVICE,FREE EVALUATION AT YOUR HOME
NURSEFINDERS	RN,LPN,HHA,LIVE,PT,HOMEMAK,OT,CNA	LIBERTYVILLE	B	
NURSEFINDERS	RN,LPN,HHA,LIVE,PT,HOMEMAK,OT,CNA	AURORA	X	
NURSES INC	RN,LPN,CNA,RT,OT	ELMHURST	B	RN: $150 BONUS AFTER 10 SHIFTS, MED/DENTAL BENEFITS
NURSES ON WHEELS HHC SERV LTD	RN,LPN,AIDE,HOME,COMP,SP,CP,OT	NCHICAGO	H	1991 ADD'N
NURSING ALERT		SCHICAGO	B	
NURSING CARE INC		SCHICAGO	B	
NURSING PROFESSIONAL POOL		NCHICAGO	B	
NURSING RESOURCE GROUP		NCHICAGO	B	
NURSING STAT		HARWOOD HTS	B	1991 ADD'N
NW MEMORIAL HOME HEALTH	RN,AIDE,LPN,SW,PT,OT,ST,BABY,YCARE,C	NCHICAGO	H	COMPLETE PROFESSIONAL HOME CARE
OMNI CARE NURSING SERVICES	RN	DCHICAGO	B	
OMNI HOME CARE		PARK RIDGE	H	AFFILIATED WITH SWEDISH COV, 1991 ADD'N
ORSINI NURSING AGENCY	RN,LPN,CNA, BATH VISITS	ARLINGTON HTS	B	CLIENTS - HOSP, NURSE HOME, PRIVATE DUTY
ORSINI NURSING AGENCY		OAK LAWN	B	EXPANDED FROM 1 TO 2 LOCATIONS, 1991 ADD'N
PACIFIC NURSING CENTER OF		MELROSE PARK	X	PLACEMENT IN HOSPITAL/NURSING HOME, 1991 ADD'N
PERSONAL NURSING SERVICE LTD		SWCHICAGO	H	
PERSONAL TOUCH HOME CARE of	RN,LPN,LIVE,COMP,HH,THER	SCHICAGO	H	RN:TOP RATES, HEALTH INS, REFERRAL BONUS
PRACTICAL NURSING AIDS		CHICAGO	X	1991 ADD'N
PRIME NURSING SERVICES		DARIEN	B	1991 ADD'N

Legend to CODE: H = home care only; I = institutional staff relief only; B = both home care and institutional staff relief; X = in fringe locality or specialty

HOSPITAL TEMPORARY AGENCIES IN CHICAGO SERVICE AREA

AGENCY	SPECIALTY	LOCATION	CODE	COMMENT
PRN H/C SERVICES	PRIVATE DUTY	OAK PARK	H	
PRO-NURSE		DCHICAGO	I	
PROFESSIONAL HHC INC		OAK LAWN	H	
PROFESSIONAL NURSES BUREAU		NCHICAGO	B	CARING FOR PEOPLE SINCE 1925
PROGRESSIVE SERVICES		CHICAGO	B	RN: MEDICAL/DENTAL PLAN, OVER 38+ HOSPITALS
RAMASEAN NURSING SERVICES	RN,LPN,AIDE LIVE	NCHICAGO	B	FREE ASSESSMENTS
REGENCY AT HOMEHEALTH SERVICE		NILES	H	
REGENCY AT HOMEHEALTH SERVICE		CHICAGO	H	
RELIABLE NURSING SERVICE	RN,CC and MED/SURGE	HOFFMAN ESTATES	B	RN: HIGHEST WAGES, HEALTH, DENTAL
RELIABLE NURSING SERVICE	RN,CC and MED/SURGE	DCHICAGO	B	RN: HIGHEST WAGES, HEALTH, DENTAL, NEW OFF. EXPANDEE TO HC
RELIEF MEDICAL SERVICES	RN,LPN,AIDE	SKOKIE	B	
RELIEF MEDICAL SERVICES	RN,LPN,AIDE	DCHICAGO	B	
RELIEF MEDICAL SERVICES	RN,LPN,AIDE	OAK PARK	B	
RELIEF MEDICAL SERVICES	RN,LPN,AIDE	EVERGREEN PARK	B	RN:HEALTH, TUITION REIM, FLEX
RENAISSANCE HEALTH CARE	RN	MI	X	RN: PROFESSIONAL AUTONOMY, REGULAR DAY HOURS, 1 ON 1
REVELL MEDICAL		DCHICAGO	B	
ROYAL HOME HEALTH INC		NCHICAGO	H	
RYAN & ASSOCIATES		NCHICAGO	X	1991 ADD'N
S C H HOME MED NORTH		NCHICAGO	H	
SECURE CARE TEMP NURSING		NCHICAGO	B	
SECURE CARE TEMP NURSING		OAK PARK	B	
SHAY NURSING SERVICE	RN,LPN,AIDE,COMP,PT,RT	PALOS HILLS	H	
STAFF BUILDERS	RN,LPN,HH,COMP,THER,HOMEMAKER	ACHICAGO	B	CONCERNED PROFESSIONALS, COMPREHENSIVE CARE
STAFF FINDERS		SCHICAGO	B	
STAFF SOLUTIONS		SCHICAGO	B	1991 ADD'N
STAT NURSES AGENCY		NCHICAGO	B	1991 ADD'N
SUMMIT HOME HEALTH INC		NCHICAGO	H	
SUNRISE ULTRA NURSING SER		NCHICAGO	B	1991 ADD'N
SUPERIOR HOME & HEALTH CARE		DCHICAGO	H	CLIENT :ELDERLY
SUPERIOR MEDICAL SERVICES	RN,CRNA,ORTECH,XRAYTECH,HOMEHEALTH	GREEN OAKS	X	OPENED 12/90; COMPETITIVE RATES
TOTAL HHC OF CHICAGO		DCHICAGO	H	
TRAVCORPS	RN		X	TRAVELING RN'S/FOUNDER BRUCE MALE
TRINITY HC		CHICAGO	X	1991 ADD'N

Legend to CODE: H = home care only;   I = institutional staff relief only;   B = both home care and institutional staff relief;   X = in fringe locality or specialty

HOSPITAL TEMPORARY AGENCIES IN CHICAGO SERVICE AREA

AGENCY	SPECIALTY	LOCATION	CODE	COMMENT
UPJOHN HEALTH CARE SERVICES		CHICAGO	H	
UPJOHN HEALTHCARE SERVICES	RN,ST,OT,PT,PSYCH, COMP. HHA	HYDE PARK	H	
UPJOHN HEALTHCARE SERVICES	RN,ST,OT,PT,PSYCH, COMP. HHA	LINCOLN PARK	H	
UPJOHN HEALTHCARE SERVICES	RN,ST,OT,PT,PSYCH, COMP. HHA	OAKBROOK	H	
UPJOHN HEALTHCARE SERVICES	RN,ST,OT,PT,PSYCH, COMP. HHA	HAZELCREST	H	
UPJOHN HEALTHCARE SERVICES		LOMBARD(NEW), NO	H	1991 ADD'N
VALLEY MED HC STAFFERS		NCHICAGO	B	1991 ADD'N
VNA		SCHICAGO	H	
VNA	HOSPICE	EVANSTON	H	
WELLSPRING		DARRIEN	I	EDGEWATER USES
WISHING WELL HEALTH SERVICES		NCHICAGO	B	

agency count   209

Legend to CODE: H = home care only;   I = institutional staff relief only;   B = both home care and institutional staff relief;   X = in fringe locality or specialty

COMPETITOR SUMMARY SHEET

NAME **ALPHA CHRISTIAN AGENCY**

CORPORATE ADDRESS   **CORPORATE OWNER** Regional

CORPORATE PHONE

LOCAL ADDRESS

LOCAL PHONE

LOCATIONS Seven local, cover WI,MI, IL, IN.

WEEKLY SHIFT VOL.   **NET PROFIT**   **GROSS MARGIN**

MARKET SHARE (EST)

MAJOR USERS Nursing home(NWCH CCC)

STRENGTHS Price competitive. Large RN pool.

WEAKNESSES Requires RN to carry malpractice insurance.

COMMENTS Claim lower prices competitive with client's "full" costs. Available 24 hours-No answering machine or service. Very religious bent. Marketing implies they have lower margin requirements. Claimed 90% placement successrate is unusually high (average is 60%).

CURRENT STRATEGY Fill all the request successfully (better than 90%). Dedicated to the spiratuality of employees and patients. Price competitive with claimed lower fees. Full services.

RN STRATEGY Adverises its rates occationaly.

ASSUMPTIONS Its spiritual mission is unique and attractive.

COMPETITOR SUMMARY SHEET

NAME	**HEALTHSTAF**
CORPORATE ADDRESS	1900 Spring Rd. suite 102, Oakbrook, IL. 60521
CORPORATE PHONE	708/571-6666
LOCAL ADDRESS	122 S. Michigan Ave., suite 1409, Chicago, IL 60603
LOCAL PHONE	312/939-6767
LOCATIONS	two, Oakbrook and Chicago
WEEKLY SHIFT VOL.	Greater than 250
MARKET SHARE (EST)	in top 5.
MAJOR USERS	Claim over 40 institutional clients. We know of: Weiss, Alexian Bros., St Francis, St. Joseph(Elgin)

CORPORATE OWNER

NET PROFIT

GROSS MARGIN

STRENGTHS Professionalism. Marketing strategy. Operational strategy. On-site orientation programs. Quality commitment.

WEAKNESSES One year RN experience requirement is weak for its pledged commitment to quality. Insufficient locations.

COMMENTS Will pay $50 if sub standard work is documented, conversely charges client $ 50 for sudden cancellation. Pays large sign on and recruitment bonuses. Claims it meets JCAHO standards. Provides a complete facility and policy description for RN. Extensive policy manual. Sends birthday and holiday wishes and other messages to the RN's and clients. One RN interviewed would be willing to work exclusively for an agency like HS.

CURRENT STRATEGY Niche: institutional staffing only. Advanced computerized system of scheduling/skill matching/assigning/records/facility documentation. Client and employee commitment; performance guarantee. Price competitive. Just raised all prices and salaries in less than 3 months.

RN STRATEGY Have large RN pool, One year experience. Recruit via regular advertising and bonuses. Intensive, extensive interviewing. Progams and commitment to RN selfworth and sensitivities. Very salary competitive. Use raffles.

ASSUMPTIONS Considers itself big and that having 40 clients is attractive. Professionalism and businesslike conduct (suit and tie) impresses RN suppliers and clients. It does provide quality.

COMPETITOR SUMMARY SHEET

NAME   **KIMBERLY QUALITY CARE**

CORPORATE ADDRESS   Kansas City, MO   **CORPORATE OWNER**   LIFETIME

CORPORATE PHONE

LOCAL ADDRESS   Skokie, IL

LOCAL PHONE   70'8/965-8150

LOCATIONS   eleven: Downers Grove, Loop(on Erie), Olympia Fields, Elgin, N. Riverside/Oaklawn

WEEKLY SHIFT VOL.   **NET PROFIT**   **GROSS MARGIN**

MARKET SHARE (EST)   in top 10 of hospital market. 340 offices in IL "?", Currently hosp. mkt. is 12 % of division sales.

MAJOR USERS   Highland Park

STRENGTHS   Large corporate know how.

WEAKNESSES   Is exiting the hospital market perhaps because it cannot compete economically.

COMMENTS   Corporate changing strategy and going to total homecare because of low profit margins in hospital segment. Limited data available about nurses. Some hospitals interviewed used this agency.

CURRENT STRATEGY   Primarily in homecare and switching out of hospital market.

RN STRATEGY

ASSUMPTIONS   Cororate believes the hospital temp market profitability is decreasing but not home care!

QHC TEMPS
QUALITY HEALTH CARE TEMPORARIES

LITERATURE SUMMARIES

EMPLOYER FOCUS-Pro Nurse (from *Spectrum*)

- Pro Nurse attempts to hire the most qualified nurses and accordingly claims to pay the the highest rates. Nancy to check this out.
- Pro-Share profit sharing program distributes profits weekly based on seniority and hours worked.
- Give gifts to needy patients and provides costumed nurses to celebrate holidays in pediatric units.
- Provide to the assigned nurse comprehensive data sheets about the specific units being staffed.

RELIABLE NURSING SERVICE:Hand-out to nurses and conversation with Lori Dorman, Pres.

- Present client hospitals are Loyola, Cook County., Good Samaritan, Humana, Rush, and U. of C.
- Presently staffing approximately 250 shifts/wk (equivalent to a gross margin of approximately $130,000 to $150,000/yr). Original goal was more like 50 shifts/wk.
- Applicants must have a minimum of three years experience. Has a pool of 150 nurses.
- In operation 21 months, but planned and organized for two years prior. Having lots of nurse friends helped the start-up
- Overtime is not scheduled. When approved, at 1.5 times day rate or currently $39.
- Cover malpractice at $million/$ 3 million and workers comp. Provide access to Health Chicago HMO at 100%; will deduct from pay at $28.22/wk, single and $72.63/wk, family. Also have Delta Dental Plan.
- Dorman suggests a good business plan (her's was 12 pages). She warns not to outgrow cash flow.

LIFETIME (KIMBERLY QUALITY CARE DIVISION)- Securities Analysis from county

- Kimberly handles Home Health (65% of sales) and institutional staffing (12%). Lifetime sees falling margins in institutional business; accordingly it projects this to be 4% of sale by 1995 (home health going to 77%.
- Home Health mkt is $9 billion vs $230 billion for the hospital mkt. Kimberly is the single largest at 5% mkt share. It is the only big public firm primarily in health comparing to Baxter, Upjohn (who just sold their home health to Olsten, Nancy, via *Modern Healthcare*), H&R Block and Kelly.
- Home health is 50 % not for profit. Most of the 11,000 agencies gross less than $250,000/yr.
- Analyst feels that market is saturated and that large hospitals are gaining mkt share(I suppose thru internal agencies?)

OLSTEN CORP.- Securities analysis from Merrill Lynch

- Olsten Health Care Division has 15% of sales at $87 million an increase of 13%
- It appears that Olsten is mainly in home health, not in institutional placements.

ADIA- Securities analysis from Merrill Lynch

- Adia claims that their lower profits in Nursefinder division are due to reduced demand. I and the analyst think they are fooling themselves because it is probably due to their poor competitive position and structure.

TEMPORARY NURSING SERVICE- *Medical Care*, 6/84

- This is probably the only study of the TNS industry. Supported by an HHS grant, They surveyed 1,133 agencies.

- 98% for-profit, 95% corporate, 85% were affiliated with a national franchisor organization. Only 15% were independent of a larger organization.
- All provide RN's; 99%, LPN's; 95%, orderlies; 56%, other. Only 18.5% mixed with other non-health care temporaries.
- Only 25% were in business prior to 1975.
- In 1981 the 3 largest firms accounted for 35% of the offices, 32% of the RN placements and 37% of the shift placements. The top 50 firms respectively accounted for 75%,75% and 77%.
- Authors feel the industry is like Bain's "low grade oligopoly" in which the large "competitive fringe" of small firms may dictate the industry and force it to perform in the competitive mode.
- The average number of RN's on the roster increased as the parent firm size decreased, independents being the largest. The overall mean/median was 61/34 and for independents 93/45. Independents could range to 300 or more.
- The average number of client institutions trended similarly. Overall mean/median was 8/6 and for independents was 10/7. A few of any size could have up to 30 or so.
- The number of RN shift placements in Oct. 1981 varied so as not to show a trend. The mean/median placements/month for independents was 260/90 ranging to 900 for a few. It does appear that the multi-firm groups may have group contracts.
- They estimate that in 1980 approximately 3% of the total RN's (1.3 million) were temporary staff (40,000). Approximately 50% did this as their primary position.

THE NURSING SHORTAGE- an analysis by Drexel Burnham Lambert

- 40% of the smaller and 75+% of the larger hospitals and nursing homes reported vacancies in 1987.
- There now over 2 million RN's; more than 80% are in the work force.
- The current average vacancy rate is over 12%. Over 50% of the community hospitals use agency nurses.
- The demand is growing exceptionally, while the supply rate is decreasing.
- TNS' and institutions entwined in a cycle that can only increase the cost of nurses out distancing the reimbursement rates to hospitals.

ONE MORE TIME-SOLUTIONS TO THE NURSING SHORTAGE. *JONA*. Nov., 1988

- A 1986 survey of RN's in Honolulu showed that 85% identified flexible staffing and scheduling to support patient care as their top priority. They suggested in-house float pools, more part-time and weekend positions, and variable shift size.
- The TNS phenomenon is not addressed by nursing research. Referred to a AHA study of 1981 which heard testimony and cited several studies on the negative effects on staff morale because of the use of "temps".
- Honolulu was a good example that higher salary is the only motivation. Temps got about the same wage as full-timers. They did it for freedom of choice and schedule. The local higher salaries are partly a result of the competition for RN's between the hospitals and the agencies.
- Some hospitals had a policy that a nurse who resigns may not return to the hospital through an agency for a year or two.
- Agency fees for placing "flying" of "traveling" nurses is a well guarded secret. Rumor has it that it may be 100/RN/month.

THE NURSING SHORTAGE-*New Eng. J. Med.*,

- The "shortage" of RN's is controversial. HHS says no; AHA studies say yes.
- 80% of RN's are actively employed compared to 54% of all American women. There are approximately a million nursing FTE's in hospitals and 400,000 in nursing homes.
- Maximum wage is only $7000 more than starting.

SUPPLEMENTAL STAFFING: CAN IT BE COST EFFECTIVE?-*Hospitals*. March, 1981

- Mentioned a 900 bed hospital study but gave no evidence for saying that a combination of regular full-time hospital personnel and planned supplemental staff from agencies is more cost effective. The author seemed to imply that agency part-time staffing is cheaper up to a point than in-house part-time staffing.

PLANNED SUPPLEMENTAL STAFFING IS A PRACTICAL ALTERNATIVE-*Hospitals*, March, 1981

- Noted that TNS has actually reduced the shortage by attracting those who would have left nursing entirely if it were not for the flexibility offered by agencies (of course these could be either internal or external).
- Mentions the consulting role of an agency through a collaborative relationship. Agency does all the employment duties; the hospital supplies the orientations and evaluations.
- Cite two 1978 studies stating that the recruitment cost of a hospital full-time nurse is $2000. When this as well as benefit and administrative costs are taken into account, the planned use of temporaries is cost-effective.
- Provides guidelines for agency use as set by the ANA.

THE COMMONWEALTH FUND STUDY on RN supply and demand for the AHA

- Of the 20% of RN's not in work force, one-third (7%) are disabled or retired and one-fourth (5%) had child care responsibilities. Only 5% of all RN's were employed outside of nursing, although 80% of the nurses with children in the 6 urban areas studied worked at nursing.
- I've seen a "rule-of-thumb" for RN's in a number of readings including this: two-thirds worked in hospitals and three-quarters of these were staff RN's.
- The two highest rated job attributes given by hospital nurses was schedule(55%) and salary(45%). For their next job 75% of full-time and 65% of part-time RN's rated salary first or second priority. Only 30% full-timers and 50% part-timers gave that rating to schedule.
- A majority of urban RN's rotate between shifts.
- Part-time RN's most often worked for agencies which paid more (1987/88) and had almost full control of their schedule.
- Areas of improvements which would entice a part-timer to work more were wages, raises, differentials, child care, schedule flexibility. However, if all those who said they might work actually did, the FTE's would increase by 6%.
- Suggest providing the choice of cash equivalents for benefits.

REPORT OF HOSPITAL NURSING PERSONNEL SURVEY:88-AHA (cat#c-154189)

- Survey showed that urban hospitals most frequently used alternative staffing (per diem.float-pool, on-call, and agency): 200-299 beds, per diem; 400-499 beds, agency and float pool.
- See their table 11 for a full break-down of agency use versus hospital location and size and rationale.

SECRETARY'S COMMISSION ON NURSING-HHS, 1988

- This was a comprehensive study of shortage and how to deal with it. It considered temporary agencies only in passing. This oversight was clearly inappropriate and most likely a result of commission selection bias. The commission were almost all nursing school educators(typically known for their heads in the sand.).
- 7% of FTE's of nursing homes are RN's and they are paid considerably less than hospital RN's.
- There is an implication that a major factor putting pressure on nursing salaries would be from agencies.
- The future economic risks for agencies would be the economic cyclic effects. Namely, hospital salaries will become competitive. The demand for nurses will go down as more less expensive non-nursing personnel are used. The supply will go up. This could also be an advantage as hospitals may find it more economical to use agency nurses for their low in-control vacancies.

NURSING IN THE 1990'S-Selected papers from a multi-sponsored Conference, 3/90

- Contains selected charts of health economics which may be helpful.

CALCULATION OF AN ESTIMATED MARKET FOR HOSPITAL TEMPORARIES
(RN'S, LPN'S and CNA'S) FOR 1989

BASED ON ERNST & WHINNEY SURVEY FOR A WEEK IN DECEMBER, 1986

	RN		LPN		CNA	
	1986	1989	1986	1989	1986	1989
Weighted average number of shifts/week for Chicago area	15.11	25.18	2.9	4.83	1.9	3.17
Percent hospitals using temporaries at time of study	30	50				
Number of hospitals in Chicago service area	98					
MARKET ESTIMATE: Average weekly temp utilization	1,481	2,468	284	474	186	310
Number of hospital staffing agencies in service area		105				
Average weekly shift placements per agency (assume even distribution)		23.504		4.51		2.96

No adjustment is made for increased utiliation of temps per hospital since the vacancy rate between 1986 and 1989 showed only a small increase and even went down slightly between 1938 and 1989.

CALCULATION OF SIZE-WEIGHTED TEMP UTILIZATION/WEEK

Number	Bed size range	shifts/ hosp	shifts/ group	shifts/ hosp	shifts/ group	shifts/ hosp	shifts/ group
8	50-99	2.2	17.6	1.2	7.2	0.7	4.2
21	100-199	4.7	98.7	1.5	28.5	0.6	11.4
47	200-399	15	705	3.5	129.5	1.5	55.5
6	400-499	25.7	154.2	2	12	6.9	41.4
16	≥500	31.6	505.6	4.5	63	3.2	44.8
98	TOTALS		1481.1		240		157.3
	Weighted average	15.113		2.9		1.9	

Only made an adjustment for the larger market to RN . Since it was an insignificant effect, it was not applied to the other 2 categories.

240

ESTIMATION OF THE NUMBER OF NURSING PERSONNEL UTILIZATION
IN CHICAGO AREA NURSING HOMES (SHIFTS/WEEK)*

LEVEL OF CARE	NUMBER OF# BEDS	MINIMUM* HRS OF CARE REQUIRED PER PATIENT/DAY	TOTAL HOURS REQUIRED PER DAY	MINIMUM SHIFTS REQUIRED FOR EACH NURSING TYPE	
				PER DAY	PER WEEK
SNF	24800	2.50	62000		
GENERAL ICF	10420	1.70	17714		
LIGHT ICF	5000	1.00	5000		
	DISTRIBUTION	TOTAL	84714		
	0.04 AS RN'S		3389	424	2965
	0.16 AS LPN'S		13554	1694	11860
	0.80 AS CNA'S		67771	8471	59300

*These calculations represent the minimum staffing as required by Illinois Dept. of Public Health regulations. Some nursing homes staff above these minimum. #Figures from nursing home data base

ESTIMATION OF UTILIZATION OF NURSING HOME TEMPORARIES
AVERAGED OVER 238 AREA NURSING HOMES

Weekly Average Shifts per Nursing Home (see above)

NURSING TYPE	TOTAL	TEMPORARIES Assume 4% use rate
RN	12.46	0.50
LPN	49.83	1.99
CNA	249.16	9.97

ESTIMATION OF MINIMUM TEMPORARY MARKET

NURSING TYPE	SHIFTS/WEEK assume 4%	AVERAGE WAGE PER SHIFT	MARKET PER WEEK
RN	119	$39.00	$37,003
LPN	474	$25.25	$95,828
CNA	2372	$14.75	$279,895
		TOTAL	$412,727
ANNUAL MARKET			**$21,461,784**

SHIFT IN CUSTOMER BASE

YEARS 1-2

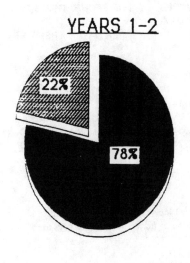

YEAR 3

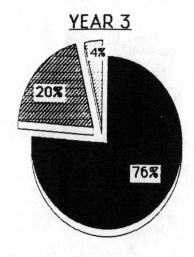

YEAR 4

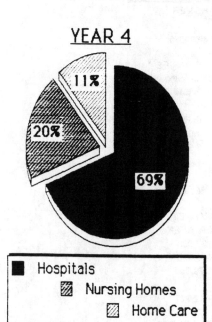

YEAR 5

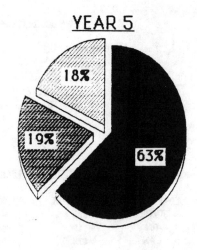

■ Hospitals
▨ Nursing Homes
▨ Home Care

Sample Business Plan A: Appendix

SCHEDULES SUPPORTING FINANCIAL STATEMENTS (PAGE 2)

REVENUE PROJECTIONS

			RN Shifts/Wk.			LPN Shifts/Wk.			CNA Shifts/Wk.			TOTAL SERVICE REVENUES		
			"Worst Case"	Median	"Best Case"	"Worst Case"	Median	"Best Case"	"Worst Case"	Median	"Best Case"	"Worst Case"	Median	"Best Case"
1st Year	HOSP.:	Shifts/wk.	15	45	75	0	9	18	0	6	12			
		Hrs./yr.	6,240	18,720	31,200	0	3,744	7,488	0	2,496	4,992			
		Avg. rate/hr.	39.00	39.00	39.00	25.25	25.25	25.25	14.75	14.75	14.75			
		Revenue/yr.	243,360	730,080	1,216,800	0	94,536	189,072	0	36,816	73,632	243,360	861,432	1,479,504
	NS. HM.:	Shifts/wk.	0	3	6	0	6	12	15	30	45			
		Hrs./yr.	0	1,248	2,496	0	2,496	4,992	6,240	12,480	18,720			
		Avg. rate/hr	39.00	39.00	39.00	25.25	25.25	25.25	14.75	14.75	14.75			
		Revenue/yr.	0	48,672	97,344	0	63,024	126,048	92,040	184,080	276,120	92,040	295,776	499,512
2nd Year	HOSP.:	Shifts/wk.	35	140	245	0	21	42	0	14	28			
		Hrs./yr.	14,560	58,240	101,920	0	8,736	17,472	0	5,824	11,648			
		Avg. rate/hr.	42.12	42.12	42.12	27.02	27.02	27.02	15.64	15.64	15.64			
		Revenue/yr.	613,267	2,453,069	4,292,870	0	236,025	472,050	0	91,058	182,116	613,267	2,780,152	4,947,037
	NS. HM.:	Shifts/wk.	0	7	14	0	14	28	35	70	105			
		Hrs./yr.	0	2,912	5,824	0	5,824	11,648	14,560	29,120	43,680			
		Avg. rate/hr.	42.12	42.12	42.12	27.02	27.02	27.02	15.64	15.64	15.64			
		Revenue/yr.	0	122,653	245,307	0	157,350	314,700	227,646	455,291	682,937	227,646	735,295	1,242,944
3rd Year	HOSP.:	Shifts/wk.	--	180	--	--	27	--	--	18	--			
		Hrs./yr.		74,880			11,232			7,488				
		Avg. rate/hr.		45.49			28.91			16.57				
		Revenue/yr.		3,406,261			324,703			124,099		3,855,063		
	NS. HM.:	Shifts/wk.	--	9	--	--	18	--	--	90	--			
		Hrs./yr.		3,744			7,488			37,440				
		Avg. rate/hr.		45.49			28.91			16.57				
		Revenue/yr.		170,313			216,469			620,497		1,007,278		
	HM. CR.:	Shifts/wk.	--	5	--	--	25	--	--	5	--			
		Hrs./yr.		2,080			1,040			2,080				
		Avg. rate/hr.		60.00			50.00			25.00				
		Revenue/yr.		124,800			52,000			52,000		228,800		
4th Year	HOSP.:	Shifts/wk.	--	200	--	--	30	--	--	20	--			
		Hrs./yr.		83,200			12,480			8,320				
		Avg. rate/hr.		49.13			30.93			17.57				
		Revenue/yr.		4,087,513			386,036			146,161		4,619,711		
	NS. HM.:	Shifts/wk.	--	11	--	--	22	--	--	110	--			
		Hrs./yr.		4,576			9,152			45,760				
		Avg. rate/hr.		49.13			30.93			17.57				
		Revenue/yr.		224,813			283,093			803,888		1,311,794		
	HM. CR.:	Shifts/wk.	--	15	--	--	7.5	--	--	15	--			
		Hrs./yr.		6,240			3,120			6,240				
		Avg. rate/hr.		64.80			53.50			26.50				
		Revenue/yr.		404,352			166,920			165,360		736,632		
5th Year	HOSP.:	Shifts/wk.	--	220	--	--	33	--	--	22	--			
		Hrs./yr.		91,520			13,728			9,152				
		Avg. rate/hr.		53.06			33.10			18.62				
		Revenue/yr.		4,855,966			454,364			170,424		5,480,754		
	NS. HM.:	Shifts/wk.	--	13	--	--	26	--	--	130	--			
		Hrs./yr.		5,408			10,816			54,080				
		Avg. rate/hr.		53.06			33.10			18.62				
		Revenue/yr.		286,943			357,984			1,007,053		1,651,980		
	HM. CR.:	Shifts/wk.	--	30	--	--	15	--	--	30	--			
		Hrs./yr.		12,480			6,240			12,480				
		Avg. rate/hr.		69.98			57.25			28.09				
		Revenue/yr.		873,400			357,209			350,563		1,581,172		

243

Sample Business Plan A: Appendix

INSURANCE PROJECTIONS

		"Worst Case"	Median	"Best Case"
		EXPOSURE HOURS		
1st Year	TOTAL NURSING STAFF HOURS Hospitals	6,240	24,960	43,680
	Nurs. homes	6,240	16,224	26,208
	TOTAL MANAGEMENT HOURS	6,000	6,000	6,000
	TOTAL OFFICE EMPLOYEE HOURS	6,000	6,000	6,000
	TOTAL EXPOSURE HOURS	24,480	53,184	81,888
	Calc. of professional/general liability premium:			
	$1,500 + $.10 (Total exp. hrs. - 16,000)	2,348	5,218	8,089
	Calc. of non-owned automobile liability:			
	$100 for each 8,000 exposure hours	306	665	1,024
	TOTAL PREMIUM:	$2,654	$5,883	$9,112

		"Worst Case"	Median	"Best Case"
2nd Year	TOTAL NURSING STAFF HOURS Hospitals	14,560	72,800	131,040
	Nurs. homes	14,560	37,856	61,152
	TOTAL MANAGEMENT HOURS	6,000	6,000	6,000
	TOTAL OFFICE EMPLOYEE HOURS	8,000	8,000	8,000
	TOTAL EXPOSURE HOURS	43,120	124,656	206,192
	Calc. of professional/general liability premium:			
	$1,500 + $.10 (Total exp. hrs. - 16,000)	4,212	12,366	20,519
	Calc. of non-owned automobile liability:			
	$100 for each 8,000 exposure hours	539	1,558	2,577
	TOTAL PREMIUM:	$4,751	$13,924	$23,097

3rd Year	TOTAL NURSING STAFF HOURS Hospitals	93,600
	Nurs. homes	48,672
	Home care	5,200
	TOTAL MANAGEMENT HOURS	6,000
	TOTAL OFFICE EMPLOYEE HOURS	9,000
	TOTAL EXPOSURE HOURS	162,472
	Calc. of professional/general liability premium:	
	$1,500 + $.10 (Total exp. hrs. - 16,000)	16,147
	Calc. of non-owned automobile liability:	
	$100 for each 8,000 exposure hours	2,031
	TOTAL PREMIUM:	$18,178

4th Year	TOTAL NURSING STAFF HOURS Hospitals	104,000
	Nurs. homes	59,488
	Home care	15,600
	TOTAL MANAGEMENT HOURS	8,000
	TOTAL OFFICE EMPLOYEE HOURS	9,000
	TOTAL EXPOSURE HOURS	196,088
	Calc. of professional/general liability premium:	
	$1,500 + $.10 (Total exp. hrs. - 16,000)	19,509
	Calc. of non-owned automobile liability:	
	$100 for each 8,000 exposure hours	2,451
	TOTAL PREMIUM:	$21,960

5th Year	TOTAL NURSING STAFF HOURS Hospitals	114,400
	Nurs. homes	70,304
	Home care	31,200
	TOTAL MANAGEMENT HOURS	8,000
	TOTAL OFFICE EMPLOYEE HOURS	9,000
	TOTAL EXPOSURE HOURS	232,904
	Calc. of professional/general liability premium:	
	$1,500 + $.10 (Total exp. hrs. - 16,000)	23,190
	Calc. of non-owned automobile liability:	
	$100 for each 8,000 exposure hours	2,911
	TOTAL PREMIUM:	$26,102

Sample Business Plan A: Appendix

DEPRECIATION SCHEDULE

Office equipment (computer system)	15,000
Office furniture and fixtures	6,000
TOTAL FIXED ASSETS TO BE DEPRECIATED	$21,000 (assuming zero salvage value)
(OVER A 10-YEAR LIFE ON A STRAIGHT-LINE BASIS)	

YEAR	DEPRECIATION EXPENSE	ACCUMULATED DEPRECIATION	FIXED ASSETS' BOOK VALUE
1	$2,100	$2,100	$18,900
2	2,100	4,200	16,800
3	2,100	6,300	14,700
4	2,100	8,400	12,600
5	2,100	10,500	10,500

LOAN AMORTIZATION SCHEDULE

YEAR	BEGINNING AMT.	PAYMENT	INTEREST (@ 12%)	REPAYMENT OF PRINCIPAL	REMAINING BALANCE
1	$200,000	$29,365	$24,000	$5,365	$194,635
2	194,635	29,365.	23,356	6,009	188,626
3	188,626	29,365	22,635	6,730	181,896
4	181,896	29,365	21,828	7,537	174,359
5	174,359	29,365	20,923	8,442	165,917
6	165,917	29,365	19,910	9,455	156,462

CHC TEMPS
INCOME STATEMENT
FOR THE FISCAL YEAR MAY 1, 1991 - APRIL 30, 1992
MONTHLY PROJECTIONS

MEDIAN PROJECTION, FISCAL YEAR		MAY, '91	JUNE, '91	JULY, '91	AUG., '91	SEPT., '91	OCT., '91
Service Revenue							
Sales							
Hospital revenues	861,432	0	23,929	23,929	47,857	47,857	71,786
Nurs. home revenues	295,776	0	8,216	8,216	16,432	16,432	24,648
Home care revenues	0	0	0	0	0	0	0
Gross Service Revenue	$1,157,208	$0	$32,145	$32,145	$64,289	$64,289	$96,434
Sales discounts (@ 3%)	$34,716	$0	$964	$964	$1,929	$1,929	$2,893
Net Service Revenue	$1,122,492	$0	$31,180	$31,180	$62,361	$62,361	$93,541
Cost of Goods Sold							
Wages							
(@70% of Gross Rev.)	810,046	0	22,501	22,501	45,003	45,003	67,504
Worker's Comp. &							
Payroll Taxes	115,431	0	3,206	3,206	6,413	6,413	9,619
Insurance	5,883	1,471			1,471		
Benefits	30,000	2,500	2,500	2,500	2,500	2,500	2,500
Cost of Goods Sold	$961,360	$3,971	$28,208	$28,208	$55,386	$53,915	$79,623
Gross Margin	$161,132	($3,971)	$2,973	$2,973	$6,974	$8,445	$13,918
Operating Expenses							
Selling							
Advertising	24,000	4,000	2,000	2,000	2,000	2,000	2,000
Mailings/other							
selling expenses	6,200	3,450	250	250	250	250	250
General & Admin.							
Licensing	500	250					
Incorporation costs	1,150	1,150					
Mgmnt. compensation	120,000	10,000	10,000	10,000	10,000	10,000	10,000
Employee comp.	48,000	4,000	4,000	4,000	4,000	4,000	4,000
Rent	9,600	800	800	800	800	800	800
Utilities	1,800	150	150	150	150	150	150
Recruitment costs	12,200	600	400	100	100	100	100
Supplies	2,400	200	200	200	200	200	200
Depreciation	2,100	175	175	175	175	175	175
Total Operating Expense	$227,950	$24,775	$17,975	$17,675	$17,675	$17,675	$17,675
Net Operating							
Income (Loss)	($66,818)	($28,746)	($15,002)	($14,702)	($10,701)	($9,230)	($3,757)
Interest Income	5,200						
Interest Expense	24,000						
Net Income (Loss)							
Before Taxes	($85,618)						
Income Tax							
Net Income	($85,618)						

QHC TEMPS
INCOME STATEMENT
FOR THE FISCAL YEAR MAY 1, 1991 - APRIL 30, 1992
MONTHLY PROJECTIONS, CONT.

	MEDIAN PROJECTION, FISCAL YEAR	NOV., '91	DEC., '91	JAN., '92	FEB., '92	MAR., '92	APR., '92
Service Revenue							
Sales							
Hospital revenues	861,432	71,786	95,715	95,715	119,643	119,643	143,572
Nurs. home revenues	295,776	24,648	32,864	32,864	41,080	41,080	49,296
Home care revenues	0	0	0	0	0	0	0
Gross Service Revenue	$1,157,208	$96,434	$128,579	$128,579	$160,723	$160,723	$192,868
Sales discounts (@ 3%)	$34,716	$2,893	$3,857	$3,857	$4,822	$4,822	$5,786
Net Service Revenue	$1,122,492	$93,541	$124,721	$124,721	$155,902	$155,902	$187,082
Cost of Goods Sold							
Wages							
(@70% of Gross Rev.)	810,046	67,504	90,005	90,005	112,506	112,506	135,008
Worker's Comp. &							
Payroll Taxes	115,431	9,619	12,826	12,826	16,032	16,032	19,239
Insurance	5,883	1,471			1,470		
Benefits	30,000	2,500	2,500	2,500	2,500	2,500	2,500
Cost of Goods Sold	$961,360	$81,094	$105,331	$105,331	$132,508	$131,038	$156,746
Gross Margin	$161,132	$12,447	$19,391	$19,391	$23,393	$24,863	$30,336
Operating Expenses							
Selling							
Advertising	24,000	1,000	1,000	2,000	2,000	2,000	2,000
Mailings/other							
selling expenses	6,200	250	250	250	250	250	250
General & Admin.							
Licensing	500			250			
Incorporation costs	1,150						
Mgmnt. compensation	120,000	10,000	10,000	10,000	10,000	10,000	10,000
Employee comp.	48,000	4,000	4,000	4,000	4,000	4,000	4,000
Rent	9,600	800	800	800	800	800	800
Utilities	1,800	150	150	150	150	150	150
Recruitment costs	12,200	1,800	1,800	1,800	1,800	1,800	1,800
Supplies	2,400	200	200	200	200	200	200
Depreciation	2,100	175	175	175	175	175	175
Total Operating Expense	$227,950	$18,375	$18,375	$19,625	$19,375	$19,375	$19,375
Net Operating							
Income (Loss)	($66,818)	($5,928)	$1,016	($234)	$4,018	$5,488	$10,961
Interest Income	5,200						
Interest Expense	24,000						
Net Income (Loss)							
Before Taxes	($85,618)						
Income Tax							
Net Income	($85,618)						

Sample Business Plan A: Appendix

MEDIAN PROJECTION		MAY, '92	JUNE, '92	JULY, '92	AUG., '92	SEPT., '92	OCT., '92
Service Revenue							
Sales							
Hospital revenues	2,780,152	198,582	198,582	198,582	198,582	231,679	231,679
Nurs. home revenues	735,295	52,521	52,521	52,521	52,521	61,275	61,275
Home care revenues	0	0	0	0	0	0	0
Gross Service Revenue	$3,515,447	$251,103	$251,103	$251,103	$251,103	$292,954	$292,954
Sales discounts (@ 3%)	$105,463	$7,533	$7,533	$7,533	$7,533	$8,789	$8,789
Net Service Revenue	$3,409,984	$243,570	$243,570	$243,570	$243,570	$284,165	$284,165
Cost of Goods Sold							
Wages							
(@70% of Gross Rev.)	2,460,813	175,772	175,772	175,772	175,772	205,068	205,068
Worker's Comp. &							
Payroll Taxes	350,666	25,048	25,048	25,048	25,048	29,222	29,222
Insurance	13,924	3,481			3,481		
Benefits	45,000	3,750	3,750	3,750	3,750	3,750	3,750
Cost of Goods Sold	$2,870,403	$208,051	$204,570	$204,570	$208,051	$238,040	$238,040
Gross Margin	$539,581	$35,519	$39,000	$39,000	$35,519	$46,125	$46,125
Operating Expenses							
Selling							
Advertising	48,000	4,000	4,000	4,000	4,000	4,000	4,000
Mailings/other							
selling expenses	12,400	3,700	3,700	500	500	500	500
General & Admin.							
Licensing	250						
Mgmnt. compensation	126,120	10,510	10,510	10,510	10,510	10,510	10,510
Employee comp.	64,296	5,358	5,358	5,358	5,358	5,358	5,358
Rent	10,080	840	840	840	840	840	840
Utilities	1,890	158	158	158	158	158	158
Recruitment costs	22,400	1,800	1,800	1,800	1,800	1,900	1,900
Supplies	4,800	400	400	400	400	400	400
Depreciation	2,100	175	175	175	175	175	175
Total Operating Expense	$292,336	$26,941	$26,941	$23,741	$23,741	$23,841	$23,841
Net Operating							
Income (Loss)	$247,245	$8,579	$12,060	$15,260	$11,779	$22,285	$22,285
Interest Income	5,250						
Interest Expense	23,356						
Net Income (Loss)							
Before Taxes	$229,139						
Income Tax (@34%)	77,907						
Net Income	$151,232						

CHC TEMPS
INCOME STATEMENT
FOR THE FISCAL YEAR MAY 1, 1992 - APRIL 30, 1993
MONTHLY PROJECTIONS, CONT.

MEDIAN PROJECTION		NOV., '92	DEC., '92	JAN., '93	FEB., '93	MAR., '93	APR., '93
Service Revenue							
Sales							
Hospital revenues	2,780,152	231,679	231,679	264,776	264,776	264,776	264,776
Nurs. home revenues	735,295	61,275	61,275	70,028	70,028	70,028	70,028
Home care revenues	0	0	0	0	0	0	0
Gross Service Revenue	$3,515,447	$292,954	$292,954	$334,804	$334,804	$334,804	$334,804
Sales discounts (@ 3%)	$105,463	$8,789	$8,789	$10,044	$10,044	$10,044	$10,044
Net Service Revenue	$3,409,984	$284,165	$284,165	$324,760	$324,760	$324,760	$324,760
Cost of Goods Sold							
Wages							
(@70% of Gross Rev.)	2,460,813	205,068	205,068	234,363	234,363	234,363	234,363
Worker's Comp. &							
Payroll Taxes	350,666	29,222	29,222	33,397	33,397	33,397	33,397
Insurance	13,924	3,481			3,481		
Benefits	45,000	3,750	3,750	3,750	3,750	3,750	3,750
Cost of Goods Sold	$2,870,403	$241,521	$238,040	$271,510	$274,991	$271,510	$271,510
Gross Margin	$539,581	$42,644	$46,125	$53,250	$49,769	$53,250	$53,250
Operating Expenses							
Selling							
Advertising	48,000	4,000	4,000	4,000	4,000	4,000	4,000
Mailings/other							
selling expenses	12,400	500	500	500	500	500	500
General & Admin.							
Licensing	250			250			
Mgmnt. compensation	126,120	10,510	10,510	10,510	10,510	10,510	10,510
Employee comp.	64,296	5,358	5,358	5,358	5,358	5,358	5,358
Rent	10,080	840	840	840	840	840	840
Utilities	1,890	158	158	158	158	158	158
Recruitment costs	22,400	1,900	1,900	1,900	1,900	1,900	1,900
Supplies	4,800	400	400	400	400	400	400
Depreciation	2,100	175	175	175	175	175	175
Total Operating Expense	$292,336	$23,841	$23,841	$24,091	$23,841	$23,841	$23,841
Net Operating							
Income (Loss)	$247,245	$18,804	$22,285	$29,160	$25,929	$29,410	$29,410
Interest Income	5,250						
Interest Expense	23,356						
Net Income (Loss)							
Before Taxes	$229,139						
Income Tax (@34%)	77,907						
Net Income	$151,232						

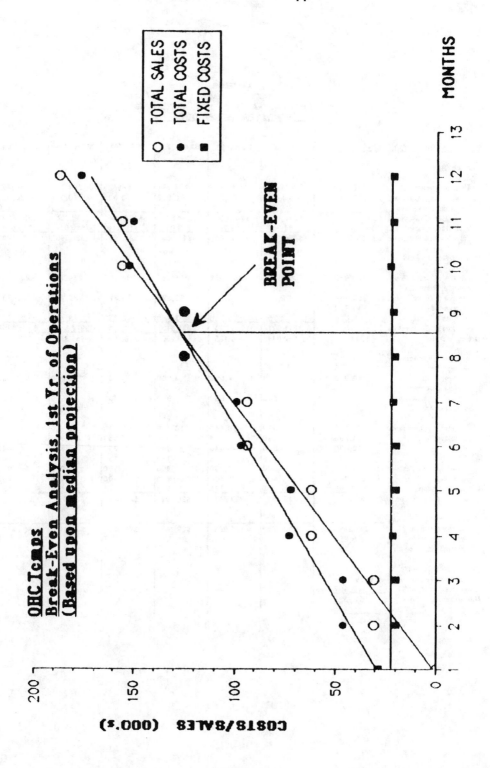

QHCTemps
Break-Even Analysis, 1st Yr. of Operations
(Based upon median projection)

BREAK-EVEN POINT

TOTAL SALES
TOTAL COSTS
FIXED COSTS

MONTHS

COSTS/SALES (000's)

CUSTOMER'S ECONOMIC JUSTIFICATION

Purpose: We use an example to demonstrate to hospital managers that there is an economic justification for using temporaries to respond to peak nursing needs rather than budgeting full-time positions. This assumes that the alternative of not meeting the peak staffing need is unacceptable because the hospital would have to turn away admissions and elective surgery. It will be neccessary for us to advise our clients on how to apply this rationale to their individual institutions.

EXAMPLE: HOSPITAL STAFFING FOR CYCLIC FLUCTUATIONS

		hourly wage	weekly hours	weekly cost	weekly savings	annual savings
Say hospital plans for variations in census and acuity by staffing for one regular, permanent full-time-equivalent		$32.00	40	$1,280		
Alternate cost for a temporary relief RN If the census, patient acuity or other factors are such that the actual need in shifts per week is:	1	$40.00	8	$320	$960	$49,920
	2		16	$640	$640	$33,280
	3		24	$960	$320	$16,640
	4		32	$1,280	$0	$0

Estimation of true hourly cost for a hospital full-time-equivalent RN

Current average RN hourly salary in Chicago metropolitan area based on 1989 survey by the Ill. Hosp. Assoc.		$18.00
Adjusted for all fringe benefits and non-productive costs (1)	44%	$26.00
Accounting for orientation, training and recruitment (including bonuses) costs for a new hiree spread over one year (2)		$6.00
Actual hourly cost incurred by hospital in first year for a new RN		$32.00

FOOTNOTES:

(1) Personal communication with Mr. Mark Lusson, Vice President and Director of Human Resources, Northwest Comm. Hosp., Arl. Hts., IL

(2) Personal communication with Ms. Phyllis Cerone, RN, Director of Nursing Education and Training at Northwest Comm. Hosp.

ORGANIZATION CHART

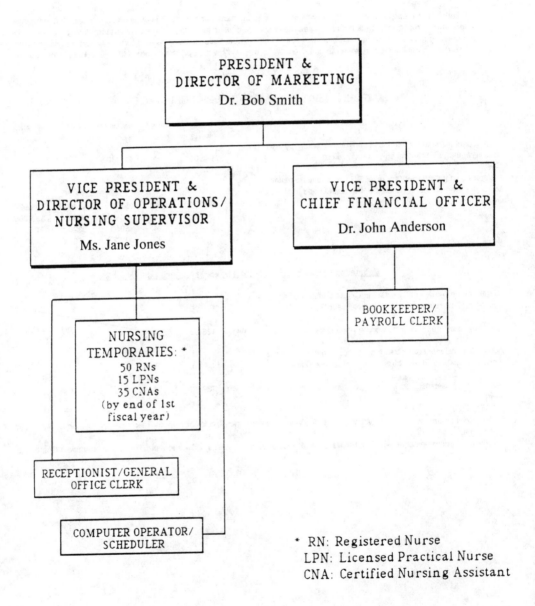

PRESIDENT &
DIRECTOR OF MARKETING
Dr. Bob Smith

VICE PRESIDENT &
DIRECTOR OF OPERATIONS/
NURSING SUPERVISOR

Ms. Jane Jones

VICE PRESIDENT &
CHIEF FINANCIAL OFFICER

Dr. John Anderson

NURSING
TEMPORARIES: *
50 RNs
15 LPNs
35 CNAs
(by end of 1st
fiscal year)

BOOKKEEPER/
PAYROLL CLERK

RECEPTIONIST/GENERAL
OFFICE CLERK

COMPUTER OPERATOR/
SCHEDULER

* RN: Registered Nurse
LPN: Licensed Practical Nurse
CNA: Certified Nursing Assistant

QHC TEMPS
QUALITY HEALTH CARE TEMPORARIES

NURSING DEPARTMENT SURVEY

Dear _____

We are developing a medical staffing service specializing in the temporary placement of fully-licensed, quality-oriented nurses. To enable us to tailor our business plan to best service the needs of the medical community, will you please take a few minutes to answer the following questions regarding your own staffing needs and your current utilization of staffing services?   Thank you.

PART A: CURRENT STAFFING NEEDS

1. Is your organization currently seeking to fill nursing staff vacancies?
   YES_____   NO_____
   (If NO, please go to part B.)

2. Are you in need of nurses with particular areas of specialization or with specific training/certification? Please be specific._____
   _____
   _____
   _____

3. How many full-time nursing positions are you presently seeking to fill?
   RN _____   LPN _____   CNA_____
   Part-time nursing positions?   RN _____   LPN _____   CNA_____

4. Are you experiencing difficulty with staffing for any particular shifts? (such as 3-11 pm, 11pm-7am, weekends, on-call, etc.) Again, please be specific.
   _____
   _____

5. What other, if any, special qualifications do you seek in the nurses you hire?
   _____
   _____
   _____

PART B: STAFFING SERVICE UTILIZATION

6. Do you have your own registry or "float pool" of nurses for temporary assignments?   YES___   NO_____

7. Is your organization currently utilizing nurses provided through the services of a temporary staffing service or agency?   YES___   NO_____
   (If NO, please go to question #13.)

8. Please give the name(s) of the service(s) or agency/agencies that you currently use._____
_____
_____

   If you prefer to use <u>one</u> of these services/agencies in particular, which is it and why?_____
_____

9. In days or weeks, what is the approximate average duration of the placement of a temporarily-placed nurse in your organization? _____

10. Are there particular shifts/positions/specialty areas that you customarily staff with temporarily-placed nurses? Please be specific._____
_____
_____

11. To what extent (as an approximate percentage of your total nursing staff) are you presently utilizing these temporarily-placed nurses? _____

12. IF YOU RESPONDED "<u>YES</u>" TO QUESTION #1:
    If our service could fully meet your supplemental nurse staffing needs, as indicated by your responses in <u>PART A</u>, <u>and</u> offer your organization an advantage in quality and costs over the temporary staffing service(s) you now use, would you be interested in contracting for our services?
    YES_____   NO_____   *(Please go to <u>question #16</u>.)*

    IF YOU RESPONDED "<u>NO</u>" TO QUESTION #1:
    If you experience nursing staff shortages in the future, and if our service could not only meet your staffing needs but could also offer your organization an advantage in quality and costs over the temporary staffing service(s) you now use, might you be interested in contracting for our services?
    YES_____   NO_____   *(Please go to <u>question #16</u>.)*

13. Can you indicate any specific reasons for your <u>not</u> utilizing nurses provided through the services of a temporary staffing service or agency?
_____
_____
_____
_____

14. What services/features would a temporary staffing service or agency have to offer in order to attract your business? _____
_____
_____
_____

15. IF YOU RESPONDED "YES" TO QUESTION #1:
   If our service could fully meet your supplemental nurse staffing needs, as indicated by your responses in PART A, and meet the other needs that you have indicated in your response to question #14, would you be interested in contracting for our services?   YES_____   NO_____

   IF YOU RESPONDED "NO" TO QUESTION #1:
   If you experience nursing staff shortages in the future, and if our service could meet not only your staffing needs but the other needs that you have indicated in your response to question #14 as well, might you be interested in contracting for our services?   YES_____   NO_____

16. We are considering the eventual expansion of our services to provide for your needs in other areas of health care staffing. Please indicate for which health care professionals your organization is in the greatest need.
   Physical therapist_____   Occupational therapist_____
   Respiratory therapist_____   Nuclear med. tech._____
   Radiology tech._____
   Other _____
   _____

17. Again, your participation in this survey will help us to tailor the specific nature of our services. May we contact you again by telephone in the near future to further discuss how your organization might benefit from those services?
   YES_____   NO_____

THANK YOU AGAIN FOR YOUR TIME AND YOUR PARTICIPATION.

HOSPITAL MARKET LISTED ALPHEBETICALLY WITH BOND RATINGS

HOSP. NAME	TOTAL BEDS	PERCENT OCCUPIED	OCCUPIED BEDS	PATIENT DAYS	LOCATION	BOND RATING
Alcholism Treatment Center of Cent. D	52	59.6	31	11312	north suburbs	
Alexian Brothers	395	66.3	262	95588	NW suburbs	Aaa
American International	87	69	60	21911	north suburbs	
Belmont Community	97	57.7	56	20429	north west	
Bethany	212	70.3	149	54398	west	
Central DuPage	338	67.2	227	82905	west suburbs	
Charter Barclay	123	87.8	108	39418	north	
Chicago Osteopathic	245	67.8	166	60630	south	
Chicago-Read Mental Health Center	607	100	607	221555	north west	
Children's Memorial	254	74	188	68605	near north	Aaa
Christ Community	824	71.4	588	214743	SW suburbs	A1,Aaa
Columbus	311	67.2	209	76282	near north	Baa1
Condell	155	61.7	96	34907	north suburbs	
Cook County	951	67.8	645	235344	loop	
Copley Memorial	201	56.2	113	41231	SW suburbs	A
CPC Old Orchard	123	70.7	87	31741	north suburbs	
Delnor Community	160	53.1	85	31010	west suburbs	Baa
Edgewater	156	69.9	109	39801	north	
Edward	155	67.7	105	38301	west suburbs	Baa1
Elgin Mental Health Center	824	97.7	805	293843	NW suburbs	
Elmhurst	392	73.8	289	105593	west suburbs	A1
Evanston	545	80.1	437	159339	north suburbs	Aa
Foster G. Mcgaw (Loyola)	567	81.5	462	168668	west suburbs	
Glenoaks Medical Center	120	62.5	75	27375	west suburbs	
Good Samaritan	311	71.1	221	80709	west suburbs	A1
Good Sheppard	162	61.1	99	36128	NW suburbs	A1
Gottlieb Memorial	275	63.6	175	63839	west suburbs	
Grant	302	69.3	209	76389	near north	
Hartgrove	99	70.7	70	25547	west	
HCA Chicago Lakeshore	110	68.2	75	27382	north	
HCA Riveredge	210	79.5	167	60937	west suburbs	
Highland Park	288	58.6	169	61600	north suburbs	
Hines VA	1111	79.7	885	323195	west	
Hinsdale	435	64.8	282	102886	SW suburbs	
Holy Cross	337	77.3	261	95083	south	
Holy Family	246	53.3	131	47858	NW suburbs	Aaa
Humana	226	57.5	130	47432	NW suburbs	
Hyde Park	176	58	102	37259	south	
Illinois Masonic	722	80.9	584	213196	north	A
Illinois State Psychiatric Institute	197	91.4	180	65721	loop	
Ingalls Memorial	579	69.8	404	147512	south suburbs	A1
Jackson Park	265	55.5	147	53682	south	
La Grange Memorial	236	68.9	163	59350	SW suburbs	
La Rabida Children's	65	70.8	46	16797	south	
Lake Forest	242	78.9	191	69692	north suburbs	
Lakeside Community	106	50.9	54	19693	near south	
Lakeside VA	354	61.6	218	79593	loop	
Lincoln West	105	38.3	40	14678	north	

Page 1

Little Company of Mary	332	71.8	238	87007	SW suburbs	Aaa
Loretto	184	77.2	142	51848	west	
Louis A. Weiss Memorial	243	79.6	193	70601	north	
Lutheran General	880	72.6	639	233191	NW suburbs	Aa
MacNeal	427	55.5	237	86500	SW suburbs	A,Aaa
Marianjoy Rehabilitation Center	100	88.4	88	32266	west suburbs	
Martha Washington	175	53.7	94	34301	north	Aaa
Mercy	477	69.5	332	121003	near south	A
Mercy Center for Health Care Services	295	63.1	186	67943	SW suburbs	
Methodist Hospital of Chicago	201	44.8	90	32868	north	A
Michael Reese	652	71.8	468	170870	near south	
Mount Sinai	356	78.4	279	101873	west	Ba
Northwest Community	407	80.6	328	119735	NW suburbs	Aaa
Northwestern Memorial	708	76.3	540	197174	loop	Aa
Norwegian-American	230	50	115	41975	west	
Oak Park	215	52.3	112	41042	west suburbs	
Our Lady of Resurrection	288	58.3	168	61285	northwest	
Palos Community	361	74.2	268	97770	SW suburbs	A1
Parkside Lutheran	88	78.4	69	25182	NW suburbs	
Ravenswood	316	78.7	249	90773	north	Baa1
Resurrection	749	74.9	561	204765	far northwest	
Roseland Community	154	64.9	100	36480	south west	Aaa
Rush North Shore Medical Center	260	60.4	157	57320	north suburbs	
Rush-Presbyterian-St. Lukes	983	77.1	758	276631	loop	Aa
Saint Anthony	142	67.9	96	35193	west	
Saint Joseph-Elgin	280	49.6	139	50691	NW suburbs	
Saint Mary of Nazareth	255	81.6	208	75949	west	
Saint Therese Medical Center	310	54.8	170	62006	north suburbs	
Schwab Rehabilitation Center	70	82.9	58	21181	south west	
Sherman	331	61	202	73697	NW suburbs	
Shriners Hospital for Crippled Childrer	60	71.7	43	15702	west	
South Chicago Community	385	59.2	228	83191	south	
South Shore Hospital	170	52.4	89	32514	south	
South Suburban	211	70.2	148	54065	south suburbs	
St Francis	446	68.2	304	111023	north suburbs	
St. Bernard	217	81.6	177	64631	south west	
St. Cabrini	200	61.8	124	45114	near west	
St. Elizabeth's	243	67.9	165	60224	near west	
St. Francis- Blue Island	294	70.6	208	75761	south suburbs	
St. James	330	59.8	197	72029	south suburbs	
St. Joseph	511	50.1	256	93444	near north	
Suburban Hosp. & Sanitarium of Cook C	122	33.6	41	14962	SW suburbs	
Swedish Covanent	200	96.5	193	70445	north	Baa1
Thorek	170	47.6	81	29536	north	
University of Chicago Hospitals	560	81.3	455	166177	south	Aaa
University of Illinois	358	72.1	258	94213	loop	
Victory Memorial	333	53.7	179	65270	north suburbs	A
West side VA	484	68.6	332	121189	loop	
West Suburban	370	43.5	161	58747	west suburbs	A
Westlake Community	288	67	193	70430	west suburbs	Baa1

	98	31474		22079.12	8058877
AVERAGES:		321	68	225	82233

Sample Business Plan B
Sports 'N Fitness USA

TABLE OF CONTENTS

Sample Business Plan B

EXECUTIVE SUMMARY

Sports 'N Fitness USA is a start-up venture offering indoor/outdoor sports activities to groups and individuals on a membership basis. Unlike current "health clubs," we will offer leagues a place to play volleyball, basketball, and hockey as well as offering individuals an opportunity to participate in a sport or fitness activity. Sports 'N Fitness USA will promote group and family participation and offer expert clinics and lessons for those who wish to learn or improve a sports skill.

Health and fitness clubs compete primarily on the basis of location, variety of activities offered, quality of staff, and condition of the physical facility. Our Libertyville location is excellent due to the high income level and the population growth which is forecasted at 2.5 times higher than the national average. Our wide range of team and individual activities and the planned preventive maintenance program of our athletic club will exceed the expectations of our membership. The staff training program will set us apart from other area facilities.

We have the basic ingredients for a successful club and, most importantly, a management team which has the experience, enthusiasm, and commitment to ensure this success (see Management Expertise). Joe Abercrombie has award-winning direct sales experience and will serve as President and Director of Sales. Susan Skelso will hold the position of Program Director and Marketing Manager. Marge McIntyre will be Facility Administrator with responsibility for staffing and training. Mr. Abercrombie, Mrs. Skelso, and Mrs. McIntyre hold M.B.A. degrees and have extensive direct management experience in the health club and recreation industry. William Weiner, a C.P.A. and financial expert with an information systems background, will be the controller and MIS Director.

The purchase of five acres of land and construction of the multi-sport athletic club will cost $4,500,000. The management team has personally raised $600,000 in equity capital. We have commitments from outside investors for $1,900,000, contingent on receiving our remaining financing. In exchange, we have given our private investors 40 percent of the company. Sports 'N Fitness USA requires a ten-year mortgage of $2,250,000. We plan to provide a 40 percent down payment to secure the mortgage. Total sales for our first year are expected to be $1,800,000. Projected net income for the start-up year is $75,500.

MANAGEMENT

THE MANAGEMENT TEAM

Joe Abercrombie, 40, received his M.B.A. from University of Texas Graduate School of Management. Mr. Abercrombie holds a bachelor's degree from the Southern Methodist University with a major in marketing. He is employed at Chicago Health Club, a Division of Bally Corporation, in the position of Vice President, Operations, and Chairman of New Site Selection Committee. He has also held the position of National Program Director. He has extensive direct sales experience through his prior employment at Signode Corporation. He is Chairman of the Chicago Chapter of the American Indoor Ice Hockey Association. A native of Texas, Mr. Abercrombie has always been active in both individual and team sports.

Susan Skelso, 39, holds an M.B.A. from Stanford Graduate School of Management and a bachelor's degree in Purchasing Management from Iowa State University. Mrs. Skelso is currently employed at New Brunswick Corporation as Purchasing Manager. She was formerly employed by the Bally Corporation as New Products Manager where she acquired key recreational equipment and supplier knowledge while working with the Midwest Operations Development Team. This team was responsible for designing the health and fitness clubs owned by Bally Corporation in the Chicago area. Mrs. Skelso serves as a member of the Board of Directors for the Playdium, a youth recreation center operated by Our Lady of Perpetual Help Parish in Glenview, IL.

Marge McIntyre, 48, also holds an M.B.A. from Keller Graduate School of Management and a bachelor's degree in Business Administration from the University of Illinois at Chicago. She is employed by the Y.M.C.A. as Manager, Facilities Administration, where she is responsible for all the units in the Greater Chicago Metropolitan Area. Mrs. McIntyre is also a licensed Commercial Real Estate Broker specializing in recreational facilities. Mrs. McIntyre belongs to a basketball and a volleyball league and is an avid jogger.

William Weiner, 40, holds a Doctorate of Finance from Harvard. Mr. Weiner holds a bachelor's degree in Finance from the University of Chicago and is a Certified Public Accountant. He is the Chief Financial Officer for the Health Corporation of America. Mr. Weiner is also a partner of a successful restaurant in the fashionable Lincoln Park area of Chicago where he oversees the restaurant's sponsored sports leagues.

Each member of our management team has several years experience in their area of expertise. We have two individuals with accounting and financial experience, and three with specific industry knowledge. This provides a back-up in the event that one of the members is no longer able to participate in the company.

Joe Abercrombie and Susan Skelso worked together for several years at Bally Corporation but neither are under any covenants not to compete. The management team has signed a contract agreeing to stay for a minimum of five years, and a covenant not to compete for an additional five years. The covenant is deemed enforceable by our attorney. It is highly unlikely that any of the four original officers will leave, due to their substantial personal and financial investment in the venture.

COMPENSATION

Each of the officers is compensated equally with an annual salary of $50,000. Stock ownership in the corporation is 14 percent apiece.

OWNERSHIP

Sports 'N Fitness USA will initially issue 100,000 shares of common stock. Mr. Abercrombie, Mrs. Skelso, Mrs. McIntyre, and Mr. Weiner will each invest $150,000 in exchange for 14 percent (14,000 shares) of the common stock outstanding. The four board members will each receive 1 percent (4,000 shares) of the common stock. Our three private investors will contribute $1,900,000 in exchange for a total of 40 percent (40,000 shares) of the business.

MANAGEMENT RESPONSIBILITIES

President, Sales Director

Joe Abercrombie is the President of Sports 'N Fitness USA. He is the driving force behind the venture. He is responsible for the direction of the management team and the training and development of the sales staff.

Program Director, Marketing Manager

Susan Skelso is responsible for monitoring trends of fitness activities and instituting the program changes desired by our membership. She is also responsible for designing the advertising and promotions as well as analyzing their effectiveness.

Facility Administrator, Personnel Director

Marge McIntyre will manage the day-to-day activities of the facility. The custodial and general staff reports to her. She is also responsible for the staffing and training of all employees except administrative and sales staff.

Controller, MIS Director

William Weiner is in charge of the financial affairs of the athletic club. He is responsible for our computer system and for designing programs to meet our current and future needs.

BOARD OF DIRECTORS

The management team realizes that they lack expertise in some relevant aspects of sports complex management. To complement their skills, agreements have been reached with an attorney, a sports medicine physician, a Jazzercise franchisee and a local, prominent sports figure to join the Board of Directors. They are particularly valuable because all are successful, self-employed entrepreneurs. They can offer insights into the business to complement the officers' management skills. The board members are given 1 percent ownership of the company. If they should choose to leave, the management team retains first right of refusal on the stock at a predetermined market price.

MARKET ANALYSIS

MARKET SEGMENTATION AND DEMOGRAPHICS

The most prominent form of market segmentation for the health and fitness industry is geographic. Eighty percent of a multi-sport center's members live within nine miles. A 15-minute average driving time is the standard used by appraisers for defining travel radius. A facility such as Sports 'N Fitness USA, which has unique features such as an indoor ice rink, sand volleyball pits, and specialized training clinics, will attract members from longer distances. Management estimates that 100 percent of their members will live or work within 13 miles of the athletic club. Sports 'N Fitness USA has chosen to locate in Libertyville, IL, due to the rapid population growth, high household income, and demand potential for sporting activities in the immediate area.

Population, age, household income ,and employment in managerial and professional occupations are the most important demographic variables in identifying the target membership. The annual growth rate of the Libertyville area is 2.1 percent. This is two- and-a-half times greater than the national average and ten times the state's annual growth rate. Approximately 290,000 residents live within nine miles of our selected site. By 1995, this figure is estimated to be over 322,000 people. "The median age of club members," states Ron Lawrence, author of *Club Location — A Site Analysis Study*, "is 34 years." Sports 'N Fitness USA's market area median age is slightly younger, at 32 years.

Income, according to a survey by the International Racquet Sports Association (IRSA), is another key element in determining who joins an athletic club. About 77 percent of the members' households had incomes greater than $25,000, compared with 61 percent of the households nationwide. Whereas 32 percent of all households had incomes over $45,000, 39 percent of members' households did. The Libertyville area had an impressive 65 percent of household income over $45,000. A larger proportion of managerial and professional employees are users of an athletic club than is true for other employment categories. Lake County exceeds the national average of managerial employees by over 100 percent.

Market potential for sporting activities in the Libertyville area scored above the 95th percentile when compared to the national average. Analysis by Medimark Research, Inc., in 1990, measured potential demand for various services within zip code tracts. Libertyville rated 122 when the median score was 103.

FEASIBILITY ANALYSIS

Market penetration analysis as developed by Arthur E. Gimmy, MAI, and Brain B. Woodworth, and described in their book *Fitness, Racquet Sorts and Spa Projects: A Guide to Appraisal, Market Analysis, Development and Financing,* is a method of estimating the overall market saturation of commercial recreational or sports clubs within a market area. It has been endorsed by a leading trade publication, and is used by real estate appraisers, financial institutions, and consultants in measuring the degree to which a market is over-built or is fertile for a new club. This set of calculations relies on demographic information relating to the target market and the square footage of current and proposed competitive facilities. (See Appendix for calculations and discussion of the results.)

The results of this industry-used analysis show that the Libertyville area with its current population can more than support the addition of a 75,000 square foot multi-sport athletic club. This market penetration analysis cannot specifically consider particular advantages or deficiencies that a project may offer. Primary market research must confirm the feasibility of a project. Our research consisted of site selection analyses, surveys involving the target market, and interviews with sports associations, directors of social and corporate leagues, and members/employees of competitive clubs.

COMPETITION

Primary competition, as defined by IRSA, comes from current and proposed facilities offering similar amenities within a six-mile radius. The major competitor is the Centre Club located in the center of Libertyville. This 70,000 square foot facility contains a weight room, extensive Nautilus and Universal equipment, a gymnasium, an Olympic sized swimming pool, an aerobics room, and a wellness and diet center. Centre Club's strength is its location and affiliation with Condell Memorial Hospital. Club membership is sold out at 2,000, with a waiting list of approximately six months. Centre Club is surrounded by the hospital. Expansion is possible, but projected by our contractor to be very expensive. By comparison, Sports 'N Fitness USA offers membership and activities for leagues and families in addition to individual fitness programs in response to our market survey.

Another competitor is the Vernon Hills Chicago Health Club. It is part of a chain owned by Bally Corporation and is located approximately five miles to the south of Sports 'N Fitness USA. Like the Centre Club, it also caters to an adults only membership. The 20,000 square foot facility boasts over 800 consistent users of the club. The health club has a weight room, exercise equipment, aerobics classes, racquetball courts, a sauna, and jacuzzi. The major advantage to members is the transferable membership to other clubs owned by Bally Corporation at a minimal additional cost. The largest disadvantage this particular facility has is its poor record on sanitation and upkeep. In 1989 it was fined by the health department for unsanitary conditions in the locker rooms and wet area.

Several members we interviewed from this club are actively seeking a new place to work out. Alternatives are limited due to the closed membership at the Centre Club. Cleanliness of facility was given a "most important" rating by over 80 percent of our survey respondents when asked about features of an athletic club. The Chicago Health Club in Vernon Hills also shows too many members per square foot (40 members) when compared to the average of 29 for multi-sport clubs as published by an IRSA survey. Sports 'N Fitness USA is ready to implement an extensive preventive maintenance program to keep our facility in top shape. Such a program will enable management to meet member requirements and keep long-term maintenance expenses in line.

The Libertyville Tennis Club consists of eight tennis courts — six indoor and two outdoor. It has such amenities as locker rooms with whirlpools, a pro shop, and a vending area. The facility is approximately four miles from our intended site. Libertyville Tennis Club relies solely on revenues generated from the one sport. Membership level at the club has stabilized after several years of decline. Although tennis received the third highest participation rate on our market survey, further investigation showed that the area has more than enough courts to meet demand. Sports 'N Fitness USA at this time has chosen not to offer tennis.

Secondary competition is considered to be facilities within a 12 mile area offering similar activities to its members. These include the Multiplex in Deerfield, Chicago Health Club in Deerfield, 41 Sports Club in Highland Park, College Park Athletic Club in Bannockburn, and the Tri-State Club in Lincolnshire. Travel times, however, all exceed the 15-minute driving time (during non-rush hour) that many appraisers consider standard for defining a market. The exception to this travel time standard is the TriState Club, located in an office complex just off of 294. This facility, however, is used only by building tenants.

There is one proposed indoor "recreation facility" in the village of Gurnee, to be built as part of Gurnee Mills, a new discount shopping mall. The mall, scheduled to open in the fall of 1991, according to the village planning office, would contain an extensive indoor playground for children to remain under supervised care as their parents shopped in the adjacent stores. This arrangement will not result in any type of direct competition. The table below illustrates our competitive position.

	Centre Club	Chicago Health Club	Sports 'N Fitness
Individual Activities	Y	Y	Y
Team/League Activities	Y*	N	Y
Offers Family Memberships	N	N	Y

* Centre Club has open gym for pick-up basketball only.

OPERATING PLAN

SITE SELECTION

The decision to build Sports 'N Fitness USA at the intersection of HWY 45 and Winchester Roads was made after a thorough examination of location, accessibility, size, zoning restrictions, and land prices in the Libertyville area. Sports 'N Fitness USA is located between a white collar business park attracting corporate clientele, and a large residential development containing upper-income housing. Planned commercial development is strong in the local area. New construction in Libertyville includes Motorola's new 1.1 million square foot facility.

A corner site was chosen because it's clearly visible from the street, allowing the club to become a reference point, and has convenient access. Convenient location was identified by International Racquet Sports Associations as one of the primary benefits an athletic club can offer its membership. The most important factor in determining the size of Sports 'N Fitness USA is the market demand for the facility.

The site that management has chosen is zoned for commercial and industrial use, enabling the contractor to begin construction immediately. By starting construction in the summer, we can take advantage of a full fall and winter season when club attendance rates are higher due to the inclement weather. Land will cost $131,000 an acre or $3.00 per square foot at the selected site. This is in line with the costs at other alternative sites shown to us by Baird & Warner's commercial property office.

FACILITY

The size of Sports 'N Fitness USA is 75,000 square feet. This size was identified as the amount of unfulfilled demand in the market penetration analysis for the target area. In order to take advantage of the forecasted population growth in the area, two acres of additional land will be purchased but left undeveloped. We will also avoid rising land costs as residential development escalates.

Robert Cleave, owner of Cleave/Cleave Architecture and Design, Inc., a firm specializing in recreational developments, has completed the design work on the facility to our specifications for $55 a square foot. Cleave/Cleave's bid was slightly higher than two others, but the award-winning firm guarantees the quality of its workmanship. Management feels the additional cost of about $1.25 per square foot is justified, as Cleave/Cleave will be able to minimize the high cost associated with construction delays and installation errors when working with the specialized mechanical systems and materials.

Maintenance of equipment and upkeep of the facility are of fundamental importance to members. Over 90 percent of the respondents gave upkeep and maintenance the highest marks possible, ranking it second of 15 items. Maintenance is a variable expense, averaging from 4 to 9 percent within the industry. Our strategy of emphasizing preventive maintenance during staff training will allow us to keep our expenses low.

Sport 'N Fitness USA will be open year round, 14 hours per day. Opening at 6:00 a.m. allows us to meet the requirements of members who prefer to use the club before work.

PRODUCTS

Sports 'N Fitness USA will be an indoor/outdoor multi-sport center offering the following activities:

- Ice Rink

- Basketball Court

- Volleyball Courts

- 18 Hole Miniature Golf Course

- 1/4 Mile Running Track

- Swimming Pool

- Batting Cages

- Two Outdoor Softball Fields

Market research of the greater Libertyville area indicated that there is a demand for a multi-sport center that would offer a variety of league activities. Our market survey revealed that 64 percent participated in more than a single league activity. Of these, 50 percent indicated they were interested and were willing to make a deposit to ensure their membership in Sports 'N Fitness USA.

Additional research confirmed that neither of our closest competitors, the Centre Club and the Chicago Health Club, offers league play for volleyball, basketball, or hockey. The Centre Club does have a basketball court but is primarily used for pick-up games and general fitness, not for league play.

Ice Rink

An ice rink was ranked by 33 percent of those surveyed as a desired activity in a multi-sports center. Ms. Jerry Krewer, Sports Center Director of the Northbrook Sports Center, said, "there is a shortage of indoor ice rinks north of Northbrook. In fact 20 percent of the people who use our ice rink come from the Libertyville area." These people are traveling in excess of 20 miles (one way). This exceeds the industry norm of nine miles and a 15-minute driving time.

The ice rink will offer figure skating, hockey (youth and men's league), as well as open time, in keeping with the demand as indicated on our research survey. Hockey leagues, figure skating lessons, and rentals of the ice rink for skating parties are estimated to account for 80 percent of the available time.

Basketball Courts

Basketball courts are primarily located in schools. They are becoming increasingly hard to rent from schools due to the spiraling insurance rates. Our market survey revealed that 43 percent ranked basketball as their primary consideration in joining a multi-sports center. The Centre Club does include a basketball court, but membership is full, with a waiting list. Basketball courts are instrumental in attracting those whose who wish to join more than one type of league, according to our studies.

Volleyball

Serious league volleyball players consider sand the only medium to play on. Our volleyball courts will have sand pits to accommodate the demand. In recognizing that high school and college tournaments are played on hardwood courts, our basketball courts can be converted for league volleyball play as needed.

Miniature Golf

Miniature golf was the number one chosen activity by both non-league and league-preferring members. In response to this demand, we have included an indoor 18 hole miniature golf course. The inclusion of the miniature golf course will allow us to further differentiate ourselves from the local park districts and health and racquet clubs. Research has shown that clubs which offer special activities will draw people from a greater distance than the industry norm of nine miles.

Running Track

The 30 percent of our market research respondents who specifically stated that the size of the track was of paramount importance to them expressed the desire for a quarter-mile track. Runners and fitness buffs expressed a dislike for the smaller tracks, as offered in the Centre Club and the Chicago Health Club, as it takes too many laps to run a mile. The large running track will allow us to host running clubs for qualifying events.

Batting Cages

Sixty percent of the people surveyed indicated that they would be more likely to join a club if batting cages were offered. Batting cages are instrumental in encouraging family members and friends of league players to frequent the center while the spouse or friend is playing, according to Pacer Manufacturing Company, the leading supplier of batting cages.

Exercise Rooms

There will also be two rooms that can be rented for aerobics and other such activities. In a canvas of the greater Libertyville area, we found that the only available rental space is that of offices and store fronts. An aerobics class for 50 students requires about 3,000 square feet and a commercial available store front of that size leases for $5,000 a month. We will be able to rent a comparable size room for $30.00 per hour. We have preleased one of the rooms to Jazzercise for $3,000 a month for two years, with a three-year extension. By insuring that Jazzercise is offered at Sports 'N Fitness USA, we have fulfilled the demand for aerobic activities as made by 50 percent of those surveyed.

Snack Bar

Sports 'N Fitness USA will operate a snack bar. The Centre Club does offer a snack bar and actively promotes it for lunch and dinner. Our research of the market area indicated that three out of five people wanted a snack bar. The snack bar represents $60,000 in annual revenue.

Softball Fields

Softball fields are in direct response to the market demand as indicated by 33 percent of those surveyed. This will allow us to better utilize the surrounding land and draw people to the facility in the warmer, slower months.

Industry trends point out that a baseball field will pay for itself in 20 tournament games with 20 teams participating. The first year we anticipate holding 15 tournaments with a minimum of ten teams participating. This will earn $18,000 in revenue during the summer months of June through August.

Swimming Pool

Multi-sport clubs offering swimming pools have an average of 40 percent more members than clubs without pools, according to IRSA Industry data. National statistics indicated that 41 percent of those who exercise participate in swimming. Twenty-six percent of the people we surveyed requested a swimming pool.

SELLING STRATEGY

The growth of the sports and recreation market in the 1990s will have a profound impact on the economy, says Thomas B. Doyle, Director of Information & Research for the National Sporting Goods Association. According to Mr. Doyle, the number of people participating in fitness activities increased by 3.2 percent, or 2.2 million people, from 1987 to 1989. The trend is expected to continue.

Mr. John Kelly, in his article "The Business of Leisure," in *Institutional Investor*, pointed out that leisure activities is now a major business segment, estimated to generate in excess of $350 billion a year in revenues.

Sports 'N Fitness USA has focused on a two-pronged selling approach to insure market penetration.

SHORT TERM

Direct Mail

It is a cost-effective way for us to reach the population in the Greater Libertyville area and it has proven successful for competition such as the Centre Club. Municipal sports facilities all use direct mail.

Executive Selling

Sales to corporations in the nine-mile geographical area will be handled by executive selling. To gain market penetration in the most economical manner during the formative stage, executive selling will allow direct contact with major corporations such as Motorola, United States Gypsum, Commonwealth Edison, etc. This will insure the timely closing of sales contracts for league play, thereby insuring their league requirements are being fulfilled by the Sports 'N Fitness USA.

To supplement the direct mail campaign, a part-time salesperson will be hired and trained to answer questions during the normal working hours. This will allow management to concentrate on the financial and operational procedures as well as public relation contacts. After construction of the building, there will be a full-time salesperson available from 8 a.m. to closing. We will not miss an opportunity for a sale.

LONG TERM

After the initial membership drive through the construction phases, we will continue to advertise in the local community paper. We will have Sports 'N Fitness USA in news letters to the various league associations: Ice Skating Institute of America, Buffalo Grove, IL; American Hockey League, West Springfield, MA; Chicago Area Runners Association, Chicago, IL; The Athletic Congress/Illinois, Elmhurst, IL; American Softball Association of America, Oklahoma City, OK; U.S. Volleyball Association, Colorado Springs, CO; and other interested league sponsors. This will build credibility for the center through association with these respected organizations and also solicit membership from their readers.

Direct Mail

A more focused approach will be used instead of mass mailings to local area residents. Next to a personal sales call, direct mail is the most effective medium one can use to put a message in front of a prospect. Average cost of direct mail is approximately $85.00 per thousand plus postage, as compared to radio at $500.00 for a 30-second spot during prime listening time. To be effective in reaching our target market, several radio stations would have to be contracted. Cost per member reached is inefficient when compared to direct mail. We will also contact various league organizations to include our advertising mail as part of their envelope stuffers.

Inside Sales

Selling after the initial corporate contacts will be handled by full-time inside sales personnel. The morning and evening operations will have one full-time salesperson with two part-time employees to assist in follow-up calls, tours of the facility, and in answering any questions.

Training of the full-time and part-time salespeople will be an on-going concern, addressing such issues as product knowledge, hours of operation, telephone skills, details of the membership contract, and general policies of Sports 'N Fitness USA. Supervision and training will be the responsibility of an owner manager.

COMPETITIVE SELLING STRATEGIES

The Centre Club primarily used direct mail. They advertised in the local newspaper, *The Daily Herald*, and participated in health awareness programs at Hawthorn Mall to generate interest and sales of preconstruction memberships. The Centre Club's success with direct mail and pre-construction publicity was evidenced by the fact that the membership was sold out and the Club had a waiting list before it opened. Sports 'N Fitness USA will use direct mail to promote the facility prior to construction. We will set up a booth at Hawthorn Mall in Vernon Hills during Health Awareness Days. We will also participate in the Summer Celebration in Vernon Hills, Libertyville Days in Libertyville, and Mundelein Days in Mundelein. This will offer us an opportunity to hand out brochures, answer questions, sign up members, and generate interest in these communities.

Chicago Health Club relies primarily on their advertisement in *The Daily Herald, The Chicago Tribune, The Chicago Sun Times,* and television. We will concentrate on direct mail and advertising in *The Daily Herald,* with spot advertisement in *Windy City Sports,* a Chicago fitness and recreation guide. These publications target our market more directly and are the best current use of our advertising dollar.

The Park Districts of Libertyville, Vernon Hills, and Mundelein (the largest in the greater Libertyville area) use catalogs to announce the different activities offered to residents for that particular season.

MEMBERSHIP SALES

Sports 'N Fitness USA will conduct a pre-opening membership drive in order to develop an initial membership base and sales revenue. Initiation fees of $300 for a family is below the $600 charged by the Centre Club. The initiation fee for Chicago Health Club is $100, but they require the signing of three-year contract. Monthly dues of $20 are less than dues at the Centre Club of $45 per person.

The initial and monthly dues allows the member to join any league sponsored by the Sports 'N Fitness USA at no additional charge and to have unrestricted use of the swimming pool, running track, and volleyball or basketball courts during non-league activities.

Revenue from the $8 walk-in fee is considered unpredictable and is not used in our financial projections.

EMPLOYEES/INSURANCE

EMPLOYEES

Sports 'N Fitness USA projects a need for six full-time and 19 part-time employees by the end of the first year of business. Full-time employees include the fitness director, maintenance staff, accounting personnel, and systems analyst. Full-time employees will be paid from $8.50 to $14.50 an hour plus benefits (group health and life insurance), depending on their position. A full-time employee receives a free family membership and becomes eligible for two weeks paid vacation after one year. Part-time employees will be supervised by the facility administrator and will be paid $5.00 an hour and receive a free family membership. Pay rates are competitive for the area, according to the Manpower Temporary Service operating out of Vernon Hills.

Management intends to provide more extensive training and orientation than most other clubs provide. The industry publication *Athletic Business* stresses that better trained employees is one way to achieve high member retention rates. Our employees will receive on-going training in the areas of physical fitness, emergency first aid, CPR, and equipment maintenance. After interviewing health and fitness employees from other facilities, it is our conclusion that the instruction part-time employees receive is minimal. Most new hires followed a co-worker around for a day or two. Sports 'N Fitness USA employees will receive their training directly from the Facility Administrator.

Benedictine College is working with us to develop a student employment program. This would allow Sports 'N Fitness USA to retain a work force of young and enthusiastic individuals wanting only part-time employment for a period of two to four years.

Some services, such as personal trainers, masseuses, and league referees will be contracted for on an as-needed basis due to the inconsistent demand during the initial months and to keep fixed payroll costs down.

INSURANCE

Insurance will be obtained through Northbrook Risk Management, Inc. Property insurance will include coverage for the real property and personal property at replacement cost. Business interruption insurance, which pays a portion of fixed cash flows during any period when the club is closed following an incident covered by the policy, will also be purchased. Fixed expenses coverage includes rent, mortgage payments, minimum utility costs, and salaries for essential employees. Business interruption insurance was recommended to us due to our high level of fixed expenses.

Liability insurance will be acquired by the club in case an injury or accident results in a personal injury lawsuit from a member. Of course, management will take preventive actions such as providing proper instructions, issuing appropriate warnings, and obtaining liability waivers from members. Sports 'N Fitness USA will insure the four members of management for death and disability.

LEGAL/SEASONALITY

LEGAL

Legal matters will be handled by William J. Provenzano and Associates of Lake Forest, a firm whose concentration is in sports law and risk management. Sports 'N Fitness USA is a corporation chartered in the state of Illinois. There are no lawsuits pending against the company or members of management. No disclosure agreements have been signed with previous employers. Sports 'N Fitness USA has obtained all business licenses required to construct a building and operate a business in the Village of Libertyville.

SEASONALITY

Seasonality is an issue within the recreation industry. A multi-sport athletic club is in the best position to minimize this due to the diversity within the facility. Sports 'N Fitness USA has taken the steps of enclosing the ice rink and swimming pool to allow for year-round use. Reduction in cash flow, because of seasonality, is minimized by the monthly membership dues and a lease agreement with Jazzercise. This income accounts for approximately 72 percent of our annual revenue. The inclusion of baseball not only fulfills a market demand but will generate just over $18,000 in revenue during June through August. During the summer season, tournaments, clinics, and sports seminars will be held, enabling members to improve their skills. Extra services and programs will be added as demand justifies, expanding the club's year-round usefulness and profitability.

CONTINGENCY PLANS

New entrants into our geographical area: It is highly unlikely that a health club or multi-sports complex would be constructed in our 9.2 mile or 15-minute drawing radius due to the fact that the population density would not support an additional facility according to industry norms. The barriers to entry are high, and a competitor would not be able to justify demand to obtain financing.

A specialty club, such as a racquetball club, would not be a serious threat. Specialty clubs draw from a greater distance than a multi-purpose club and our members choose Sports 'N Fitness USA because of the range of activities offered.

If a competing club were proposed, we would respond by attempting to prohibit construction through the Libertyville City Council on the grounds that it could not succeed. If the club were constructed in spite of our efforts, we would offer deals on extended memberships to lock our current members in longer, and promotions to attract more people.

Changing trends of sports and fitness activities: Our building is designed with open spaces and courts which can be adapted to current trends. We have planned for flexibility and can capitalize on popular sports easily and quickly. We plan to monitor trends both nationwide and in our area to be able to provide innovation and keep our clients interested.

Failure to attract the projected number of members: If we did not obtain the planned number of members, we would lower the initial membership fee or offer additional benefits, such as free towel service, to entice potential members. Two-for-one promotions and group discounts would also be offered until we obtained the necessary revenue to make up for the shortfall. The monthly dues paid by members make up the bulk of our annual income, so a special offer involving a temporary reduction of the initiation fee would have little effect on our long-term revenues.

FINANCIAL PROFILE

ASSUMPTIONS FOR PROJECTED MEMBERSHIP

The International Racquet Sports Association (IRSA) estimates the average multi-sport athletic club membership at 29 members per 1,000 square feet of club space. Based on our 75,000 square feet, we will use a potential membership of 2,175. A recent IRSA survey showed that newly constructed facilities have an absorption rate of new members of six to 24 months. Absorption is the time it takes a club to reach full capacity. Sports 'N Fitness USA has decided to use a conservative absorption figure of 24 months when preparing the financial projections.

Based on the information received from our interviews with fitness club marketing managers, we estimate the pre-sale of memberships at 50 percent of full capacity. The IRSA survey of multi-sport clubs that include a swimming pool show membership growth for the next five years at 7 percent, with attrition (membership turnover) of 30 percent annually. Based on these numbers, Sports 'N Fitness USA estimates our membership to be as follows:

Year One

Pre-sold membership	870	
Membership through absorption	432	
Total Membership Year One		1,302

Year Two

Prior-year membership	1,302	
Membership through absorption	432	
Annual membership growth less attrition	91	
Total Membership Year Two		1,825

Year Three

Prior-year membership	1,825
Annual membership growth less attrition	127
Total Membership Year Three	1,952

Year Four

Prior-year membership	1,952	
Annual membership growth less attrition	137	
Total Membership Year Four		2,089

Year Five

Prior-year membership	2,089	
Annual membership growth less attrition	146	
Total Membership Year Five		2,235

MEMBERSHIP PRICING

Based on the competitors in the target market area of nine to 12 miles, industry data, and our market research, Sports 'N Fitness USA has selected the following prices for membership fee schedule:

Initiation Fees

Family membership	$300
Single membership	$200

Monthly Dues

Family membership	$35
Single membership	$20

League Dues

Because none of the fitness clubs in our primary market area offer any type of league play, we have used the fee schedules of the park districts as a guideline for our rate structure. The dues for local park districts range between $250 and $375, depending on the activity. After much discussion with several league managers, Sports 'N Fitness USA has decided on a flat league fee of $300 per team.

FINANCIAL ASSUMPTIONS FOR INCOME STATEMENT AND BALANCE SHEET

The following assumptions are based on the receipt of a mortgage of $2,225,000 at an 11 percent interest rate. This is the current borrowing rate for commercial development. After conferring with Rick Dorsette, a mortgage banker at Mortgage Masters, we learned that a 40 percent down payment would be required for this type of venture, due to the present economic conditions. The remaining $250,000 of the capital, raised from the management team and outside investors, will be used to fund inventory, working capital, and start-up expenses.

1. Membership dues were calculated using the previously mentioned pricing schedule. In Year Three, we forecast that league play will consist of two leagues per night. (We will use the two-year absorption figure to calculate our increases in leagues.) The two league per night calculation is very conservative, since we can accommodate three or more leagues nightly.

2. Revenues for the ice rink, miniature golf and swimming pool were all estimated using percentages of sales based on industry averages. Batting cages revenues were estimated at 35 percent of capacity per hour, which is $8.75 per hour. Pacer Corporation, the vender supplying the equipment, provided the information. Softball revenue was calculated conservatively, assuming that during the three-month period of June to August we would host one tournament per week at $150 per team. Each tournament has ten teams. We have commitments from various sponsors to host their tournaments, so expenses will be kept to a minimum.

3. We plan to lease the Pro Shop as a concession, charging $4,000.00 monthly rent. To entice a renter, we will hold rent constant for the first two years. Future increases will be 5 percent annually.

4. Exercise rooms will rent for $30 per hour. Rates will increase after the second year at 5 percent annually.

5. General and administrative expenses include owners' salaries, payroll taxes and benefits. Each member of our management team will draw an annual salary of $50,000. This salary is justified because all members have left their current jobs and have taken out substantial home equity loans.

6. Pay scale for full-time employees is $10.00 per hour. Part-time workers will earn $5.00/hour.

7. Direct expense is estimated at roughly 87 percent of total revenues.

8. Income taxes were calculated at 40 percent of income and will be paid quarterly.

9. The cost of the land is $653,000. The building and equipment cost is $3,900,000. The interest rate of our ten-year mortgage will be 11 percent. We are using the double declining depreciation method, taking advantage of the current tax laws, to depreciate the building over a 30-year period. Construction costs were estimated by using the figures supplied by the *Means Costing Book* and through consultation with Cleave/Cleave Architecture & Design.

10. Multi-sports facilities' accounts receivables are about 11 percent of sales. Inventory is 2 percent of sales. This is typical of the industry, according to *Fitness, Racquet Sports and Spa Projects,* published by the American Institute of Real Estate Appraisers.

11. Prepaid expenses will consist of insurance premiums.

12. Accounts payable will be paid within 30 days. We will take advantage of any discounts offered.

FINANCIAL ASSUMPTIONS FOR MONTHLY STATEMENT OF INCOME AND CHANGES IN FINANCIAL POSITION

1. Revenues will flow evenly throughout the year, because 72 percent of the revenues are obtained through monthly membership dues and lease agreement.

2. Operating expenses are incurred uniformly on a monthly basis. Additional activities offered during the summer compensate for the seasonal decreases in some league play.

3. Break-even revenues were calculated using the following equation:
(actual revenues × fixed costs) / (actual revenues − direct costs)

4. Interest will be paid on a monthly basis.

Sample Business Plan B

SPORTS 'N FITNESS USA
FORECASTED STATEMENT OF INCOME
For the years ending December 31

	YEAR 1	YEAR 2	YEAR 3	YEAR 4	YEAR 5
REVENUES					
Membership/League Fees	1,327,040	1,402,420	2,077,300	2,131,520	2,298,060
Ice Rink	105,000	120,100	138,000	158,790	182,500
Miniature Golf	90,000	97,000	107,000	118,000	130,000
Swimming Pool	15,000	15,750	16,538	17,365	18,233
Pro Shop (RENT)	48,000	48,000	53,000	55,000	58,000
Food and Beverage	60,000	63,000	66,000	69,700	72,765
Exercise Room Rentals	87,360	87,360	96,314	101,130	106,186
Batting Cages	77,175	81,033	85,085	89,339	93,806
Softball	18,000	19,800	21,780	23,958	26,353
TOTAL INCOME	1,827,575	1,934,463	2,661,017	2,764,802	2,985,903
DIRECT EXPENSES					
Miniature Golf	13,707	14,508	19,958	20,736	22,394
Pro Shop	6,397	6,771	9,314	9,677	10,451
Ice Rink	25,586	27,082	37,254	38,707	41,803
Food and Beverage	47,517	54,165	74,508	77,414	83,605
Exercise Roon Rentals	9,321	9,866	13,571	14,100	15,228
Batting Cages	11,500	12,000	12,600	13,400	13,900
TOTAL DIRECT EXPENSES	114,028	124,393	167,205	174,034	187,381
INCOME BEFORE INDIRECT EXPENSES AND FIXED CHARGES	1,713,547	1,810,070	2,493,812	2,590,768	2,798,522
INDIRECT EXPENSES					
General Repairs	91,379	96,723	133,051	138,240	149,295
Energy and Utilities	118,792	125,740	172,966	179,712	194,084
Marketing and Sales	109,655	108,330	149,017	154,829	167,211
General and Administrative	694,479	735,096	1,011,186	1,050,625	1,134,643
TOTAL INDIRECT EXPENSES	1,014,305	1,065,889	1,466,220	1,523,406	1,645,233
INCOME BEFORE FIXED CHARGES	699,242	744,181	1,027,592	1,067,362	1,153,289
FIXED CHARGES					
Real Estate Taxes	45,689	48,362	66,525	69,120	74,648
Property and Business Insurance	29,241	30,951	42,576	44,237	47,774
TOTAL FIXED CHARGES	74,930	79,313	109,101	113,357	122,422
INCOME BEFORE INTEREST, DEPRECIATION AND TAXES	624,312	664,868	918,491	954,005	1,030,867
Interest Expense	241,031	225,885	208,985	190,129	169,092
Depreciation	262,500	245,000	228,667	213,422	199,194
INCOME BEFORE TAXES	120,781	193,983	480,839	550,453	662,581
Income Taxes	48,312	77,593	192,336	220,181	265,033
NET INCOME	72,469	116,390	288,503	330,272	397,548

287

SPORTS 'N FITNESS USA
FORECASTED STATEMENT OF CHANGES IN FINANCIAL POSITION
For the years ending December 31

	YEAR 1	YEAR 2	YEAR 3	YEAR 4	YEAR 5
Cash Provided:					
Net Income (Loss)	72,469	116,390	288,503	330,272	397,548
Depreciation	262,500	245,000	228,667	213,422	199,194
Changes in Working Capital Components:					
Accounts Receivable	(201,033)	(11,758)	(106,531)	(12,454)	(26,532)
Inventory	(91,379)	(5,344)	3,588	(3,632)	(7,739)
Prepaid Expenses	(54,827)	16,138	(14,531)	(2,076)	(4,422)
Accounts Payable	109,655	6,413	43,593	6,227	13,266
Income Tax Payable	48,312	29,281	114,743	27,845	44,852
Current Portion of Debt	0	(130,894)	(146,041)	(162,941)	(181,796)
NET CASH PROVIDED BY OPERATIONS	145,697	265,226	411,990	396,663	434,372
Cash Flows from Investing Activities					
Sale of Common Stock	2,500,000	0	0	0	0
Increase in Long Term Debt	(2,250,000)	0	0	0	0
NET INCREASE (DECREASE) IN CASH	395,697	265,226	411,990	396,663	434,372
CASH BALANCE–BEGINNING OF YEAR	0	395,697	660,923	1,072,913	1,469,576
CASH BALANCE—END OF YEAR	395,697	660,923	1,072,913	1,469,576	1,903,948

SPORTS 'N FITNESS USA
PROJECTED NET INCOME BREAKEVEN ANALYSIS
For the years ending December 31

	YEAR 1	YEAR 2	YEAR 3	YEAR 4	YEAR 5
REVENUES	1,827,575	1,934,463	2,661,017	2,764,802	2,985,903
DIRECT COSTS					
Miniature Golf	13,707	14,508	19,958	20,736	22,394
Pro Shop	6,397	6,771	9,314	9,677	10,451
Ice Rink	25,586	27,082	37,254	38,707	41,803
Food and Beverage	47,517	54,165	74,508	77,414	83,605
Exercise Room	9,321	9,866	13,571	14,100	15,228
Marketing and Sales	109,655	108,330	149,017	154,829	167,211
Batting Cages	11,500	12,000	12,600	13,400	13,900
Repairs	91,379	96,723	133,051	138,240	149,295
TOTAL DIRECT COSTS	315,062	329,446	449,273	467,103	503,887
FIXED COSTS					
Utilities	118,792	125,740	172,966	179,712	194,084
General and Adminstrative	694,479	735,096	1,011,186	1,050,625	1,134,643
Real Estate Taxes	45,689	48,362	66,525	69,120	74,648
Property and Business Insurance	29,241	30,951	42,576	44,237	47,774
Interest Expense	241,031	225,885	208,985	190,129	169,092
Depreciation	262,500	245,000	228,667	213,422	199,194
TOTAL FIXED COSTS	1,391,732	1,411,034	1,730,905	1,747,245	1,819,435
BREAKEVEN REVENUES	1,681,635	1,700,663	2,082,505	2,102,446	2,188,808

SPORTS N' FITNESS, USA
FORECASTED MONTHLY STATEMENT OF CHANGES IN FINANCIAL POSITION

	MONTH One	MONTH Two	MONTH Three	MONTH Four	MONTH Five	MONTH Six	MONTH Seven	MONTH Eight	MONTH Nine	MONTH Ten	MONTH Eleven	MONTH Twelve	TOTAL
CASH PROVIDED:													
Net Income(Loss)	6,039	6,039	6,039	6,039	6,039	6,039	6,039	6,039	6,039	6,039	6,039	6,039	72,469
Depreciation	21,875	21,875	21,875	21,875	21,875	21,875	21,875	21,875	21,875	21,875	21,875	21,875	262,500
Changes in working capital components													
Accounts Receivable	(16,753)	(16,753)	(16,753)	(16,753)	(16,753)	(16,753)	(16,753)	(16,753)	(16,753)	(16,753)	(16,753)	(16,753)	(201,033)
Inventory	(7,615)	(7,615)	(7,615)	(7,615)	(7,615)	(7,615)	(7,615)	(7,615)	(7,615)	(7,615)	(7,615)	(7,615)	(91,379)
Prepaid expenses	(4,569)	(4,569)	(4,569)	(4,569)	(4,569)	(4,569)	(4,569)	(4,569)	(4,569)	(4,569)	(4,569)	(4,569)	(54,827)
Accounts payable	9,138	9,138	9,138	9,138	9,138	9,138	9,138	9,138	9,138	9,138	9,138	9,138	109,655
Income tax payable			12,078			12,078			12,078			12,078	48,312
NET CASH PROVIDED BY OPERATIONS	8,115	8,115	20,194	8,115	8,115	20,194	8,115	8,115	20,194	8,115	8,115	20,194	145,697
Cash flows from Investing Activities													
Sale of common stock	2,500,000												2,500,000
Increase in long term debt	(2,250,000)												(2,250,000)
NET INCREASE (DECREASE) IN CASH	258,115	8,115	20,194	8,115	8,115	20,194	8,115	8,115	20,194	8,115	8,115	20,194	395,697
CASH BALANCE —BEGINING OF YEAR	0	258,115	266,231	286,424	294,540	302,655	322,849	330,964	339,079	359,273	367,388	375,504	0
CASH BALANCE —END OF YEAR	258,115	266,231	286,424	294,540	302,655	322,849	330,964	339,079	359,273	367,388	375,504	395,697	395,697

FORECASTED MONTHLY STATEMENTS OF INCOME

REVENUES	MONTH One	MONTH Two	MONTH Three	MONTH Four	MONTH Five	MONTH Six	MONTH Seven	MONTH Eight	MONTH Nine	MONTH Ten	MONTH Eleven	MONTH Twelve	TOTAL
Membership Dues	110,587	110,587	110,587	110,587	110,587	110,587	110,587	110,587	110,587	110,587	110,587	110,587	1,327,040
Ice Rink	8,750	8,750	8,750	8,750	8,750	8,750	8,750	8,750	8,750	8,750	8,750	8,750	105,000
Miniature Golf	7,500	7,500	7,500	7,500	7,500	7,500	7,500	7,500	7,500	7,500	7,500	7,500	90,000
Swimming Pool	1,250	1,250	1,250	1,250	1,250	1,250	1,250	1,250	1,250	1,250	1,250	1,250	15,000
Pro Shop (RENT)	4,000	4,000	4,000	4,000	4,000	4,000	4,000	4,000	4,000	4,000	4,000	4,000	48,000
Food and Beverage	5,000	5,000	5,000	5,000	5,000	5,000	5,000	5,000	5,000	5,000	5,000	5,000	60,000
Exercise room rentals	7,280	7,280	7,280	7,280	7,280	7,280	7,280	7,280	7,280	7,280	7,280	7,280	87,360
Batting Cages	6,431	6,431	6,431	6,431	6,431	6,431	6,431	6,431	6,431	6,431	6,431	6,431	77,175
Softball						6,000	6,000	6,000					18,000
TOTAL INCOME	150,798	150,798	150,798	150,798	150,798	156,798	156,798	156,798	150,798	150,798	150,798	150,798	1,827,575
DIRECT EXPENSES													
Miniature Golf	1,142	1,142	1,142	1,142	1,142	1,142	1,142	1,142	1,142	1,142	1,142	1,142	13,707
Pro Shop	533	533	533	533	533	533	533	533	533	533	533	533	6,397
Ice Rink	2,132	2,132	2,132	2,132	2,132	2,132	2,132	2,132	2,132	2,132	2,132	2,132	25,586
Food and Beverage	3,960	3,960	3,960	3,960	3,960	3,960	3,960	3,960	3,960	3,960	3,960	3,960	47,517
Exercise room rentals	777	777	777	777	777	777	777	777	777	777	777	777	9,321
Batting Cages	958	958	958	958	958	958	958	958	958	958	958	958	11,500
TOTAL DIRECT EXPENSES	9,502	9,502	9,502	9,502	9,502	9,502	9,502	9,502	9,502	9,502	9,502	9,502	114,028
INCOME BEFORE INDIRECT EXPENSES AND FIXED CHARGES	142,796	142,796	142,796	142,796	142,796	142,796	142,796	142,796	142,796	142,796	142,796	142,796	1,713,547
INDIRECT EXPENSES													
General Repairs	7,615	7,615	7,615	7,615	7,615	7,615	7,615	7,615	7,615	7,615	7,615	7,615	91,379
Energy and Utilities	9,899	9,899	9,899	9,899	9,899	9,899	9,899	9,899	9,899	9,899	9,899	9,899	118,792
Marketing and Sales	9,138	9,138	9,138	9,138	9,138	9,138	9,138	9,138	9,138	9,138	9,138	9,138	109,655
General and Administrative	57,873	57,873	57,873	57,873	57,873	57,873	57,873	57,873	57,873	57,873	57,873	57,873	694,479
TOTAL INDIRECT EXPENSES	84,525	84,525	84,525	84,525	84,525	84,525	84,525	84,525	84,525	84,525	84,525	84,525	1,014,305
INCOME BEFORE FIXED CHARGES	58,270	58,270	58,270	58,270	58,270	58,270	58,270	58,270	58,270	58,270	58,270	58,270	699,242
FIXED CHARGES													
Real Estate Taxes	3,807	3,807	3,807	3,807	3,807	3,807	3,807	3,807	3,807	3,807	3,807	3,807	45,689
Property and Business Insurance	2,437	2,437	2,437	2,437	2,437	2,437	2,437	2,437	2,437	2,437	2,437	2,437	29,241
TOTAL FIXED CHARGES	6,244	6,244	6,244	6,244	6,244	6,244	6,244	6,244	6,244	6,244	6,244	6,244	74,930
INCOME BEFORE INTEREST, DEPRECIATION AND TAXES	52,026	52,026	52,026	52,026	52,026	52,026	52,026	52,026	52,026	52,026	52,026	52,026	624,312
Interest expense	20,086	20,086	20,086	20,086	20,086	20,086	20,086	20,086	20,086	20,086	20,086	20,086	241,031
Depreciation	21,875	21,875	21,875	21,875	21,875	21,875	21,875	21,875	21,875	21,875	21,875	21,875	262,500
INCOME BEFORE TAXES	10,065	10,065	10,065	10,065	10,065	10,065	10,065	10,065	10,065	10,065	10,065	10,065	120,781
INCOME TAXES		12,078	12,078					12,078	12,078				48,312
NET INCOME	6,039	6,039	6,039	6,039	6,039	6,039	6,039	6,039	6,039	6,039	6,039	6,039	72,469

SPORTS 'N FITNESS USA
FORECASTED BALANCE SHEET
December 31

	YEAR 1	YEAR 2	YEAR 3	YEAR 4	YEAR 5
CURRENT ASSETS					
Cash	395,697	660,923	1,072,913	1,469,576	1,903,948
Receivables(net)	201,033	212,791	319,322	331,776	358,308
Inventory	91,379	96,723	93,136	96,768	104,507
Prepaid Expenses	54,827	38,689	53,220	55,296	59,718
TOTAL CURRENT ASSETS	742,936	1,009,126	1,538,591	1,953,417	2,426,481
FIXED ASSETS					
Building and Land	4,500,000	4,500,000	4,500,000	4,500,000	4,500,000
Less Acc.Depreciation	262,500	507,500	736,167	949,589	1,148,783
TOTAL ASSETS	4,980,436	5,001,626	5,302,424	5,503,828	5,777,698
LIABILITIES					
CURRENT LIABILITIES					
Accounts Payable	109,655	116,068	159,661	165,888	179,154
Income Tax Payable	48,312	77,593	192,336	220,181	265,033
Current Portion of Debt	130,894	146,041	162,941	181,796	202,833
TOTAL CURRENT LIABILITIES	288,861	339,702	514,938	567,865	647,020
Long Term Debt	2,119,106	1,973,065	1,810,125	1,628,329	1,425,497
Common Stock	2,500,000	2,500,000	2,500,000	2,500,000	2,500,000
Retained Earnings	72,469	188,859	477,362	807,635	1,205,183
TOTAL LIABILITIES AND NET WORTH	4,980,436	5,001,626	5,302,425	5,503,829	5,777,700

Sample Business Plan B: Appendix

The inclusion of authoritative support for the business plan in essential. Because the reader will not want to rely solely on the author's plan, the appendix should contain detailed documentation that helps to substantiate statements made or positions taken. Due to space limitations, this plan uses only a representative sample of the types of support documents that should be included.

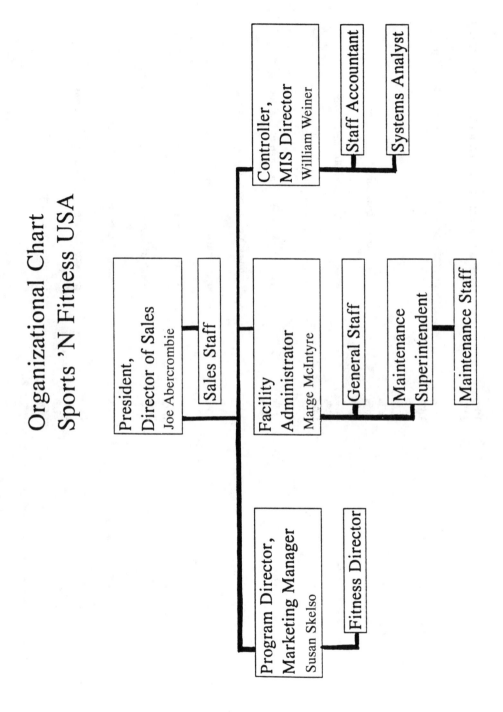

Organizational Chart
Sports 'N Fitness USA

President, Director of Sales
Joe Abercrombie

Sales Staff

Facility Administrator
Marge McIntyre

General Staff

Maintenance Superintendent

Maintenance Staff

Controller, MIS Director
William Weiner

Staff Accountant

Systems Analyst

Program Director, Marketing Manager
Susan Skelso

Fitness Director

Age and socioeconomic status are positively correlated with health club membership. About one in ten Americans age 24 – 44 belong to a fitness center. For those adults under the age of 30, membership is almost twice as high as the national percentage. The percentage of health club memberships is even higher among the upper-income population groups. Given that income increases with age, the relative youth of health club members combined with their high income is very striking and presents numerous growth opportunities for the fitness industry.

Table   Health Club Membership Demographics

Total Adults	11%
Men	10%
Women	11%
Age	
Under 30 years	19%
18-24 years	18%
25-29 years	22%
30-49 years	12%
50 & older	3%
50-64 years	5%
65 & older	1%
Household Income	
$50,000 & over	23%
$40,000-$49,000	18%
$25,000-$39,000	10%
$15,000-$24,999	11%
$10,000-$14,999	6%
Under $10,000	4%
Education	
College graduates	17%
College incomplete	15%
High school grad.	10%
Less than HS grad.	2%
Occupation	
Profess. & business	16%
Clerical & sales	20%
Manual workers	8%
Non-labor force	8%
Young Urban Professionals	24%
Region	
East	12%
Midwest	11%
South	7%
West	14%

Source: Gallup Opinion Polls, *Gallup Leisure Activities Index 1986* (Princeton: 1986), p. 91.

Demographics of Target Market

Table 7.1 Relationship of Club Membership to Market Area Population

	Distance Miles	Members	Population	Mem./Pop.
NO. CLUBS AT 50%				
6 Racquet Clubs	5.5	5,312	792,602	.67
7 Tennis Clubs	5.9	4,288	475,832	.90
9 Multisport	5.5	8,009	992,890	.81
TOTAL 22 CLUBS	5.6	17,609	2,261,324	.78%
NO. CLUBS AT 60%				
6 Racquet Clubs	7.0	5,910	920,648	.64
7 Tennis Clubs	6.7	4,756	553,578	.85
9 Multisport	6.2	9,858	1,530,224	.64
TOTAL 22 CLUBS	6.6	20,524	3,004,450	.68%
NO. CLUBS AT 70%				
6 Racquet Clubs	7.9	6,563	1,194,384	.55
7 Tennis Clubs	7.6	5,123	820,526	.62
9 Multisport	7.0	10,176	1,718,972	.59
TOTAL 22 CLUBS	7.4	21,862	3,733,882	.59%
NO. CLUBS AT 80%				
6 Racquet Clubs	9.0	7,390	1,838,430	.40
7 Tennis Clubs	8.6	5,497	1,005,639	.55
7 Multisport	8.2	11,063	2,302,779	.48
TOTAL 20 CLUBS	8.6	23,950	5,146,848	.47%

Source: Ron Lawrence, *Club Location—A Site Analysis Study* (Brookline: IRSA, 1984), 21-22.

Population

Table 7.1 shows relevant populations of the areas surrounding the surveyed clubs corresponding to the 50%, 60%, 70%, and 80% membership levels. For the average of all clubs at the 50% membership level, these data reveal that members constitute 0.78% of the general population within a 5.6 mile radius of the subject. This conclusion is based on a large sample that encompassed over 17,600 members and a general population of over 2.2 million people. In addition, the variation of percentages between categories of clubs is relatively small for the population variable.

Age

The correlation between membership and the 25 to 34 age bracket is much stronger than overall population figures. Nationwide surveys reveal that 39% of health club members are between the ages of 24 and 35 compared with 17% of the nationwide population in 1985. Similarly, 31% of members are between the ages of 35 and 44 compared with 18% of the national population.[2] The proportions of members to the population aged 25 to 34 living within the areas of specified percentages of membership are shown in Table 7.2. These data demonstrate that members represent 4.10% of the 25 to 34 population at the 50% membership level. Members of multisport clubs tend to comprise a smaller proportion of the 25 to 34 population (3.16% at the 50% level) than do members of tennis clubs (5.88%). Median age data are included so readers can compare the area data for the surveyed clubs with their own subject markets.

Table 7.2 Club Membership As a Proportion of the Age 25 to 34 Population

	Distance Miles	Members	Pop. 25-34	Mem.%/ Pop. 25-34	Med. Age
NO. CLUBS AT 50%					
6 Racquet Clubs	5.5	5,312	128,701	4.13	36.7
7 Tennis Clubs	5.9	4,288	73,711	5.82	33.9
9 Multisport	5.5	8,009	227,198	3.53	33.9
TOTAL 22 CLUBS	5.6	17,609	429,610	4.10%	34.9
NO. CLUBS AT 60%					
6 Racquet Clubs	7.0	5,910	151,295	3.91	36.1
7 Tennis Clubs	6.7	4,756	87,121	5.45	33.5
9 Multisport	6.2	9,858	347,249	2.84	34.0
TOTAL 22 CLUBS	6.6	20,524	585,665	3.50%	34.6
NO. CLUBS AT 70%					
6 Racquet Clubs	7.9	6,563	199,499	3.29	34.8
7 Tennis Clubs	7.6	5,123	131,030	3.91	33.5
9 Multisport	7.0	10,176	382,402	2.66	35.5
TOTAL 22 CLUBS	7.4	21,862	712,931	3.07%	34.8
NO. CLUBS AT 80%					
6 Racquet Clubs	9.0	7,390	322,032	2.29	33.2
7 Tennis Clubs	8.6	5,497	163,230	3.37	33.3
7 Multisport	8.2	11,063	507,899	2.18	34.9
TOTAL 20 CLUBS	8.6	23,950	993,161	2.41%	34.0

Source: Ron Lawrence, *Club Location—A Site Analysis Study* (Brookline: IRSA, 1984), 21-22.

Managerial and Professional Employees

Another characteristic of health club members that distinguishes them from the overall population is their type of employment. Similar to the income and age characteristics, a larger proportion of managerial and professional employees are health club members than is true for older employment categories. Table 7.4 illustrates the proportions of members to the number of managerial and professional employees within their respective market areas. At the 50% membership level, the average ratio of members to these employees is 4.03%. Similar to the age and income variables, tennis club members represent a higher proportion of management and professional employees (5.88% at the 50% membership level) than do members of multisport clubs (3.16%).

Table 7.4 Ratio of Club Membership to Managerial and Professional Employees

	Distance Miles	Members	No. Mgr. & Prof.	Mem. % No. Mgr. & Prof. Emply	No. Employed
NO. CLUBS AT 50%					
6 Racquet Clubs	5.5	5,312	110,234	4.82	387,907
7 Tennis Clubs	5.9	4,288	72,961	5.88	221,929
9 Multisport	5.5	8,009	253,611	3.16	560,849
TOTAL 22 CLUBS	5.6	17,609	436,806	4.03%	1,170,685
NO. CLUBS AT 60%					
6 Racquet Clubs	7.0	5,910	135,152	4.37	454,767
7 Tennis Clubs	6.7	4,756	90,074	5.28	257,236
9 Multisport	6.2	9,858	376,103	2.62	850,973
TOTAL 22 CLUBS	6.6	20,524	601,329	3.41%	1,562,976
NO. CLUBS AT 70%					
6 Racquet Clubs	7.9	6,563	164,639	3.99	586,196
7 Tennis Clubs	7.6	5,123	121,612	4.21	371,167
9 Multisport	7.0	10,176	407,386	2.50	942,927
TOTAL 22 CLUBS	7.4	21,862	693,637	3.15%	1,900,290
NO. CLUBS AT 80%					
6 Racquet Clubs	9.0	7,390	249,754	2.96	910,867
7 Tennis Clubs	8.6	5,497	148,836	3.69	454,241
7 Multisport	8.2	11,063	543,452	2.04	1,245,099
TOTAL 20 CLUBS	8.6	23,950	942,042	2.54%	2,610,207

Source: Ron Lawrence, Club Location—A Site Analysis Study (Brookline: IRSA, 1984), 21-22.

Demographics of Target Market

Table 7.3 Club Market Area Income Characteristics

	Distance Miles	Members	H.H. W/>$25K	Mem.% H.H. W/ Inc. W/ 25K	Med. Income	Per Capita Income
NO. CLUBS AT 50%						
6 Racquet Clubs	5.5	5,312	111,708	4.76	23,536	9,857
7 Tennis Clubs	5.9	4,288	65,776	6.52	27,254	9,703
9 Multisport	5.5	8,009	203,221	3.94	22,317	13,331
TOTAL 22 CLUBS	5.6	17,609	380,705	4.63%	$23,600	$11,350
NO. CLUBS AT 60%						
6 Racquet Clubs	7.0	5,910	134,022	4.41	23,746	10,002
7 Tennis Clubs	6.7	4,756	80,895	5.87	28,142	10,249
9 Multisport	6.2	9,858	299,054	3.30	22,070	13,360
TOTAL 22 CLUBS	6.6	20,524	513,971	3.99%	$23,472	$11,750
NO. CLUBS AT 70%						
6 Racquet Clubs	7.9	6,563	168,595	3.89	22,832	9,548
7 Tennis Clubs	7.6	5,123	109,357	4.68	24,538	9,388
9 Multisport	7.0	10,176	327,475	3.11	22,840	13,390
TOTAL 22 CLUBS	7.4	21,862	605,427	3.61%	$23,163	$11,282
NO. CLUBS AT 80%						
6 Racquet Clubs	9.0	7,390	249,350	2.96	22,699	9,417
7 Tennis Clubs	8.6	5,497	132,095	4.16	23,260	9,212
9 Multisport	8.2	11,063	424,346	2.61	22,281	12,814
TOTAL 20 CLUBS	8.6	23,950	805,791	2.97%	$22,589	$10,897

Source: Ron Lawrence, Club Location—A Site Analysis Study (Brookline: IISA, 1984), 21-22.

Household Income

Health club members tend not only to be younger, but also to have greater incomes than the general population. According to the IRSA survey, about 77% of club members' households had incomes greater than $25,000 compared with 61% of households nationwide in 1985. Whereas 32% of all households had incomes over $45,000, 39% of members' households did. Considering that members are relatively younger than the overall population and that they have not yet reached their prime earning years, this finding is even more impressive.[3] At the 50% membership level, the ratio of all club members to households with incomes greater than $25,000 was 4.63%. Higher household incomes, but not per capita incomes, were observed in the market areas for tennis clubs in comparison with market areas for other fitness facilities. These data are summarized in Table 7.3.

298

MARKET PENETRATION ANALYSIS - Supportive Calculations

The first step involves summarizing the demographic characteristics of general population, population aged 25 to 34, households with incomes greater than $35,000, and management and professional employees. Appropriate sizes of market areas are determined in terms of a radius surrounding the subject in miles, census tracts or zip codes.

The second step is to determine the total size of all existing and proposed clubs in the primary market area. Third, the market penetration rates resulting from all competitive facilities with the subject's primary market area are calculated. This calculation is performed both with and without the subject. The general formula for this calculation is:

Market	Total Existing & Proposed		Market
Penetration =	Competition (with and	+	Demand
Rate	without subject)		Variable

The benchmark penetration rates have been derived from survey data published by IRSA. These rates provide a useful tool for market feasibility analysis when comparing market data relevant to a particular sit with averages from a nationwide sample of clubs.

Market penetration rates can be measured by the number of competitive clubs, total existing memberships or total square feet within the market area. It is the opinion of IRSA that market

299

penetration rates based on the total size of competitive facilities in the market area provide a superior analytical tool to rates based on the gross number of competitors. Penetration rates derived on a per club basis may be skewed in a market area with a small number of large clubs or a large number of small clubs. Adjusting these rates for a particular market area based on the total floor area would yield more meaningful results.

Our analysis is to determine whether a new health club containing 75,000 square feet should be built. A 8.6 mile radius of analysis has been selected, which corresponds with the 80% membership level. Within the area, there are three comparable competitive clubs containing a total of 135,000 square feet. The demographic characteristics of this market are described in the table below.

Demographics of Target market

Zip Code	Post Office Name	Population	25 to 34 Year Olds	Households with incomes over $35K (1)	Managerial & Professional Em	Market Potential Index Sporting Activites
60030	Grayslake	13,306	2,155	2,706	2,450	118
60031	Gurnee	25,673	4,255	6,202	5,788	115
60095	Lincolnshire	5,048	853	1,096	1,453	110
60048	Libertyville	30,709	4,606	7,573	7,672	122
60047	Kildeer	18,189	2,673	4,411	4,173	116
60060	Mundelien	20,381	3,566	4,343	4,192	112
60045	Lake Forest	18,660	3,452	4,926	4,892	121
60044	Lake Bluff	18,636	4,677	2,203	5,538	117
60064	North Chicago	21,235	5,096	1,867	6,311	94
60078	Round Lake	24,755	3,837	4,106	3,243	119
60088	North Chicago	7,927	2,378	368	1,760	118
60061	Vernon Hills	7,988	1,885	1,821	2,028	117
60087	Waukegan	19,784	3,383	4,445	3,882	102
60085	Waukegan	57,630	10,315	9,014	8,362	85
60069	Praire View	5,940	980	1,403	1,539	119
60020	Fox Lake	3,417	560	609	998	106
TOTAL MARKET		299,278	54,671	57,093	64,278	

Penetration Analysis in the Sports 'N Fitness Target
Market Area Based on Sizes of Competitive Clubs

Demographic Variables	Benchmark Penetration*	Existing Market**	% Difference w/Benchmark	Proposed Market***	% Difference w/Benchmark
Population	1,348	2,216	64.4%	1,425	5.7%
Age 25-34 Population	260	404	55.4%	260	0%
Household Income Over $35K	211	422	100.0%	271	28.4%
Managerial & Professional Employees	247	476	92.7%	306	23.8%

*   @ 80% membership per 1,000 sq. ft. basis.

**   135,000 sq. ft.

*** 210,000 sq. ft.

The resulting percentage differences for the existing market range
from 0% to +28%. These percentages showing positive differences
indicate the potential for supply expansion in the market.
Conversely, negative percentage differences, or calculated
penetration ration lower than the benchmark figures, indicate that
a market may be over-built. With the addition of Sports 'N Fitness
USA in the proposed market the resulting penetration ratios are
still above the benchmark ratios showing that the market area can
support the addition of our new club. Note that the smallest
percentage difference with the benchmark figure were for the
variables general population and age 25-34 population. A club much
larger than 75,000 square feet could not be supported at the
present time in this area.

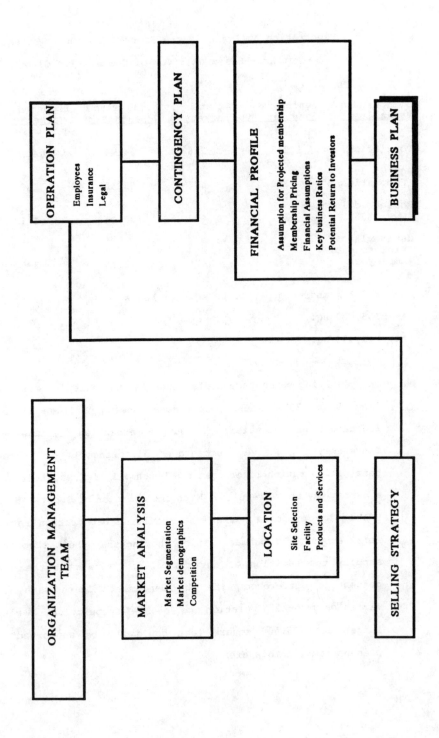

SPORTS 'N FITNESS USA

FLOW CHART OF THE BUSINESS PLAN

OPERATION PLAN

Employees
Insurance
Legal

CONTINGENCY PLAN

FINANCIAL PROFILE

Assumption for Projected membership
Membership Pricing
Financial Assumptions
Key business Ratios
Potential Return to Investors

BUSINESS PLAN

ORGANIZATION MANAGEMENT TEAM

MARKET ANALYSIS

Market Segmentation
Market demographics
Competition

LOCATION

Site Selection
Facility
Products and Services

SELLING STRATEGY

SPORTS 'N FITNESS USA
PROJECTED FINANCIAL RATIOS

	YEAR 1	YEAR 2	YEAR 3	YEAR 4	YEAR 5	Industry Average
Profit Margin on Sales	3.97%	6.02%	10.84%	11.95%	13.31%	6.00%
Current Ratio	2.57	2.97	2.99	3.44	3.75	1.20
Quick Ratio	2.26	2.69	2.81	3.27	3.59	0.80
Times Interest Earned	1.50	1.86	3.30	3.90	4.92	6.10
Debt to Total Assets	48.35%	46.24%	43.85%	39.90%	35.87%	21.00%
Debt to Equity	93.61%	86.01%	78.09%	66.40%	55.94%	89.80%
Return on Total Assets	1.46%	2.33%	5.44%	6.00%	6.88%	6.40%
Return on Equity	2.82%	4.33%	9.69%	9.99%	10.73%	10.30%
Earnings per Share	$0.72	$1.16	$2.89	$3.30	$3.98	

SPORTS 'N FITNESS USA
PROJECTED NET INCOME BREAKEVEN ANALYSIS
Based on Best Case – Worse Case Scenario

	1991	+20%	–20%
REVENUES	1,827,575	2,193,090	1,462,060
DIRECT COSTS			
Miniature Golf	13,707	16,448	10,965
Pro Shop	6,397	7,676	5,118
Ice Rink	25,586	30,703	20,469
Food and Beverage	47,517	57,020	38,014
Exercise Rooms	9,321	11,185	7,457
Repairs	91,379	109,655	73,103
Batting Cages	11,500	13,800	9,200
Marketing and Sales	109,655	131,586	87,724
TOTAL DIRECT COSTS	315,062	232,688	252,049
FIXED COSTS			
Utilities	118,792	142,550	95,034
General and Adminstrative	694,479	833,375	555,583
Real Estate Taxes	45,689	54,827	36,552
Property and Business Insurance	29,241	35,089	23,393
Interest Expense	241,031	289,237	192,825
Depreciation	262,500	315,000	210,000
TOTAL FIXED COSTS	1,391,732	1,670,079	1,113,386
BREAKEVEN REVENUES	1,681,635	2,017,962	1,345,308

INDEX

INDEX

INDEX

INDEX

INDEX

INDEX

INDEX

ABOUT THE AUTHOR

Gregory I. Kravitt has sixteen years of experience in corporate finance, banking and venture capital. He has structured, negotiated, financed, conducted due diligence and developed business plans for portfolio acquisitions in numerous industries. Currently, Mr. Kravitt is Managing Director and Co-Founder of Joraco, a Chicago-based investment banking firm, and an instructor at the Keller Graduate School of Management. He is the former President of North American Venture Group, Ltd., a venture capital firm specializing in turnaround situations. Mr. Kravitt earned his M.B.A. with distinction from Northwestern University and a B.A. in psychology from the University of Denver. He is the author of *How to Raise Capital* (Dow Jones, 1984).

For those of you who would like to further streamline the process of writing your business plan, we are pleased to announce the availability of a computer software product that was developed to be used in conjunction with *Creating a Winning Business Plan*. *The Business Plan Writer* is a full featured software application. We believe that you will find this program to both save you time and improve the quality of your business plan.

To order *The Business Plan Writer,* please send your check for $99.95, plus $5.00 for shipping and handling to:

Joraco, Inc.
Software Division
1149 Laurel Avenue
Deerfield, IL 60015

(708) 948-0404